T0374786

Convergent Teaching

REFORMING HIGHER EDUCATION: Innovation and the Public Good

William G. Tierney and Laura W. Perna, *Series Editors*

Convergent Teaching

Tools to Spark Deeper Learning in College

Aaron M. Pallas *&* Anna Neumann

Johns Hopkins University Press

BALTIMORE

© 2019 Johns Hopkins University Press
All rights reserved. Published 2019
Printed in the United States of America on acid-free paper

2   4   6   8   9   7   5   3   1

Johns Hopkins University Press
2715 North Charles Street
Baltimore, Maryland 21218-4363
www.press.jhu.edu

Library of Congress Cataloging-in-Publication Data

Names: Pallas, Aaron M., author. | Neumann, Anna, author.
Title: Convergent teaching : tools to spark deeper learning in college /
    Aaron M. Pallas and Anna Neumann.
Description: Baltimore : Johns Hopkins University Press, 2019. |
    Series: Reforming higher education : innovation and the public good |
Includes bibliographical references and index.
    Identifiers: LCCN 2019005187| ISBN 9781421432939 (hardcover : acid-free paper) |
    ISBN 9781421432946 (electronic) | ISBN 1421432935 (hardcover : acid-free paper) |
    ISBN 1421432943 (electronic)
Subjects: LCSH: College teaching—United States. | Education, Higher—Aims and
    objectives—United States.
Classification: LCC LB2331 .P343 2019 | DDC 378.1/25—dc23
LC record available at https://lccn.loc.gov/2019005187

A catalog record for this book is available from the British Library.

*Special discounts are available for bulk purchases of this book. For more information,
please contact Special Sales at 410-516-6936 or specialsales@press.jhu.edu.*

Johns Hopkins University Press uses environmentally friendly book materials,
including recycled text paper that is composed of at least 30 percent post-consumer
waste, whenever possible.

CONTENTS

A great many friends and colleagues offered insightful comments on a draft version of the book. We are grateful to Greg Anderson, Lesley Bartlett, Liza Bolitzer, Steve Brint, Audrey Bryan, Milagros Castillo-Montoya, Corbin Campbell, David Cohen, Katie Conway, Margaret Cuonzo, Jonathan Gyurko, Tom Hatch, Don Heller, Mary Taylor Huber, Melissa McDaniels, KerryAnn O'Meara, Rebecca Natow, Usha Rao, Judith Raymo, Jim Spillane, Aimee LaPointe Terosky, Lois Trautvetter, Dan Willingham, and Lauren Young. We also thank anonymous reviewers for Johns Hopkins University Press. None of these individuals bears any responsibility for the contents of the book.

We thank series editors Laura Perna and Bill Tierney, who invited us to pursue this project as part of their series Reforming Higher Education: Innovation and the Public Good; they provided sound advice on an earlier draft, along with persistent encouragement as we wrote. We are also grateful to Greg Britton, Editorial Director of Johns Hopkins University Press, who leads acquisitions in the field of higher education, for his guidance and support. MJ Devaney was a superb copyeditor, enhancing the manuscript's consistency and clarity.

Portions of the book are reused with permission of the American Academy of Arts and Sciences from *Policies and Practices to Support Undergraduate Teaching Improvement*, a 2017 white paper we coauthored with our colleague Corbin Campbell for the American Academy of Arts and Sciences Commission on the Future of Undergraduate Education. In addition to the many debts we owe Corbin, we also owe much to Mike

McPherson, commission cochair, and Francesca Purcell, commission director and program director for education and the development of knowledge at the academy, who supported us and provided comments on the white paper.

An earlier version of a portion of the book also previously appeared in "Staking a Claim on Learning: What We Should Know about Learning in Higher Education and Why," Anna Neumann's 2012 presidential address to the Association for the Study of Higher Education, published in the *Review of Higher Education* in 2014.

The middle of the book has its roots in MetroCITI (Metropolitan Colleges Institute for Teaching Improvement), Anna Neumann's initiative to improve and enrich teaching in the general/liberal education curricula of diversity-intensive colleges and universities throughout the New York metropolitan area. We thank the Teagle Foundation for their support of MetroCITI. The three cohorts of MetroCITI fellows were our collaborators in illuminating what convergent teaching might look like in the college classroom; we thank these thoughtful and very hard-working teachers for what they taught us. We are especially grateful to the fellows whose teaching we spotlight in the book: Tony Acevedo, Allison (Allie) Bach, Scott Carlin, Eryn Klosko, Lauren Navarro, and the pseudonymous "Sofia." A very special thank-you to Liza Bolitzer, Jolie Woodson, and Dianne Delima, who worked closely with Anna to make MetroCITI happen through the 2014–15 and 2015–16 academic years and whose collaboration in the initial carving out of teaching cases helped jump-start our work. We thankfully acknowledge Lucy Tam for her support of all that we do.

Katie Conway and Aimee LaPointe Terosky kept us laughing as we continually barraged them with questions about all aspects of the book, from its start through its completion. Their intellectual companionship kept us going.

Tom James, provost and dean of Teachers College, took an interest in this project from its inception and offered those most valuable of faculty resources: time and money. We are in his debt.

Finally, we thank the staff of Joe, a specialty coffee shop on the Columbia campus a block from our offices and just a few blocks from where we live. Writing a book requires a great deal of discipline. At times, that meant setting aside two hours a day to read, write, and hold each other accountable, often while camped out at a table at the coffee shop sipping a single-origin medium coffee. Once the staff figured out that we were married, they were generous in anticipating our coffee needs and kept us coming back. Our students and colleagues knew enough to leave us alone, but occasionally a college president would wander by and ask pesky questions.

PART I

A ROADMAP

Coming out of graduate school, Chris Felton was thrilled to secure a tenure-track job at Roseville University, a small, private institution in the Midwest.[1] On the strength of his job-market paper, he joined five colleagues in Roseville's political science department. Though he'd TA'd for his advisor a few years earlier, Chris had no formal preparation for college-level teaching. Rather, he'd learned as a doctoral student what research methods in political science research were defensible and why, through taking courses, participating in his advisor's research group, attending conferences, and reading the scholarly political science journals.

Other than the chair of his new department's request that he teach introductory American politics and his own desire to teach a seminar in his specialization in comparative politics, there wasn't much guidance about what to do in the classroom. The department didn't discuss teaching in its monthly faculty meetings, and what his colleagues hoped that students would learn in the introductory courses or even as undergraduate majors was never addressed publicly. He'd heard that there was some kind of teaching center on campus, but it seemed to be directed at faculty who'd been flagged as weak teachers. That's not how he saw himself.

Chris understood the key contradiction of faculty life: he was hired to teach, but his prospects for promotion and tenure, appraised on a tight timeline, would be judged primarily on the basis of his research productivity. There were no incentives to be a great teacher—only incentives not to be an awful one. He mainly kept to himself, working in isolation in his office, surfacing mostly to maintain a veneer of collegiality with his senior colleagues. Though he was friendly with some of the other junior faculty on the Roseville campus, he was busy trying to keep up with his research, his classes, and the line of students outside his door seeking academic advising. He and his new friends might relax over a beer a few times a month, but by the time the weekend rolled around, they were pretty exhausted, and the last thing they wanted to talk about was work. Chris didn't know how much in common he'd have with a microbiologist or a philosopher, anyway. Even if others at his college were having similar teaching experiences, they rarely discussed their problems or small victories with one another.

Though Chris took his teaching seriously, thinking carefully about class readings and course assignments, he was mainly flying blind. He worried especially about how to translate complex political ideas so that they would be comprehensible to students who, as best as he could tell, had never been exposed to political science. Which topics should he start with? How could he get to concepts and theories without turning off his students? Were there good ways to assess if students were picking things up in the middle of a class without disrupting the flow of discussion?

Chris was dimly aware that there were journals that dealt with teaching political science, such as the *Journal of Political Science Education*, but he'd skimmed the table of contents of a few issues and didn't see anything relevant to the issues he was struggling with. And what he did see raised questions for him: a stream of articles proclaiming the "best" way to teach about a particular topic but with relatively little evidence to support claims about student learning of the topic or musings about how new technologies might affect the modern political science classroom. Could he trust articles such as these? If not, where could he turn?

Perhaps, he thought, Roseville's mandatory teaching observation system could help. Once a year, a senior colleague came to Chris' classroom to observe him teach. The visits weren't a surprise, but they made Chris nervous and self-conscious, even though he was beginning to feel comfortable as a lecturer and seminar leader. He wasn't really sure what his colleague was looking for—there were no written guidelines or training for the observer that he knew of—but Roseville's policies required that the junior faculty be observed once annually. The senior colleague would smile and nod as she walked out of the classroom, which was encouraging, but Chris got no formal feedback from her on the class, and the observation went virtually unmentioned at Chris's annual meeting with his department chair. Roseville encouraged undergraduates to fill out course evaluations, and Chris's ratings fell in the satisfactory range, though in some classes, he looked stellar. Students commented on how much reading he assigned and the number of papers, among other features of Chris's teaching that they liked or did not like, but these provided little insight into whether and what his students learned. At a loss for insight into his teaching, Chris wondered if he should be doing something fundamentally different in the classroom. The uncertainty nagged at him, but he wasn't sure what, if anything, to do.

———

There are tens of thousands of Chris Feltons teaching in American colleges and universities, alongside other college teachers we introduce later. The American higher education system is failing them. And in so doing, it is also failing our students.

This book is about undergraduate college teaching, which we argue is at the heart of undergraduate education. Americans have long looked to colleges and universities as the conveyors of the American dream. We ask a lot of our higher education system, and it simply is unable to shoulder all of the hopes and dreams we place on it. But if education cannot do all that we ask, solving the complex set of social, economic and political problems that define our country, what *can* it do?

Our answer is simple: colleges and universities can do that which historically we have charged them to do, namely, cultivate students' knowledge and skills so that they can promote their own, their communities', and the nation's well-being. In brief, educational institutions, and the educators in them, can teach their students well. That means positioning students to examine and understand subjects that matter for their lives and for the lives of all those around them. There is no one best way, however, to promote this laudable goal. Although higher education is highly decentralized in the United States, institutions of higher education are frequent targets of broadly spanning public policy, and they shift their behavior in response to mandates and incentives originating in federal, state, and local governments. Institutions of higher education also act autonomously; they can create and respond to markets that pop up to manage the supply of and demand for educational credentials, pursuing entrepreneurial efforts that promise to give them an edge on competitors.

There's a lot that can be and has been done to improve higher education. But most reform initiatives do not aim for the center of the target: college teaching and student learning. In this book, we make the case that good college teaching matters and that we can do better at identifying, cultivating, and rewarding it. We acknowledge that other things matter too. Without access to affordable higher education, no one will be learning. And without high-quality counseling, advisement, and other support systems, students may be derailed from learning. Moreover, there's a widespread view that students learn as much outside the classroom as within it.[2] We leave the thorny problems of access, affordability, and student support to experts in those domains.[3] Here, we make claims solely about college teaching as the heart of undergraduate education.[4]

In chapter 1, we build an argument for the importance of undergraduate teaching and explore why it has not yet captured the attention of stakeholders in higher education. We consider the paradox of declining confidence in higher education even as demand continues to rise. Going to college is seen as the engine of the American dream, but there is much more attention to the acquisition of credentials that can be exchanged for jobs and a comfortable standard of living than to the learning of anything in particular. We consider three approaches to the reform of undergraduate education, which we term "powering it up," "staying the course," and "blowing it up." None of these, we argue, gives teaching, a critical determinant of what students learn, its due. We conclude the chapter with an introduction to the concept of convergent teaching, which draws extensively on the rich research literature on teaching in K–12 classrooms.

The second section of the book is divided into three chapters, each of which addresses a principle of convergent teaching and provides concrete examples of teachers enacting the principle. Chapter 2 takes up the principle of targeting. Targeting involves identifying and specifying the disciplinary or field-based concepts, modes of thought, and other knowledge to be taught in a particular course, with attention to what students need for related and advanced learning later in the course, in other courses, in the field, or in life.

Chapter 3 describes the principle of surfacing. Surfacing includes unearthing what students know already—culturally, personally, and academically—that may offer a bridge to understanding subject-matter concepts new to them. Chapter 4 explains the principle of navigating. Navigating consists of steering instruction between what students know already (their prior knowledge) and what they need to learn (subject-matter concepts). Navigating can take many forms, including planning lessons, interacting with students about content, creating and discussing assignments, and informally assessing students' understandings of course content.

The third and final section of the book consists of two chapters that address policies and practices to promote undergraduate teaching improvement. Chapter 5 considers campus-based policies and practices that promote a broad conception of good undergraduate teaching, of which convergent teaching is but one component. Chapter 6 outlines policies and practices to support convergent teaching beyond the campus, concluding with an account of some of the risks and promises of what we propose and suggestions for individual faculty who seek to improve their undergraduate teaching practices.[5]

We are not the first to call for a renewed commitment to undergraduate teaching nor to offer guidance on how to get from our current state—indifference—to one of focused attention, supported by adequate resources. The field of higher education in the United States is extraordinarily complex, with multiple organizations and institutions acting and reacting, often in loosely coupled patterns. What we offer breaks new ground in several ways. First, we situate our interest in undergraduate teaching and its improvement in an account of higher education in contemporary America, exploring the demographic, social, and economic forces that shape our present and our likely future. Second, we center our approach to undergraduate teaching improvement in the learning sciences, drawing on knowledge about how people learn as a guide to the work that college teachers must undertake to assist students in learning new concepts and ideas. Third, we offer novel approaches that institutions of higher education and the other organizations that make up postsecondary education in the United States can use to pursue the improvement of undergraduate teaching. There are some excellent monographs on specific initiatives, such as campus teaching centers, or Preparing Future Faculty programs, but we are not aware of any other books that "go wide" in thinking about the problems of undergraduate teaching practice and possible solutions to them.

CHAPTER ONE

American Ambivalence and College Teaching

What is good college teaching? How is it best supported and rewarded? In this chapter, we explore why good undergraduate teaching is at the margins of conversations about the future of higher education. We begin with a phenomenon we call "American ambivalence": The demand for higher education in the United States remains robust, but there is declining confidence in higher education and its ability to deliver on the American dream. We then describe the American higher education system, its students, and its faculty. The populations of students and faculty are changing rapidly, and our policies and practices continue to lag behind these changes.

Next, we review three policy avenues that seek to respond to recent changes in the American higher education system, which we summarize here, metaphorically, as "powering it up," "staying the course," and "blowing it up." None of these proposals, we argue, gives college teaching its due, especially in light of the evidence we present that good college teaching matters. Though often well meaning, none actually is grounded in the notion of teaching as efforts crafted intentionally to advance students' learning of ideas and subjects and ways to think deeply and thoughtfully about them. Without good college teaching, students are unlikely to acquire the knowledge and ways of knowing that can enable them to live the kinds of lives to which they aspire. Nor will they likely be able to contribute as richly as we might wish to society's well-being and our economic recovery.

We conclude the chapter with a discussion of the centrality of teaching to human learning and develop an expansive and flexible definition of convergent teaching that is illuminated in part II of the book. We rely on the rich and elaborate body of knowledge developed in recent decades by learning scientists, sociocultural researchers of education, and researchers of K–12 subject-matter teaching to breathe life into the definition. We position convergent teaching as an aspirational ideal in higher education and as a starting point for future research, professional development, and policy development.

American Ambivalence

Americans have long expressed ambivalence about schooling in ways that go well beyond caricatures of bookish, eggheaded nerds stumbling through daily life or contrasts between being "school smart" or "book smart," on the one hand, and "street smart" or "motherwise," on the other.[1] Half a century ago, when sociologist James Coleman criticized what he called an "adolescent society," separate from adult society, that saw academic prowess as subservient to being popular, good looking, or athletically talented, fellow sociologist Bennett Berger responded by challenging the argument that adolescent values were something distinct and separate from the anti-intellectualism observed among their parents and running throughout American society.[2] Not long after, historian Richard Hofstadter chronicled how anti-intellectualism had surged in American life.[3] It continues to this day.[4] Americans admire education but see school as work and drudgery. Most do not have vivid memories of learning something exciting or important in the classroom.[5] Achievement is measured in terms of credentials that can be exchanged in the labor market, not by learning anything in particular.

This view is emblematic of a set of tensions around American education described well by sociologist and historian David Labaree.[6] Labaree identifies three major purposes that have steered public education in the United States since its inception: democratic citizenship, social efficiency, and social mobility. Democratic citizenship pertains to education's power to create politically equal citizens prepared to act and participate in our democracy. Social efficiency represents the mechanism by which individuals whose knowledge and skills are honed through education are matched with the positions in the nation's economy that drive and sustain it in a global and connected world. Social mobility is the promise of the American dream, namely, that by hard work, one can attain the educational credentials that allow individuals to leap over others and move up in society or, for those who are already advantaged, to sustain their privileges.

Labaree argues that because social mobility is so tied to credentials, learning has been decoupled from the acquisition of educational credentials. Because social mobility dominates the landscape, education policies and practices render the schools a competitive battleground for advantage. Very few people *want* to go to school; they go because they feel that they *have to*. Credentials are key; learning is incidental.

The American populace has viewed education as the engine of the American dream for much of the country's history. We hope and believe that individuals can, by virtue of talent and hard work, move up in society and surpass the accomplishments of their parents. And indeed, across many generations, better-educated individuals have been less likely than their parents to hold unskilled blue-collar jobs and more likely to live longer and healthier lives than their ancestors. This is in good part due to the dual promise of higher education: that it will grow the human capital that generates the workforce productivity and economic prosperity that benefits us all and provide all individuals with opportunities to learn, to develop their capacities to the fullest, and move up in the world. The anticipated synergy is unmistakable: as the nation supports individual educational pursuits, so will individuals uplift the nation and its civic, economic, scientific, and social potential. Education in this view is the route to the nation's enhanced well-being.

This grand promise, even in its most basic terms, has not and perhaps cannot be realized. For one thing, it asks—and assumes—a lot about education's ability to shape the larger social good. But education is not the sole driver, or orchestrator, of macrolevel economic booms and declines, nor can it, on its own, regulate social change. Nor should it be expected to do this. Education, by itself, cannot spur our nation's social, political, economic, and scientific growth and development; this effort must be shared broadly by the full range of social institutions that underpin American life: the political and governmental, the medical, the financial and industrial, the legal, and others. Nor can education alone be tasked with achieving the nation's historic aim of overcoming structural inequalities that locate individuals and the social groups to which they belong in more or less advantaged social and economic positions,. There is far more in play than what education can deliver.

Even if a rising educational tide lifts all boats, some start out ahead of others. Individuals born with advantages can capitalize on them to go further through school. Carefully crafted policies and practices can indeed do much to equalize educational opportunity. But our problems are far bigger. For example, among children and youth aged 18 or younger, 18% were living below the official poverty line in 2016.[7] In 2013, 30% of households headed by a Black person and one in four households headed by a person of Hispanic origin had zero or negative net worth.[8] Among households where the head holds a four-year college degree, the median net worth of households headed by whites is three to four times greater than of those headed by Blacks.[9] Even if we were to equalize access to education across racial groups, the gaps in wealth among these groups would persist. Education may produce individuals who can help work on these larger problems, thereby shifting the larger societal scene (i.e., "lifting all boats"), but it will take far more than education alone to do that.

The promise of American higher education has not yet been realized. College retention and graduation rates are far too low, individual students have been let down, and public resources have been squandered. Most students who start college as full-time students do not finish in a timely way (i.e., within three years for a two-year associate's degree or certificate or six years for a bachelor's degree). Among entering full-time students seeking a degree from a two-year postsecondary institution in 2000, only 30% had graduated from that institution in three years. That figure has not budged; only 30% of first-time, full-time students entering two-year schools in 2013 had graduated in three years. The numbers are depressingly low across all of the major racial and ethnic categories of students.[10]

The figures are more promising for students entering four-year institutions as full-time students. About 55% of those entering four-year schools as first-time, full-time students in 1996 had graduated from their entering institution in six years. That figure has risen to 59% for the 2009 cohort of first-time enrollees. Nevertheless, the figures for students of color, especially Black and Latino students, lag behind those of white students. Just 40% of Black students enrolling in four-year schools on a full-time basis for the first time in 2009 had graduated from their initial school in six years. Slightly over half (54%) of Latino students did so.[11] Both percentages fall well short of the 63% of white students who had graduated within six years.

To be sure, students may transfer to other institutions and receive degrees, and such students would not be reflected in these figures. But adding these students in doesn't change the overall story: of the 44 million Americans aged 25–34 in 2017, 37% held a bachelor's degree or higher, 10% held an academic or vocational associate's degree, and 18% had attended college for some amount of time but not obtained a degree.[12] The glass is at once half empty and half full.

Social Change and the Demand for Higher Education

Sociologists Ulrich Beck and Anthony Giddens argued that the industrial revolution and the rise of modernity, with their focus on science, rationality, and technology, have reduced uncertainty in daily life, for example, by enabling the creation of large firms and trade unions that provide structure to work lives and careers.[13] During the nineteenth century, Western nation-states expanded, giving rise to civil service bureaucracies (such as those associated with compulsory education, marriage laws, and military service) that came to regulate the timing and sequencing of important life events and providing social safety nets (such as Social Security, Medicare, and Medicaid in the United States) for the most vulnerable members of society. Although wars and economic downturns have continued to create sharp discontinuities amid this emerging large-scale regularity, the mass of people have, to date, been able to foresee the arc of their lives.

In the United States, as in the rest of the Western world, schooling was seen as the surest route to personal success. As the economy expanded, new careers and job opportunities emerged, and education, as the institution for preparing people for them, became the key to getting ahead, and perhaps to survival itself. As many social scientists have pointed out, the playing fields of education and career gradually shifted. Whereas a high school diploma was a solid credential offering opportunity for surviving and getting ahead in the middle decades of the twentieth century, gradually a college degree became the minimum credential in guaranteeing a comfortable way of life with some security.[14]

Beck's key insight is that technology can backfire, hurtling modern society forward in unpredictable ways, some favorable and others downright terrifying.[15] His vision bears out today. Technological changes, in the form of computers and the social interconnectedness created by the internet, allow us to do things that were unimaginable just fifty years ago—consider, for example, international collaborations in fighting disease, enhancement of educational and other service delivery to remote areas, and abilities to connect far-flung families and communities, among others.

Conversely, some technological innovations have hastened the damage we have done to the earth: human-produced tools have enabled climate change, ignited nuclear power plant calamities, and supported unfettered gene technology, to name just a few. Beyond such physical dangers lie the social, political, and economic risks stemming from the rise of global terrorism and the fragility of a global economy that hums along to high-speed computers carrying out billions of trade and other financial transactions daily. Computer viruses—which of course did not exist prior to computers—can grind us to a halt. Boasts about who has the biggest nuclear button are terrifying. And modern technologies allow information about these new risks, and collateral anxiety, to circulate immediately and effortlessly. This flow of information also facilitates the dissemination of "fake news," to which those who have not been educated to think critically are particularly susceptible.

Amid such changes, we must confront the fact that those who already possess wealth and power are best positioned to benefit from social change and to buffer themselves from the risks of negative outcomes. The most vulnerable—the residents of Flint, Michigan, or Puerto Rico, for example—face illness, disability, and other hardships due to endangered water supplies and a crumbling infrastructure for food, shelter, and medical care. All save those ensconced in the elite are right to worry about their futures. The risks to maintaining one's place, or to getting ahead, are palpable.

Anxieties about College and Career

Educational attainment is scarcely in the same ballpark as these technological and infrastructural hazards, but the state of education does play into the uncertainty and anxiety of the era. For example, we periodically see mismatches between available jobs and individuals' educational aims and pursuits and the credentials they eventually earn.[16] It's hard to know how to prepare for a world of work driven by new technologies, many of which continue to evolve. Fears that one will be undereducated—or overeducated—abound. Yet in study after study, demographers demonstrate that college attendance is a sound investment. After footing the bill for college attendance, a typical four-year college graduate will earn about $200,000 more during the course of his or her working life than a similar young person who stops at high school.[17]

The economic benefits don't stop with earnings, as education has a broad reach in its payoffs in adulthood and old age, promoting healthy behaviors, reducing exposure to hazardous jobs, and promoting saving for the future.[18] But most people do not function as econometricians, calculating the costs of education and likely long-term returns on investments in it. They lack the information and tools to do so, and there are few norms and established methods that would support their so doing. Information about the payoffs of higher education attendance and acquisition of postsecondary credentials remain distributed unevenly, with those who are already advantaged having the best grasp of how the system works and how to bend it to their advantage.

Why might a college education not seem like a great investment in this new era of heightened occupational risk and anxiety? Perhaps the economic and social security a college degree historically has provided is eroding. As evidence for this hypothesis, labor statisticians point to increasing levels of job turnover, including changes in the kinds of work in which Americans engage. It's estimated that baby boomers born between 1957 and 1964 held an average of twelve jobs between the ages of 18 and 50, a figure that was as high for those with a bachelor's degree or even with more schooling as for those with less than a high school diploma.[19] Naturally, some of these jobs included short-term spells of youth employment, hard to view as a career step. Nevertheless, college-educated baby boomers held approximately eight different jobs, on average, between the prime adult years between the ages of 25 and 50. Job changes can, of course, serve as steps upward, and earnings may grow as individuals, especially the highly educated, move from young adulthood to midlife.[20]

But job changes also can sacrifice individuals' accumulated retirement and other job benefits and thus reduce future security and well-being; they can also take individuals outside their preferred careers, derailing their trajectories. Baby boomers embarking on a new job between the ages of 35 and 44 were not likely to persist very long in those jobs; 36% stayed in these jobs for less than a year, and more than half held a new job for less than two years.[21] If at one time people could believe that a college education would prepare them for a predictable work future, that is no longer the case. The pattern has, of course, surfaced questions in the minds of prospective college students and their families about the value of a college degree in a world of evolving and diffusing career lines. Higher education cannot inoculate us against all work-related risks.

Alongside the effects of new technologies on the predictability of work and careers, we see changes attributable to the shape of the new economy. It's no surprise that these changes have intensified worries about how best to prepare emerging adults for the work worlds to come and how to organize postsecondary education to support workforce development. One feature of this new work world is the "gig economy," featuring work arrangements that differ greatly from the idealized career of a full-time job with a single employer who provides a desirable living wage and benefits. Economists Lawrence Katz and Alan Krueger have found that the percentage of US workers whose main job involved "alternative work arrangements"— that is, employment as temporary help agency workers, on-call workers, contract workers, and independent contractors or freelancers—increased from about 10% in 2005 to 16% in 2015.[22] This growth amounted to about nine million jobs, which was about the same increase in overall employment over this ten-year period. The uncomfortable inference is that virtually all the growth in employment in the United States between 2005 and 2015 was due to increases in the gig economy.

Using different datasets, McKinsey Global Institute (MGI) came to similar conclusions with regard to what's referred to as "independent work," marked by high autonomy; payment by task, assignment, or sales; and short-term relationships between workers and clients.[23] According to MGI, independent workers can be classified in one of several ways: as "free agents" whose primary livelihood is derived from independent work that they undertake voluntarily, as "casual earners" who choose to supplement their primary income with independent work, as "reluctants" who engage in independent work as a primary source of income and thus out of necessity, or as "financially strapped," individuals who supplement a primary income with independent work, not because they want to, but because they feel they must.

In the United States, MGI estimates, about one in eight workers are "free agents" or "reluctants" whose primary income is from independent work, and a similar fraction rely on independent work as a supplemental source of income ("casual earners"). All told, approximately sixty million workers in the United States are independent workers. About two-thirds of these independent workers are between the ages of 25 and 65 and thus in their prime working years, and only one in five resides in a low-income household (defined as one in which the annual household income is below $25,000).[24]

It seems inevitable that the rise of the gig economy will threaten workers' sense of security, if it has not already done so. The United States has historically depended on employers to provide economic security and a safety net for their workers in the form of defined-benefit or defined-contribution pension plans, unemployment insurance, workers' compensation, and disability insurance, among other job benefits. To be sure, independent workers, who in effect have no employers, and those who work for employers pay Social Security and Medicare taxes that eventually provide the benefits. However, independent workers, unlike their counterparts, must pay both the employee and the employer amounts. And these benefits generally are not large enough to provide economic security during retirement.[25]

All told, the rise of the gig economy appears to be weakening an idealized and historically forged bond between employers and employees, as long-term contracts and trusting relationships come to be replaced by shorter-term, transient interactions. Both policy makers and the general public are awakening to the realization that a college education cannot and will not inoculate most workers from this societal shift.

Although the consequences of this shift are still emerging in the United States and in much of the world, Japan has already completed the transition, and so its experience is suggestive. For decades, Japan relied on long-term employment relationships between firms and workers. Once hired, workers would typically remain with the firm for their entire careers. Moreover, it was expected that an employee's commitment to the firm would be matched by the firm's commitment to the employee, and that this would be manifested in a reluctance by employers to lay off or terminate long-term employees, even during tough economic times. For many white-collar workers, known as salarymen, entry into a firm was largely structured by informal agreements between schools and colleges and particular firms. Educational institutions would agree to identify and provide graduates to particular employers in exchange for an expectation that the employer would hire a certain number of these graduates each year, who were then guaranteed a respectable long-term career.[26] Such a position conveyed a *ba*, a Japanese term that refers to one's comfortable place in the world. However, in the 1990s, the Japanese economy plummeted, and employers drew back from these long-term contractual relationships with workers. Young people were obliged to find jobs on their own, and many struggled to secure positions that promised a stable career with a respectable salary.

Sociologist Mary Brinton has shown that for a generation of Japanese youth, the economic downturn eroded trust in education and work as sources of identity and security.[27] Although the US economy remains surprisingly robust, the shift to a gig economy could have a similar consequence, as individuals come to count more on themselves and their talents to make their way, occupationally and career-wise, than on educational institutions and large employers. Over time, it may make less sense for emerging adults to count on a college education to anchor their livelihoods and their lives.

Declining Public Confidence in Higher Education

These changes in the technologies of work and in the shape of the economy have spurred anxieties about how best to create the workforce of the future. Accompanying worries as to whether higher education, in its current form, can do the job is a larger problem: confidence and trust in American higher education have declined from their historic high.

Public Opinion

On average, American adults believe that colleges and universities have a positive effect on the way things are going in the country, more so than other social institutions, such as labor unions, banks, and the national news media.[28] But the public is highly divided along party lines. In 2017, 58% of self-reported Republicans and Republican-leaning independents reported that colleges and universities have a negative effect on the way things are going, a sharp increase of thirteen percentage points over the preceding year and a twenty-six percentage point rise since 2010. Coupled with relative stability in the favorable and unfavorable ratings offered by Democrats and Democratic-leaning independents, the overall percentage of American adults who think that colleges and universities are having a negative effect on the way things are going in the country has risen from 26% in 2010 to 36% in 2017. When asked if colleges and universities are beneficial, a substantial plurality agrees, but in recent years, support has waned.[29]

How one asks the question matters, too. A Gallup poll conducted in August 2017 asked American adults about the degree of confidence that they personally had in colleges and universities.[30] At that time, 44% of US adults reported that they had a great deal or quite a lot of confidence in colleges and universities, whereas 56% claimed that they had some or very little confidence. The partisan divide was very clear here, with 56% of Democrats or those leaning Democratic expressing a great deal or quite a lot of confidence, and only 33% of Republicans or those leaning Republican doing so. At best, a slight majority of those on the left are confident in American colleges and universities, and a clear majority of those on the right are not. The overarching pattern yields a less than optimistic view: American higher education appears to be under indictment in the court of public opinion. Its unresolved status is uncomfortable.

What might account for declining confidence in higher education? It's a puzzle, as declining support for higher education as a long-standing social institution nonetheless remains joined to strong beliefs in the benefits of higher education to individuals. Americans have long viewed education as the engine of social mobility, and as the education system has expanded, many have come to see postsecondary credentials as a passport to a better life. The belief is not without support. Individuals who attend and graduate from a postsecondary institution are more likely to be employed than youth who never attend college, and their projected lifetime earnings far outstrip those of terminal high school graduates and high school dropouts.[31] Whatever the weaknesses of US institutions of higher education and whatever the source of declining confidence, Americans still clamor for college degrees, and for good reason.

The US economy counts on a supply of educated workers, especially those with postsecondary training or a degree. Of the fifty occupations with earnings above the 2015 US median income of $36,000 expected to have the largest number of openings in the coming years due to growth and replacement needs, thirty have a typical entry-level education of postsecondary training or a bachelor's degree. These occupations include registered and licensed practical nurses, managers, elementary and secondary schoolteachers, accountants, and software developers and computer systems analysts.[32]

Clamor and demand are one thing, but uptake is quite another. With regard to college enrollment and completion, the United States has lost ground to other countries. Among US individuals aged 25–34 in 2000, 38% had completed some postsecondary academic, advanced vocational, or professional education, well above the average of 26% in this age group in Organisation for Economic Co-Operation and Development (OECD) countries. Although the US figure had risen by nine percentage points to 47% by 2015, other OECD countries showed more rapid growth, moving from 26% to 42%. In countries as diverse as Canada, Ireland, Japan, Korea,

Lithuania, Luxembourg, and the Russian Federation, at least 50% of those aged 25–34 had completed some tertiary schooling.[33] In short order, many other countries will eclipse our rates of college participation.

Cost and Affordability

Anxieties about college affordability surface in virtually all discussions of US higher education, be they about access, quality, or simply the pursuit of credentials. The vast majority of undergraduates attend public two-year and four-year institutions whose budgets hinge critically on state appropriations. Although state and local funding for public institutions has increased about 10% over the past twenty-five years, funding has not kept pace with the 34% increase in student enrollments in these schools. Together, these trends amount to a 17% decline in per-student state expenditures from 1991 to 2016.[34] There appears, then, to be less state government financial support for higher education than ever before.

As state dollars decline, tuition costs fall increasingly on students and their families, with economically advantaged families better positioned to absorb them than the poor. Although grants and tax benefits offset the cost of tuition, fees, and room and board, the net costs of college attendance are substantial, and approximately 60% of four-year college graduates take out federal and/or nonfederal loans to cover the cost of attendance.[35] On average, students at public and private four-year colleges borrow more than 25% of the net cost of each year of college (i.e., net tuition, fees, room and board).[36] A typical graduate of a public two-year institution who has borrowed will incur about $12,000 in cumulative loan debt, and a typical graduate of a public or private four-year school who has borrowed will have taken out a total of $27,000 or $33,000 in loans, respectively.[37] The overall costs of college attendance are high, even at institutions that pride themselves in offering wide access to all who desire to learn.

These various threads taken together weave a complex tale: as a nation, we appear to retain faith in the value of higher education, and Americans' demand for it remains clear. But internally, our doubts may be increasing, perhaps more so on the conservative than the liberal end of the political spectrum. From a global perspective, however, American performance falls, at best, near the middle of the pack. The emergent pattern—declining internal confidence in higher education, coupled with mediocre performance internationally—raises important questions. What *are* students learning in college, and how well is that going?

What Do Students Learn in College? And What *Should* They Learn?

Enrollments and educational credentials are only part of our collective anxiety about higher education. We treat credentials as proxies for the knowledge, skills, and dispositions that enable people to be productive on the job and to participate in civil society. Yet the knowledge and skills acquired via education matter much more so than the possession of a sheepskin. The US education system could quadruple postsecondary enrollments or double the number of degrees awarded without students learning anything. Effecting links between teaching and learning and between learning and usable knowledge is no small matter; making these connections strikes at the very heart of educational purpose, including what's gained in college. One might wonder how well we are doing on this count.

If we look to the basic literacy and numeracy skills of young adults who are participating in or have completed some postsecondary schooling, the United States falls in the middle, trailing some countries and ahead of others. Among thirty-four countries in an OECD survey, US youth aged 20–24 who are participating in or have completed postsecondary schooling are significantly behind eight countries in literacy skills, are statistically indistinguishable from sixteen, and are significantly ahead of nine. But US youth fare less well in numeracy, with seventeen countries significantly ahead of the average performance of the US cohort and only four countries significantly behind. The average performance of college-educated US youth in literacy is indistinguishable from the OECD average, but mathematical proficiency is significantly lower.[38]

The reasons that the United States is lagging in young adult numeracy skills are manifold and include variations across countries in poverty rates, the relative influence of markets and the state, and the quality of elementary and secondary education. We know, for example, that since the 1960s, US adolescents have generally scored lower on international assessments of academic performance than other adolescents from around the world.[39] All the more reason to puzzle over a pattern in which the educational attainment of young adults in the United States outstrips their academic performance: We have higher levels of postsecondary enrollment and continue to outpace most of the world in the proportion of young adults with postsecondary credentials. Shouldn't our students then be learning more, too? The data indicate that this is not the case, and the finding has set off alarms.

Are American College Students Academically Adrift?

Concerns about what students learn in college escalated with the 2011 publication of *Academically Adrift*, one of the rare books on higher education with broad appeal. The drifting to which authors Richard Arum and Josipa Roksa refer pertains both to students and to institutions of higher education. The book's most striking claim is that a majority of today's college students are not learning critical thinking skills in college, a finding that strikes at the heart of long-held narratives about the purpose of a college education. If going to college doesn't cultivate students' critical thinking, what *is* it good for? And why go?

Critics pounced on this dramatic finding, in some cases with good reason. Arum and Roksa relied on the Collegiate Learning Assessment (CLA), an assessment developed by the Council for Aid to Education, to measure students' critical thinking performance. The heart of the current version of the assessment, the CLA+, is a sixty-minute performance task in which test takers are asked to address a hypothetical real-world problem and present viable solutions to it with the help of a set of reference documents and information sources that might bear on the problem. Responses are scored via a rubric that assesses the quality of analysis and problem solving, writing effectiveness, and writing mechanics, each on a six-point scale ranging from one (low) to six (high).[40]

Arum and Roksa administered the CLA to a sample of about twenty-three hundred entering college freshmen enrolled in four-year institutions and again in the spring of their sophomore year. Students' scores on the CLA increased by .18 standard deviations from the first to the second test, which the authors deemed a small amount. More damning, they concluded, was the finding that the scores of 45% of their sample in the sophomore spring assessment were not statistically distinguishable from their scores in the fall of the freshman year. Although their interpretation that nearly half of their sample showed no gains on the CLA was faulty due to the imprecision of individual students' scores, it quickly became part of the lore justifying the book's subtitle: "Limited Learning on College Campuses."[41]

In search of explanations for this apparent pattern of limited learning in college, the authors analyze data derived through surveys they had administered to study participants alongside the CLA critical thinking performance task. Zeroing in on the amount of effort that students said that they devoted to their studies, Arum and Roksa report that more than a third of participating students spent less than five hours a week studying and that only one half had taken a course that required twenty pages of writing throughout the term in the previous semester. Many had not taken even a single course in the previous term that had required reading forty or more pages a week. The conclusion was inescapable: across a wide range of institutions and among students of diverse backgrounds, colleges were not demanding much of their students. Little wonder, then, that students did not display much growth in the critical thinking skills that many colleges proclaim as their raison d'être.

Arriving amid growing concerns about government efforts to hold colleges and universities accountable for student outcomes, *Academically Adrift* touched a nerve in the higher education community. The book continues to anchor many researchers' and policy makers' discussions about the weak impact of colleges and universities on what their students learn and can do. The general public, in contrast, wavers in this concern, often reverting to people's faith in the power of the college degree, more so than specific knowledge, to grant access to "the good life." The distinction between learning achieved and degrees earned is subtle but important.

What Should Students Learn in College?

Moreover, the exchange value of educational credentials obscures important questions about what students should learn in college. Is it the ubiquitous "twenty-first century skills"?[42] We are reluctant to engage in a debate about what skills will be required for the jobs that will evolve over the course of this century, and where they should be taught and learned. Perhaps the most distinctive twenty-first century skills are those that are specifically dependent on technology, such as digital literacy, and the ability to use information and communication technologies effectively in daily life and for learning other knowledge and skills. And perhaps these skills that will be valuable in the workplace are not easily acquired in discipline-based college courses. But few are calling for minimizing the learning of disciplinary subjects, and indeed proponents of the teaching of twenty-first century skills are often sharply critiqued by those favoring the teaching of disciplinary knowledge and discipline-anchored modes of thought. Rather than supplanting disciplinary study, they argue, the teaching of disciplines can be supplemented with what are sometimes referred to as "learning and thinking skills," such as how to think critically, problem solve, communicate, and collaborate, and "life skills," such as how to assume personal and social responsibility, behave morally and ethically, and learn to adapt.

All of these are important, but we do want to make a particular pitch for disciplinary knowledge, as it is higher education's unique offering to society and something that no other current social institution can offer in depth. To learn a discipline is only partly about gaining knowledge for use in school or elsewhere. It also involves learning to think in ways that are unique to a discipline. Beyond that, deep learning in a particular discipline, in line with its internal knowledge structure, sensitizes learners to be alert to the existence of such structures across disciplines, hence heightening their sensitivity to interdisciplinary thought, including that in professional endeavor.

Disciplines are broad categories of knowledge produced, taught, and learned in colleges and schools. As a category of knowledge, a discipline typically highlights some sense of within-category coherence, though as most disciplinarians report, usually internal differences reign.[43] Disciplinary categories are substantive, consisting of the content of knowledge associated with a discipline, *and* social, comprising disciplinary communities made up of expert practitioners, as well as symbolic, each discipline's identity being distinct from that of others.[44] They can be described simultaneously as "academic territories" and the "academic tribes" that populate them, in Tony Becher's colorful terms.[45] The social terrain is inherently interesting to college faculty, as disciplines struggle for legitimacy in the eyes of the general public and within specific educational institutions, all with regard to the material resources associated with prestige and status. Moreover, most college faculty have themselves been socialized within disciplinary communities, and their professional and personal identities are rooted in these communities.[46] The communities, in turn, have specialized vocabularies and practices that are shared among the members but are often opaque to those outside of the community.[47]

We are concerned here, primarily, with disciplines as ways of structuring academic knowledge. The structure of a discipline is defined by the phenomena, including problems, it deems significant; the ways of knowing and thinking and forms of argument used to make knowledge claims; and the methods and/or instrumentation, or approaches, used to generate the evidence, itself variously construed, for those claims.[48] We view most disciplines as having a set of core ideas or concepts that serve as building blocks, or stepping-off points, for more advanced learning, both within the discipline and in other domains of knowledge.[49]

Typologies of disciplines, such as the well-known Becher-Biglan scheme, which classifies disciplines as hard or soft and pure or applied, identify some differences across disciplines in the structuring of knowledge. Hard-pure disciplines, such as physics, for example, see knowledge as concerned with universals and simplification and as cumulative; in these disciplines, there are clear criteria and consensus about what counts as evidence. In contrast, soft-pure disciplines value particulars and complication, and practitioners do not agree on which problems are most important to address and what methods are best.[50] Disciplines thus vary too in their representations of exemplary scholarship. For example, if a problem is believed to have a single right answer, the simplest route to that answer will be the most "elegant" solution. If, on the other hand, problems are viewed as addressable in multiple and different ways, then unearthing a heretofore unseen angle on a topic of interest could be inherently interesting and important.

The point here, of course, is not to argue that any one discipline's approach is superior to that of others. Rather, we contend that students benefit from exposure to *any* discipline's approach to structuring knowledge and that they can also capitalize on the nature of a known disciplinary structure to advance their learning in other disciplines or in settings that privilege disciplinary mixes. In learning a particular disciplinary structure thoroughly, students are positioned to anticipate encounters with new disciplines and to recognize that they need to learn them deeply or else rely on experts in those fields to guide their way through.

Every discipline can make a claim to the social value of the knowledge that its practitioners create, codify, and disseminate to students and to society. What is important for students to comprehend is that knowledge is not a random list of knowledge bits (e.g., facts) but rather a set of patterned regularities reflecting core ideas that recur via elaboration and critique.[51] As Jerome Bruner noted more than fifty years ago, "The teaching and learning of structure, rather than simply the mastery of facts and techniques, is at the center of the classic problem of [knowledge] transfer."[52]

Another argument for shifting attention away from learning in service to work and toward preparation for daily life pertains to civic life. In his book *Flunking Democracy*, legal scholar Michael Rebell makes a convincing case that young Americans are not being prepared to participate in our democracy. Productive citizenship, he argues, requires that Americans understand our government institutions and how they work and that they feel empowered to vote and participate in civic and community organizations. But voting rates and other metrics for civic engagement are low, and political apathy is widespread. Moreover, civic engagement is distributed unevenly in the population, with the poor and people of color feeling that they have less of a voice in public affairs and displaying more distrust of government institutions than those who are more advantaged.

Rebell sees education as the central mechanism our society has for ensuring that young people are prepared to be competent and active citizens in our democracy. As education is primarily defined as a state responsibility in our nation's constitution and those of the fifty states, he has directed his attention to the state and federal courts as sites for holding states accountable for providing K–12 schools and school districts with the resources they need to meet their responsibilities for civic preparation. Rebell is the lead attorney in a federal lawsuit alleging that the state of Rhode Island has violated these students' constitutional civil rights by not providing them with the skills they need to function productively as civic participants.[53]

Yet the division of labor between K–12 education and postsecondary education is arbitrary, especially as more and more young people attend colleges and universities. Legal actions to compel states to provide resources for an adequate education are directed at elementary and secondary schooling because all of our states have compulsory schooling laws that require school attendance from roughly ages 6 to 17. But we should hope that going to college expands students' knowledge and worldviews in ways that make them better prepared for adult civic life. The health of our democracy depends on it. The American ideal cannot survive without a populace educated to participate in our political and community institutions.

We turn now from these lofty aspirations to the realities of where teaching lives: the US higher education system, which includes thousands of campuses and capital structures; millions of students, faculty, staff, and administrators; rapidly expanding arrays of knowledge for research, teaching, and service; processes for activating and coordinating these and other resources; and distinctive norms and cultures that make day-to-day life in colleges and universities meaningful.

The US Postsecondary Teaching Enterprise Today: Students and Faculty

Close your eyes and think about the American college. What do you see? You probably envision a bucolic campus teeming with young people milling around with backpacks, moving across a quad from one class to the next, or perhaps heading back to a dormitory or nearby off-campus apartment. You may also see faculty members—some in tweed and others perhaps in jeans—leaning back in chairs in well-appointed offices, thinking about their research and their teaching.

But American college students are probably not who you think they are. And neither are American college teachers.

The American College Student

US college students are spread across four-year, two-year, and less-than-two-year institutions.[54] Of the seventeen million students enrolled in undergraduate programs in degree-granting postsecondary institutions in the fall of 2017, about 63% were enrolled in four-year institutions and 37% in two-year or less-than-two-year institutions. The National Center for Education Statistics expects total undergraduate enrollments to grow by about 12% by 2026, with slightly faster growth in two-year enrollments than in four-year enrollments.[55]

It is common to classify colleges and universities according to institutional level (i.e., whether they offer two-year or four-year credentials) and control (i.e., public or private). Most students attend public institutions. About two-thirds of student enrollments in four-year institutions are in public colleges and universities, as are 95% of those in two-year institutions. At the turn of the twenty-first century, about 3% of undergraduates were enrolled in for-profit institutions; this figure increased to 5% in 2016, representing a moderate uptick.[56]

Level and control are fundamental institutional features, but there are many ways to describe US colleges and universities. The well-known Carnegie classification breaks them down into doctoral universities, master's colleges and universities, baccalaureate colleges, baccalaureate/associate's colleges, associate's colleges, special focus institutions, and tribal colleges.[57] A number of these categories comprise subcategories; all told, there are thirty-three Carnegie designations.[58] Other classification schemes yield similar numbers of categories, defined by internal institutional characteristics such as control, degrees offered, forms of instruction, student demographics, and institutional mission statements.[59]

We are reluctant to refer to US higher education as a system, because that term, as an ideal, implies intelligent design—not the supernatural form, of course, but at least the idea that someone thought things through in advance of their coming into being and also that someone, or some assemblage, is in charge. Public higher education within states can, to varying degrees, take the form of a system. However, the most prestigious colleges and universities in the country are private, not public, and are subject only to modest oversight by states.[60] The various segments in American higher education are stratified in the shape of a pyramid, with the most selective and prestigious institutions, serving a relatively small number of students, at the top of the pyramid and the least selective institutions, serving the masses, at the base. Historian and sociologist David Labaree has argued persuasively that this shape satisfies political demands for equal access to higher education while reserving socioeconomic advantages to those who are at the top. Though it's clear that those who attend the most elite institutions fare best in the labor market, we don't know if that's because attending an elite school produces better outcomes or because the kinds of students who select and are selected into elite schools are already on a trajectory for socioeconomic success.[61]

Part of Labaree's argument is that the strata describing the more than four thousand American postsecondary institutions expand or contract in response to market forces, most commonly by adding additional layers of mass education at the base of the pyramid, to satisfy growing demand. Total enrollments in higher education increased 131% from 1970 to 2016, and the growth was somewhat higher—163%—in the two-year sector.[62] In contrast, the US population aged 18–24 increased by just 25% over this period.[63] Even though this comparison does not account for growth in enrollments among those over the age of 25, or among international students, it's clear that growth in the demand for higher education has outstripped increases in the size of the traditional college-going population. More people than ever seek to reap the rewards of a college education.

Moreover, the college-going population has become more diverse over the past several decades, with increasing numbers and proportions of racial and ethnic minority students enrolling in two-year and four-year institutions. In 1976, 83% of domestic undergraduate students identified as white. By 2016, only 56% did, a drop spurred by sharp increases in the number and proportion of Latino college students and continued growth among students who identify as Black, Asian, or two or more races.[64] But students from underrepresented racial and ethnic backgrounds are not evenly distributed across American institutions of higher education. Whereas about 33% of white undergraduates are enrolled in a two-year institution, 39% of Black students and 47% of Latino students attend two-year schools, which are broad access, admitting almost all applicants regardless of prior academic preparation.[65] As of 2017, among four-year undergraduates, 58% of those identifying a racial or ethnic group are white only, and 42% are students of color. In contrast, two-year and less-than-two-year institutions are now "majority minority," as 51% identify as students of color and 49% as white only.[66]

The undergraduate population is becoming more diverse in other ways, as well. Increasingly, students are enrolling at ages older than the "traditional" ages of 18–22. In the fall of 2017, about one-third of American undergraduates were 25 or older; that was true both of students in four-year and in two-year institutions.

These older college students have complex lives outside of school. Among participants in the 2015–16 National Postsecondary Student Aid Study aged 19–23 at the end of 2015, approximately 8% were financially independent from their parents and had dependents, mostly children, living with them. Among older college students, the figures are sharply higher, with 32% of students aged 24–29 and 63% of those aged 30–39 reporting one or more dependents.[67]

Another aspect of current college students is that they may be ready for college, but not college ready. Domestic undergraduates are the product of an American elementary and secondary schooling system that is routinely criticized for its inability to educate children and youth adequately. The configuration of unpredictable personal and school resources, a weak technology for teaching and learning, and ambiguous and conflicting educational goals has overwhelmed education policy makers, practitioners, and researchers for generations.

For reasons beyond their control, many students emerge from high school ill prepared for the traditional academic demands of college. The institutions in which they enroll take on the responsibility of educating them, but there may be a gap between the students they desire and the ones they serve. A 2012 federal survey found that only 15% of first-year undergraduates enrolled in private, four-year institutions offering a doctorate—a relatively selective type of institution—had ever enrolled in a remedial course in college. In public two-year institutions, the figure was

40%. Across all institutional types, 33% of first-year undergraduates reported having taken a remedial course in college.[68] Even if some of these remedial enrollments are due to overzealous application of placement tests and other screening tools, US colleges and universities must devote significant resources—an estimated $7 billion per year—to help get their incoming students up to speed.[69] Some students never escape remediation and drop out. More commonly, though, students enrolled in remedial classes simply are diverted away from college-level coursework during their first semesters of enrollment.[70]

One last feature worth noting is that college students today study at a distance. Whereas most of our images of college continue to draw on brick-and-mortar residential or commuter institutions, distance education has become much more prominent. In the fall of 2017, about one-third of US undergraduates enrolled in two-year or four-year institutions took at least one distance education course. This figure was about the same for the four-year and two-year sectors. In both cases, about 13–14% of undergraduates were enrolled exclusively in distance education courses and 19–20% were enrolled in some distance education courses. The vast majority of students taking distance education courses were not enrolled in institutions that are exclusively distance education.[71]

The American College Faculty

These changes in the college-going population are accompanied by a different kind of dynamic in the professoriate. About three-quarters of the faculty in US degree-granting postsecondary institutions in the early 1970s were full-time. Just a quarter century ago, in 1995, 42% of instructional positions in US postsecondary institutions were full-time, tenure-track positions, and 41% were part-time positions. The proportion of faculty who are full-time, tenure-track has shrunk to about 29% today.[72]

In 2011, there were about 1.5 million total instructional positions at all postsecondary institutions nationwide. Of these, 29% were full-time, tenure-track positions and about 20% were full-time contingent (i.e., non-tenure-track) positions. One-half of all instructional positions in 2011 were part-time positions. Overall, then, more than 70% of instructional positions in US institutions are filled by contingent faculty, although some of these may have recurring, multiyear appointments. The figures are even starker if we count the roughly 350,000 graduate students employed part time as graduate teaching assistants outside of medical schools. If we treat graduate teaching assistants as holding instructional positions, 77% of instructional positions in US higher education are held by contingent faculty in the form of full-time contingent faculty, part-time faculty, and graduate teaching assistants. This is likely an upper bound, as not all graduate teaching assistants are the instructors of record in the courses they teach and the federal IPEDS data that are the primary source of information do not distinguish between graduate teaching assistants who are instructors of record and those who assist in the classroom in other ways (e.g., by grading or leading discussion sections).[73]

These figures represent a continuing shift in the nature of the professoriate in the United States. What we have seen is a displacement of full-time positions characterized by long-term relationships between institutions and faculty, a hallmark of the tenure system. Such positions increasingly have been supplanted by part-time positions and full-time positions that do not provide long-term job security.

This is especially true in the two-year sector, where part-time contingent positions represent more than 66% of all instructional positions. In contrast, among four-year institutions, part-time contingent faculty are 40% of all instructional positions.[74]

While faculty headcounts tell part of the story, instructors with differing kinds of appointments may have differing teaching responsibilities, often indicated by the number of courses and students they teach. The US Government Accountability Office examined teaching patterns at four-year public institutions in Georgia, North Dakota, and Ohio between 2014 and 2016. Because most contingent faculty are part time, they teach a smaller fraction of courses than their headcount might indicate. In these three states, contingent faculty—including full-time and part-time contingent faculty and instructional graduate assistants—represented 55–63% of the instructional positions in public four-year schools, but they taught 45–54% of the courses offered and 50–60% of the total student credit hours taught.[75] The four-year public institutions in Georgia, North Dakota, and

Ohio rely on contingent faculty extensively in the teaching of developmental (e.g., below the freshman level) and lower-level (e.g., freshman- or sophomore-level) classes. Contingent faculty taught 59–93% of developmental courses at these institutions and 54–74% of lower-level courses. In contrast, contingent faculty taught 37–53% of the upper-level courses offered at four-year public institutions in these three states.[76]

The trend toward part-time and other contingent faculty is relevant to policies and practices regarding improving undergraduate teaching. The fundamental problem is that part-time faculty typically are not full institutional "citizens" in the institutions they serve, often barred through custom or regulation from access to the same resources full-time faculty do. Kevin Eagan, Ellen Stolzenberg, Jennifer Lozano, Melissa Aragon, Maria Suchard, and Sylvia Hurtado's 2013–14 survey of undergraduate teaching faculty found that of the nearly twenty-six hundred part-time faculty they surveyed at 168 institutions, more than a quarter did not have access either to a private office or shared office space, and about 60% were not provided access to a personal computer or to a phone or voicemail. Only about one in seven part-time undergraduate teaching faculty reported receiving professional development funds.[77] Moreover, contingent faculty often get little advance notice about course assignments, which makes it harder for them to prepare for the courses they are to teach. Nearly 40% of part-time faculty in public four-year colleges reported getting less than a month's advance notice about course assignments, and the modal amount of advance notice across all institutional types was one, two, or three months.[78]

Our work is cut out for us: beset by public and policy maker demands to become more efficient and responsive, higher education institutions are shaving costs, and their leaders are claiming organizational agility by increasing institutional reliance on contingent faculty. But the system, overall, has given little attention to the question of how best to prepare these faculty to teach. At the same time, these contingent faculty and their tenure-track colleagues, many educated at elite institutions, face rapidly expanding and diversifying student populations with interests, goals, and needs that differ, more and more, from their own. If leaders and policy makers are serious about improving teaching, their efforts will need to address the classroom practices of this expanding professional corps and in light of the learning needs and goals of today's students.

We have now pointed to a number of problems that together create a troubling picture: the future of American higher education is less than assured. As the economy evolves, consumers of higher education question whether postsecondary credentials can truly grant access to a secure and prosperous future. In a word, public trust and confidence in our postsecondary system is waning. Yet at the same time, desire and demand for college degrees run high. As the tension between these two strains of the public voice has intensified, so has the public's tendencies to conflate degrees (i.e., earned credentials and certifications) and substantive learning (i.e., the knowledge and skills gained in college). The two are not the same thing. Ideally, they would be aligned, but the messy and complex realities of education in our volatile times are not only likely to prevent that but also at times to push them farther apart.

Growing realization of this gap has inspired policy makers to question the meaning and validity of the college degree and to ask whether our students are learning what they need to in order to be productive adult workers and citizens. Doubts raised by analysis of CLA data as to whether college is adequately contributing to US students' critical thinking skills have further fed these concerns, as have international markers of postsecondary success: other countries are doing a better job of improving their college attendance rates than is the United States. Still more worrisome are OECD data indicating that in the United States, young adults display literacy and numeracy skills that are undistinguished. As costs of college attendance rise, so do concerns about higher education's quality and functioning, all in a time of growing societal need and equally high demand for knowledge that promotes the social good.

Policy Responses: Where's College Teaching?

These patterns suggest that there's trouble ahead, for the economy, for society, and for higher education. Thus it is no surprise that a variety of proposals for changes to our current system of higher education have been made, many more than we can begin to account for here, offering solutions to any number of perceived problems. In this section, we highlight several proposals for change that have, in recent years, captured the public's and policy makers' attention, each representative of a broader reform category. Though neither exhaustive nor mutually exclusive, the broad groupings provide a sense of the range of policy and entrepreneurial activity currently in play. We refer to these three classes of proposed reform to the current state of education as powering it up, staying the course, and not least, blowing it up. The "it" in each refers to the current state of higher education. None, in our view, promises success. Pointedly, none addresses teaching as central to the student experience in general and to students' learning of subject matter in particular. We introduce an alternative perspective, albeit less glossy and dramatic, at the end of this chapter.

Powering It Up

We say that those higher education reformers championing technology for learning are seeking to "power it up," and refer to adherents, metaphorically, as "techno-optimists." Some in this group focus on technology as promising a "rebundling" of the disciplines, the curriculum, or other features of academic knowledge. Others promise to expand any one faculty member's reach, which would call for a teacher having to address the needs of more students than any one teacher could. Still others promise that technology can increase the efficiency of student learning through data analytics. Technological change in contemporary society can be swift and decisive, and it's tempting to imagine higher education as a target for the kind of disruptive innovation that has led to remodeling of other enterprises—retail shopping, for example, or news and communications.

Institutions compete for scarce resources—students, talented faculty, and dollars, to name just a few—and new technologies may allow for more efficient uses of these resources. But potential advantages can overshadow points of slippage, including on major issues of mission and policy. Technology, for example, can't tell us what the purpose(s) of higher education *should* be, but if we know what we value, technology may help us create campuses, programs, and relationships that reflect our values, possibly at lower cost.

The arguments that the techno-optimists offer are cheerful and relentless in the belief that technological change—for example, the modern internet, artificial intelligence, and big data—will fundamentally transform what higher education will look like in the near term. They emphasize vocational outcomes and preparation for work and frequently attend to learning—but not to teachers and teaching.

Kevin Carey is perhaps the most strident of this group. He espouses a radical individualization in higher education, predicated on individual differences in what he refers to as "neural patterns" in the functioning of the brain. Technological advances in big data and artificial intelligence, he says, will enable providers of higher education to customize students' learning experiences. It's a sophisticated form of computerized adaptive learning in which machines quickly gauge students' responses to educational stimuli and respond to students' histories of success and failure by providing feedback to students and selecting the new content to which they should be exposed.

We worry that it also is pop neuroscience, a dream more so than a grounded possibility. A small bit of knowledge, coupled with high hopes and calls for deep investments, can be dangerous, especially when it feels like anything is better than standing pat. The fact is that at this time, education researchers have but limited knowledge about the links between the physical features of the brain and student learning.[79]

Although we know, for example, that socioeconomic status is related to physical features of children's brain development, such as the thickness of the cerebral cortex and the volume of white matter in portions of the brain that support executive function, and although advances in neuroimaging promise continued strides in mapping the functioning of the brain (it already is possible to see patterns in brain activity and connectivity associated with learning tasks), that is a far cry from claims that a particular pattern represents particular knowledge.[80] Technologies for identifying and tracking the array of thoughts that individual students may have as they engage with new materials have not yet been developed; instructional protocols for use of such technologies are not yet on the horizon. Carey's vision of college as highly individualized on-line learning experiences might well be enacted in the future—but probably not in the first half of this century. Relying on it now as a guide to address the range of pressing concerns we've laid out is not, in our view, a viable near-term strategy.

Ryan Craig drinks from the same well as Kevin Carey. In *College Disrupted: The Great Unbundling of Higher Education*, Craig champions technological advances as the key not only to improved student learning but also to the system by which individuals can be matched to jobs.[81] Like Carey, he foresees a highly individualized stream of instruction, noting that "combining adaptive learning with competency-based learning is the killer app of online education."[82] The content of higher education, he argues, is currently bundled into large "modules" that represent discrete functions—remedial coursework, general education coursework, and the more advanced courses that comprise a college major. But this bundling, he adds, is inefficient, as it blocks students from access to the specific modules that are of most value to them and plumps their course schedules with courses they neither want nor need.

For Craig, an "unbundled" education will consist of smaller learning modules that engage students and provide them with learning challenges calibrated to what they already know as well as help in addressing those challenges. Like the most popular computer games, these smaller modules will provide students with rewards and recognition that instill motivation to master difficult subject matter. According to Craig, gamification, coupled with adaptive learning and timely and customized help and driven by data on student performance, will yield learning gains that far outstrip those pursued in the traditional face-to-face classroom. Moreover, on-line learning technologies can record information about learning modules and the competencies that students have mastered, bringing a college transcript to life for employers seeking to hire well-prepared students.

The endgame Craig envisions is an information system that will "incorporate intelligent, data-driven portfolio applications that tag student work with competency metadata and dynamically create portfolios for each job." In brief, the curriculum and transcript will become as one, as curricula, majors, and courses as we know them come undone; most of the knowledge that is now conveyed by them will be dropped and only the most essential bits retained, configured in light of students' interests and employers' needs. This picture, of course, misses a sense of the structure of disciplinary knowledge as an entity incorporating distinctive ideas that are fluid and interconnected and revealed at multiple levels of complexity. Engaging with disciplinary knowledge and working across disciplines are more complex learning tasks than Craig's predictions allow.

In contrast to Craig, Richard DeMillo is largely indifferent to what is taught in college, though he believes that whatever that is can be done better. In his book *Revolution in Higher Education*, DeMillo argues that technological innovations such as artificial intelligence can level the playing field, providing students access to higher education regardless of their socioeconomic status or prior academic performance.[83] Drawing on cognitive science research, he suggests that we can design instructional tools that can increase the likelihood that students will retain what they've learned, moving information from working memory into long-term memory. Our success in doing so, he argues, may depend on how well technology can simulate effective face-to-face teaching. Can the virtues of personal attention, as ideals of classroom interaction, be simulated so as to support repeated presentation of digestible information and provide frequent assessment and feedback to the student? Only the market can determine this, DeMillo believes.

The resulting increase in productivity, he adds, could easily lead to shifts in faculty responsibilities. "A single professor must be able to touch tens of thousands of students at a time," he states, which can only happen if much of what faculty currently do in the name of instruction is delegated to other college and university staff.[84] But beyond this reconstruction of teaching roles and responsibilities, only technology can increase the reach of a single professor, ideally to the point that each professor is in essence tutoring thousands of students one-on-one. Whether this is possible is not clear; big data and artificial intelligence, he notes, have not yet addressed the problem of scaling up a personalized college experience to the masses.

These three authors' ideas, exemplary of many other technology enthusiasts, are provocative, but their claims are subject to question. First, the proposed innovations are predicated on technological changes yet to be realized. They are more persuasive as forecasts of what higher education might look like several decades from now than as recipes and toolkits for the present day. Reallocating the current funds directed at students' needs toward the development of technologies whose viability and future effectiveness is unassured is risky. Certainly, many administrative activities central to institutional functioning today could be carried out more efficiently with appropriate investments in technology, and technological change *can* reduce costs, though this is by no means guaranteed.[85]

Second, although the proliferation of on-line programs, courses, and modules acclaimed by the techno-optimists may have opened up opportunities for nontraditional learners, these can have mixed, and sometimes disturbing, consequences for undergraduates.[86] In a series of studies, higher education researchers Di Xu and Shanna Smith Jaggars found that students enrolled in an online section of a course were less likely to persist in the course and received a lower final course grade than students enrolled in a face-to-face section.[87] Males, younger students, Black students, and those with lower grade point averages were even more likely to withdraw from and to earn a lower grade in online sections, suggesting that on-line education was in many respects especially harmful for the most vulnerable undergraduates.[88]

Third, as we have already suggested, the economics of online education are not straightforward. Economist Caroline Hoxby has found that online postsecondary education is not substantially less expensive than traditional face-to-face education and that the economic returns to online postsecondary education are overshadowed by the direct costs incurred by individuals and the social costs borne by governments.[89]

Staying the Course

Standing in stark contrast to the techno-optimists are the defenders, theorists of reform that urge educators and learners, literally, to "stay the course," thus casting reform as "antireform." The narrow vocational focus espoused by the techno-optimists grates on defenders of liberal education, who envision a broader set of purposes to higher education. In their view, higher education is about the search for meaning in life and the cultivation of habits of mind that allow individuals to think critically about the world and how they might act in and on it. These values are espoused by contemporary writers as disparate as Wesleyan University president Michael S. Roth, essayist William Deresiewicz, and journalist and author Fareed Zakaria, among many others.[90] Roth is a particularly articulate spokesperson for this view, contrasting it sharply with what he refers to as radical instrumentalism, which position higher education in service to the economy.[91] Technology itself is neutral, he argues; what matters is what students are asked and invited to learn. Drawing on the ideas of W. E. B. Du Bois and John Dewey, he claims that the meaning of actions in the world arises from the critical thinking that is at the heart of a liberal education.[92]

Embedded in this view is a critique of the rampant consumerism in higher education often linked to the techno-optimists. Institutions of higher education do need students to survive (though calling them "customers" is jarring for those who yearn for college to yield higher learning). But the defenders of liberal education contend that giving students exactly what they want, as many technology enthusiasts seek to do, is counterproductive. Encountering new ideas that differ from what one has learned from experience may be uncomfortable. Worse, the fact that faculty are assessed frequently on the basis of course evaluations can lead to a trade-off in which faculty offer a curriculum that is relatively free of challenges in exchange for the high student evaluations that promote their job security. And at the level of the institution, focusing too narrowly on what local employers say they want and need may sacrifice a trajectory of long-term learning for knowledge and skills with a short shelf life.

Roth and other defenders of liberal education want all students to experience "the life of the mind," since in the long run that experience evokes the personal and social good. Habits of mind encoded in deep study of the liberal arts and sciences need not be decoupled from careers; liberal education can assist young people both in choosing a career that is imbued with meaning and mastering the practical skills needed to succeed in that career. Adherents of liberal education often view careers as experiences in lives; careers can be mindfully chosen and cultivated toward a crafting of the social good. One lives a career inasmuch as one lives a life. Roth refers to this as "pragmatic liberal education" and with other defenders points to the ways in which a liberal education prepares individuals for a lifetime of learning.[93]

This claim about the purpose of higher education, emphasizing the way liberal education cultivates humanity, is of course far from new, but it takes a slightly different form in what is sometimes referred to as "late modernity."[94] It may well be that the defenders' distancing of liberal education from instrumental job, career, industrial, and economic concerns has already positioned their case as lost in the court of public opinion. Despite insiders' efforts to promote higher education as an opportunity to initiate or deepen engagement with the life of the mind, the fact is that most young people go to college to acquire credentials essential to getting a good job. Sociologist Paul Attewell makes the point that American college students are not really academically adrift; rather, they are strategic in pursuing vocational goals that differ from those of their professors.[95]

Blowing It Up

Another reform proposal, quite different from that of the techno-optimists and the defenders and currently voiced by the economist Bryan Caplan, maintains that students should bypass higher education and that employers should ignore postsecondary credentials, thereby in effect arguing for "blowing up" American higher education overall. In his book *The Case against Education,* Caplan goes beyond arguing that limited learning is taking place in college, claiming that with few exceptions, students learn virtually nothing in college that contributes to their workplace productivity.[96] Employers reward highly educated workers, he claims, largely because education signals the presence of desirable workforce skills and habits that are already present before students enter college. Citing Arum and Roksa's claims, Caplan adds a dollop of evidence from the learning sciences on transfer, a topic we take up in the next section. He appeals to common sense in contending that much of what is learned in school, excluding basic literacy and numeracy skills, is soon forgotten and has little connection to adult work. Schools and colleges, he contends, continue to teach esoteric subjects in the hopes that what students learn will transfer to the workplace, despite evidence that this kind of transfer of knowledge is exceedingly rare and unpredictable.

Critics of Caplan have pointed out that he is single-mindedly focused on schooling's contributions to workplace productivity, a narrow conception of the purpose of schooling. As we have already noted, debates about the purposes of schooling date back to the founding of American society, and there is no national consensus on our policy goals for education.[97] For Caplan, what is learned in school is relevant only to the extent that it prepares an individual for work. Thus, vocational education, cast narrowly, might be defensible, but the vast majority of school subjects—including history, government, foreign languages, and the arts—are "ossified" and at best a route to a hobby, not a career.

Commonalities and Differences in Reform Strategies

The contrast between Carey and Craig, on the one hand, and Caplan, on the other, could not be more clear. All three see a tight coupling of higher education and the labor market. But Carey and Craig claim that the connection lies in the specific skills and competencies that students acquire in college, which can then be certified through microcredentials and portfolios of student work. Credentialing is central to both their views. In contrast, Caplan, who believes that virtually nothing of value is learned in college, sees credentials as but crude signals of the skills and competencies that employers want in their workers. Neither side has much patience for the less vocational features of college life, such as learning broadly about the world and deeply about one's self, coming to appreciate the diversity of human knowledge, and preparing for citizenship and service for the social good.

The defense of such learning falls to those who promote liberal education, seeking to stay that course; many in this group believe that faith in technology is misplaced. Their argument is not so much that technology is harmful (although it might be) but rather that it misses the point. Instead, these reformers believe that technology is a means to an end and that the major task at hand is figuring out what that end is. Once we've agreed on what we value, they argue, we can imagine what the content of higher education should consist of and how best to undertake the teaching and facilitate the learning of subjects that matter.

As a society, we can hope that higher education will promote learning for both life and career—that it will motivate students to become better, wiser, more thoughtful persons and also help them create and benefit from successful careers. For the techno-optimists, these educational aims overlap: being successful in the labor market *is* being a better person. One's productive role in the economy trumps all. Individuals move from job to job not because of a clash of values but rather because the skill demands of the economy dictate job movement. For the defenders of liberal education, the knowledge and skills cultivated through study of rich and difficult disciplinary concepts are valuable in and of themselves and are bound to lead to the satisfaction won from insight.

Is there a common ground? One key question is whether technology can be configured to promote the goals of a liberal education. The Minerva Project, which launched in 2012 with a $25 million seed investment from Benchmark Capital, seeks to be a proof of concept. Minerva subsequently partnered with the Keck Graduate Institute of the Claremont Colleges to offer a four-year bachelor's degree in five majors: social sciences, computational sciences, natural sciences, arts and humanities, and business.[98] Minerva's curriculum seeks to provide students with practical knowledge undergirded by the liberal arts, paying particular attention to core competencies in critical thinking, creative thinking, effective communication, and effective interactions, which in turn are represented in approximately one hundred habits of mind and foundational concepts. Each course in the curriculum, and indeed each lesson in each course, is designed to engage students in what Minerva's creators refer to as "fully active learning" of the outlined habits of mind and foundational concepts. In the first year, this is accomplished through a set of four cornerstone courses. In the second and third years of study, this process is reinforced through core and concentration courses in the students' majors. In the final year, students pursue a capstone project, take remaining electives, and participate in two senior tutorials, modeled on the tutorials in the Oxbridge tradition.

Minerva is distinctive in the design and delivery of its curriculum. Every course is offered on line in a seminar format, and each class has no more than twenty students; the school has no physical campus, and students rotate among seven cities during their four years of study. Each course seeks to capitalize on the science of learning, drawing on it to design on-line classroom activities that promote comprehension, reasoning, memory, and pattern perception. Minerva prohibits its faculty from lecturing, and memorization does not figure largely in the learning process. The on-line Active Learning Forum facilitates instructors' delivery of lesson plans, maintaining a video repository of each student's class participation that instructors can use to evaluate student performance and provide written feedback. Courses are designed by teams and undergo extensive review, and lesson plans are highly structured, ensuring comparability across different sections of the same course. The largely full-time faculty, hired initially for a one-year term and then offered a renewable three-year appointment based on their performance, undergoes an intensive month-long training to learn how to use the Active Learning Forum and its tools, delivering lessons to peers and students and receiving feedback on their performance before "going live" in the classroom.

We suggest that this is probably not, as the subtitle of the book-cum-sales-pitch describing Minerva's accomplishments to date extols, "the future of higher education." Minerva may indeed take its place as an elite niche institution, but it is hard to see how it could be scalable in American higher education. Because Minerva is so selective—admitting approximately 2% of its applicants—its students are extraordinarily well prepared for an instructional delivery system that demands high levels of engagement.[99] Moreover, Minerva's efforts to have a global presence have yielded a student body that is far from representative of young Americans. As of fall 2017, there was but 1 Black or African student enrolled among Minerva's 468 undergraduates and just 5 Latino students. More than three-quarters of the undergraduate enrollees were nonresident aliens.[100]

As reform proposals continue to be put forward—the innovation window remains wide open—we note just how little attention the trends we've described here give to teaching. There is, to be sure, some attention to learning, and educators continue to debate who is to learn what and why. Teaching is taken for granted, and college teachers rendered largely invisible. This, in our view, is a serious mistake.

Why does teaching matter for innovations like those we've described? Teaching matters because it is deeply entwined with most people's learning of subject matter. Few people learn all they need to know, as deeply as needed, without a teacher joining them mindfully, following the ins and outs of their perceiving, thinking, feeling, imagining, and questioning of the subject under study. As a guide and intellectual mentor, a teacher watches closely what learners do with new knowledge; they help learners discern problems and obstacles, possibilities, resources, new thoughts; they nudge, correct, and support with an eye to learning in process, including ways to ignite it.

Creators of the technologies we have described have promised to approximate this vision of good teaching more fully and affordably than it is at present. We question their claim for two reasons: First, we are unable to locate data indicating that the technologies are sufficiently developed to do this without leaving out something of import. They may fail to grasp and share the complexity of what it means to understand a subject (mathematics, history, philosophy) as subject-matter experts do, much less what's entailed in helping novices develop comparable expertise or get started on the road to so doing. And second, they may not address *all* learners, with their particular needs and unique background knowledge, thus raising serious equity concerns. Both, in our view, are central to good teaching. It is possible that some of the technologies described will, at some point, be functional, but probably within a limited number of niches.

But it's unlikely that any one, or any one set, will be able to respond in comprehensive ways to the larger and rapidly diversifying ecology of higher education providers. This is not to say that technology cannot be better interwoven into higher education as we know it, strengthening its best-functioning and most promising parts; nor does it mean that ineffective features of US postsecondary education should not be pared away. It does mean that we need to tread more carefully than many of the proposed reforms would.

Good College Teaching Matters

Does college teaching matter? "Good teaching matters. It *really* matters," write Matthew Mayhew and his fellow authors of *How College*

Affects Students, the third of a renowned series of research syntheses. "Across all outcomes reviewed in this volume (including those related to persistence and degree attainment), results confirmed that good teaching is the primary means through which institutions affect students. In addition, high-quality instruction was generally more effective in promoting the learning, cognitive, and educational attainment outcomes of students from historically underserved populations than those from majority groups."[101]

We could just take their word for it, but we want to provide evidence for this claim, which is so fundamental to our argument. First, we draw on the literature on K–12 teaching and argue that the patterns of teacher and teaching effects that researchers have found should apply to postsecondary teachers and teaching as well. Second, we point to an influential meta-analysis about college teaching practices and student performance in the science, technology, engineering, and mathematics (STEM) fields, showing that teaching practices shape how much students learn. Finally, we provide a particular case study of a college teacher's influence on the lives of his students. Together, these details provide additional support for the claim that good college teaching really matters.

K-12 Teacher and Teaching Effects

Starting in the 1970s, labor economists and economists of education turned to K–12 schooling as a site for studying a fundamental analytic problem: how can we estimate a worker's productivity independent of his or her wages? Theories assumed that employers paid workers proportional to their productivity, but there were few direct measures of worker productivity. The economists' insight was that the productivity of K–12 classroom teachers, as workers, could be estimated by their effects on their students' learning. Looking at changes over time in students' performance on standardized tests, they found that some teachers were more effective at boosting test scores than others, a finding that came to be described as "teacher effects."[102]

Research on teacher effects gained momentum in the late 1990s and early 2000s, especially with the passage of the landmark federal No Child Left Behind act, which obliged states to test virtually all of their third to eighth grade students annually in English language arts and mathematics. The finding that some teachers were more successful at raising their students' test scores than others was the centerpiece of a variety of policy initiatives that sought to identify high- and low-performing teachers by using complex statistical models and to reward or punish these teachers as appropriate. Without doubt, there were questions about the ability of these models to identify an individual teacher's "productivity," including whether test scores were an appropriate measure of what teachers sought to accomplish in the classroom, the ability of the statistical models to take account of the fact that different teachers taught different batches of students, and how precisely the models could locate a teacher in relation to other teachers. The algorithms for calculating teacher "value-added" have occasionally been subject to legal challenges, some of which have been successful and others not. But few observers have questioned the notion that some teachers are more skilled than others and that those differences can have consequences for their students' later academic experiences and adult lives.

The pinnacle (or nadir, depending on one's point of view) of value-added research to date is a longitudinal analysis of the long-term consequences of a student's being taught by a high value-added teacher. Economists Raj Chetty, John Friedman, and Jonah Rockoff used school district data and administrative records to examine teacher value-added effects on college attendance, the probability of becoming a teen parent, annual income, retirement savings, and the quality of the neighborhood in which a student lives. Based on their findings of value-added effects on annual income at age 28, they estimate that replacing a teacher in the bottom 5% of the value-added distribution with an average teacher would boost the lifetime earnings of a class of about thirty students by about $250,000.[103]

More recent research has shown that K–12 teachers also can influence student attributes beyond test scores and that changes in these attributes can convert into longer-term advantages or disadvantages. Teachers who are good at raising their students' test scores may not be as skilled at boosting "noncognitive" attributes, as indexed by absences from school, suspensions, and course grades (for high school students), or academic self-efficacy, happiness in class, or classroom behavior.[104] The implication is that K–12 teachers differ from one to another in how they influence their students, and these differences are largely not captured by differences in easily measured teacher characteristics, such as the types of teaching credentials they hold or the length of time they've been teaching.[105] Although postsecondary teaching differs from K–12 teaching in ways that we discuss in detail, it is not a huge leap to assume that the same dynamics are in play: college teachers differ in their contributions to undergraduate students' learning and development, and having a string of good teachers is likely to pay off in both the short and long run. These insights from K–12 education research offer hope that cultivating good college teaching can pay dividends in what and how much undergraduate students learn.

College Teaching Practice and Student Learning

Assessing how college teaching practices influence students' academic performance is challenging. Some of the standardization observed in K–12 schooling—common subject-matter assessments administered widely to students and the relative ease of linking student performance to particular teachers—has no parallel in higher education. We won't dwell on the challenges but instead highlight a complex study that addresses them in thoughtful ways. In 2014, a team of researchers led by biologist Scott Freeman of the University of Washington published a meta-analysis of 225 different studies that contrasted two different college teaching styles in undergraduate STEM courses, termed "traditional lecturing" and "active learning." The researchers defined active learning as engaging students "in the process of learning through activities and/or discussion in class, as opposed to passively listening to an expert. It emphasizes higher-order thinking and often involves group work."[106] Operationally, the active learning practices that are contrasted with lecturing include group problem solving, in-class personal response systems (e.g., "clickers"), peer instruction, in-class worksheets and tutorials, and studio course designs. This is a wide variety of practices, and of course lecturing is not monolithic either.

In selecting studies to analyze, the authors sought contrasts between traditional lecturing and alternative active-learning practice(s) in regularly scheduled undergraduate courses in a set of fields roughly corresponding to STEM. They chose studies in which the students were similar in the two conditions, either due to randomization or matching on prior general academic performance or a course pretest. They also limited their analyses to studies in which the instructors were similar in the two conditions, either because they were identical or randomly assigned to the course or because there were three or more instructors in each condition. Finally, they required that the assessments of student learning in the course be identical, based on either a third-party observer's judgment or the use of a random subset of questions from a common item bank. The two outcomes they considered were a measure of the average difference in student assessment performance for the traditional lecturing and active learning conditions and the percentage of students receiving either a D or an F in the course or withdrawing from it before completion (commonly referred to as the DFW rate).

The authors' analyses provide strong support for the claim that a college teaching approach emphasizing active learning can generate better academic outcomes for students than traditional lecturing. A common metric for comparing the performance of two groups is the effect size, a standardized measure of how far apart the two groups are, on average, in relation to the spread of individual performance.[107] The estimated average effect size for active learning undergraduate teaching interventions in the STEM fields was .47, which historically has been referred to as a moderately large effect.[108]

The metric for the average group difference in the percentage of D, F, and W grades is a bit more complicated, because we are talking about probabilities. The average DFW rate in traditional lecturing classes in the studies was 34% but just 22% in the active learning classes. This difference means that 55% more students in traditional lecture courses are likely to receive a D or F grade or withdraw from the class than similar students in active learning courses. The policy implications for the STEM fields are substantial, as DFW rates are a natural break in the pipeline leading to STEM majors and careers. This meta-analysis is widely cited as evidence of the power of teaching interventions to improve undergraduate learning in STEM fields, and appropriately so. As one might surmise from the description of the study, though, it provides little guidance about what specifically teachers might do in the undergraduate STEM classroom, as there is so much variability across studies in what counts as active learning (a term that by now has expanded to the point that it is nearly meaningless).[109] It nevertheless is another building block for our claim that good college teaching matters.

The "Pock Effect"

Earlier, we pointed to research by economists about the impact of particular K–12 teachers on their students' lives. An example from higher education bolsters the claim that good teaching matters. In 2012, sociologist John Pock passed away at the age of 86. He had spent most of his career at Reed College, a highly selective liberal arts college in Portland, Oregon. Historically, Reed has ranked among the highest colleges and universities in the country in the proportion of its graduates who go on to earn a doctorate, propelled by a challenging curriculum, small, conference-style classes, and a mandatory senior thesis.[110] But that doesn't explain the influence of John Pock. Over the course of his forty-three-year career at Reed, he mentored more than one hundred students writing senior theses in sociology. More than seventy of these went on to get PhD's in sociology and become professional sociologists.

This is an extraordinary accomplishment, heightened by the fact that Reed truly is an undergraduate institution, having but one small program leading to a master of arts in liberal studies. Pock never taught graduate students at Reed, and the undergraduates he mentored did not have a clear pathway to advanced study there. Stimulated by Pock's teaching, they enrolled elsewhere, at places such as the University of Chicago, University of California–Berkeley, University of Wisconsin, University of California–Santa Barbara, University of California–Los Angeles, and Stanford University, among many others.

Pock was awarded the American Sociological Association's Contributions to Teaching Award in 1982, and in 1996, three of his former students edited a festschrift entitled *Social Differentiation and Social Inequality: Essays in Honor of John C. Pock*. In 2007, Pock's former students established an endowed professorship at Reed in his honor, pledging more than $1.5 million to establish the chair.

It seems trite to reduce Pock's contributions to a series of anecdotes, but there's little doubt that he had a profound impact on the intellectual lives of a wide range of individuals—some now retired, and others still in the bloom of their careers. "John combined the highest and most demanding standards of scholarship with a fierce loyalty and passion for his students," wrote sociologist Neil Fligstein of the University of California–Berkeley in an obituary published in the American Sociological Association newsletter *Footnotes*. "John asked that each of us take responsibility for ourselves and our intellectual lives. He challenged us to take ourselves seriously if we wanted others to take us seriously."[111] Martina Morris, now a sociology professor at the University of Washington, recalled Pock's use of the conference method as a tool to engage students in presenting an author's position as revealed through a text assigned to the class and then challenging it. Having each student bring a precis of a different chapter of a text is "extremely efficient," she said, "but you are now totally dependent on other people. It's a little bit of field work, participatory observation, where you say, 'Oh, this is what Marx means when he's talking about the division of labor. This is what Durkheim means by the difference between mechanical solidarity and organic solidarity.' I've never run across anybody who has taught that way since. It was eye-opening."[112]

Even his students who did not pursue graduate study in sociology never forgot the lessons they learned while studying with him. "John treated his students as graduate students," said Matthew Bergman, now a successful attorney, philanthropist, and entrepreneur in Seattle. "There was no coddling involved. At the conclusion of my thesis-writing process, I foolishly asked John what he thought of it. He said it was 'boring shit.' John was right: It was. But that kind of unsparing honesty and intellectual integrity helped me—working through John—to develop additional academic work and get several [legal] articles published. I asked him what I thought of one piece, and he said, 'Well, that was pretty good.' With that kind of honesty, I knew that it really was pretty good, and I knew that I had achieved something I hadn't thought possible."[113]

In a separate interview, Bergman said, "Reed did nothing to prepare me for law school—with its intellectual drudgery—but it did everything to prepare me for a career in law." He noted how his studies at Reed, including his time with John Pock, taught him to analyze arguments from multiple sides, a critical skill for an attorney best known for negotiating a nationwide $5.1 billion asbestos settlement with Owens Corning and a $4.3 billion asbestos settlement with the multinational oil company Halliburton.[114]

The memories of John Pock's teaching shared by his students are just one more piece of evidence that good teaching matters in higher education, much as a variety of writings have shown that it does in K–12 education.

The Centrality of Teaching

Virtually all American institutions of higher education engage in significant teaching of undergraduate and, where appropriate, graduate/professional students, even though the fame and public status of many schools are associated with research. Although we strongly applaud American higher education's contributions to the greater public good via institutions' research and public service missions, we think it odd that teaching remains peripheral in debates about the future of US postsecondary education. Clearly the debates address costs, the value of the college degree, economic impact, and the usefulness of what students learn, but teaching, as a distinctive and complex professional activity and as the lifeblood of American postsecondary education, gets little attention, even though every enrolled student will be exposed to it. Although American higher education counts well over one million college teachers in its ranks, we have not developed a common vocabulary for describing good undergraduate teaching practice or a shared base of professional knowledge that allows us to identify it when we see and hear it in action. This is in spite of the fact that there is good evidence that college teaching really does matter when it comes to the learning and development of American college students.

As is often the case, though, we can draw on parallel challenges and efforts to address them in the more standardized and regulated world of K–12 education. Though these two sectors vary, our reviews of research on teaching in K–12 classrooms suggest that some of what's been learned there is applicable to higher education. In this section, we describe some of the big ideas derived from research on K–12 teaching, and we summarize what we've learned from our own long-term effort to import and shape them for college teaching. Our discussion culminates in the presentation of a framework for defining what we see as at the heart of good college teaching, which we refer to as "convergent teaching." We see this concept as offering a foothold for future research and improving teaching in higher education.

Professional Knowledge for Teaching

Efforts to professionalize K–12 teaching got a major boost in the work of psychologist Lee Shulman, who in the 1980s began writing about the knowledge needed for K–12 teaching. Among Shulman's most notable achievements is the identification of seven forms of knowledge that school teachers need to teach subject matter effectively to students. Six were already well worked out and commonly discussed by educational researchers, policy makers, and teachers, as well as broadly in the public sphere. Important both to new instructors just learning to teach and more experienced teachers, these six familiar forms included knowledge of the content or subject matter to be taught; approaches to organizing and managing classrooms (Shulman called this "general pedagogical knowledge"); curriculum and curricular materials; learners and their characteristics; educational contexts (including "workings of the group or classroom," "the governance and financing of school districts," and the "character of communities and cultures"); and broad educating aims (referred to as "educational ends, purposes, and values, and their philosophical and historical grounds"). Shulman's seventh form of knowledge for teaching, which he termed "pedagogical content knowledge," breathed new life into the study of teaching and into models for K–12 teacher professional development.

Pedagogical content knowledge represents the knowledge that teachers need to teach particular subject matter to particular learners in a particular context. The concept recognizes that good teaching cannot be reduced to a set of general teaching practices applicable equally to all subjects, students, and situations. The other six forms of knowledge give little attention to the larger issue of how to put them together and do not differentiate between general patterns (e.g., features of a population of students, curricula as broad organizing principles) and particular and contingent features (e.g., the interests, goals, and needs of students enrolled in a particular class at a particular time, the unique concerns and structures of a given discipline, a local curricular imperative and its effects on local teachers and students). Nor do the other forms of knowledge offer instructors ways of getting into students' heads, following their thoughts about what's being taught, responding to them on the basis of what they know, and helping them build out from there.

The former six forms of knowledge for teaching also are relatively discrete and disconnected; logics and means for linking them were not built into them. Pedagogical content knowledge—a broad amalgam of disciplinary knowledge, insight into what one's students know already and how they think, and facility with instructional methods—is of a different order altogether.[115] Beyond the knowledge of a subject and a teacher's general teaching skills, pedagogical content knowledge emphasizes how students come to learn particular subject-matter concepts—for example, through their existing conceptions and misconceptions, which teachers can excavate and use to advance students' understandings.

Asset-Based Pedagogies

In short order, several scholars developed a contrasting approach that challenged some of the assumptions of Shulman's exposition of professional knowledge for teaching. Collectively, these researchers sought a different balance between the knowledge taught and learned in school and the knowledge students learn in their homes and communities. Writing against the grain of Shulman's thinking, they challenged some of the assumptions of his approach to professional knowledge for teaching, offering a perspective now known as "asset-based pedagogy."

Among the first of these was educational psychologist Luis Moll, who with his colleagues developed the idea of "funds of knowledge" residing in students' households and communities.[116] Their projects trained teachers to visit students' households and interview parents to learn about family histories and their jobs and hobbies. Teachers could use the family practices revealed in these interviews as classroom resources to promote students' learning of school subjects. Introducing household funds of knowledge into the classroom motivated students via the familiarity of home and community value of this knowledge and served as a source of prior knowledge teachers could draw on in introducing their students to the less-familiar and abstract school knowledge.

Using the Southwest as their research base, Moll and his colleagues were keenly aware of the common perception that poor, immigrant families were "deprived" or "deficient," especially if the adults were fluent in Spanish but not in English. The prevailing politics—which have not budged much over the past thirty years—saw public schooling as a means for assimilating immigrants into American society, even at the cost of family linguistic and other practices that were a powerful source of identity. By creating a dialogue between teachers and parents and validating home knowledge as a school resource, the funds of knowledge projects were intended to reduce the social and political distance between home and school. Nevertheless, household and community funds of knowledge were in service to the learning of school subjects.

Others engaged Shulman more directly. For example, Gloria Ladson-Billings argued that pedagogical content knowledge shortchanged culture's role in teaching in at least two ways. First, Shulman's acknowledgment of the importance of the knowledge of learners and their characteristics and of contexts did not adequately pick up the importance of students' identities and how these identities originate in their distinctive family and community cultures. These cultures are laden with meaning, shaping ideas, values, and ways of knowing that students bring to class. In placing subject matter at the center of his framework, they argued, Shulman pushed the cultural knowledge a teacher needs to connect with her students and to advance their thinking to the margins. Second, Shulman's approach took for granted that there was consensus about the subject matter to be taught in school subjects such as literature, mathematics, and social studies. But whose knowledge counts is often contested, and formulations of good teaching that do not acknowledge community cultural knowledge, alongside disciplinary knowledge, as central to teaching are necessarily incomplete.

Ladson-Billings cast her gaze specifically on the education of Black children and youth and teaching practices that can support them. She termed her approach "culturally relevant pedagogy," a set of teaching practices designed to produce students who can achieve academically, demonstrate cultural competence, and understand and critique the existing social order. Academic achievement was explicit in Shulman's formulation, but neither cultural competence—competence in multiple language and interaction styles and pride in self and one's cultural heritage—nor a critical political and moral sensibility poising students to confront social injustice were addressed.[117]

Ladson-Billings and those who have followed her place learning the culture of one's home community on the same plane as learning the school subjects deemed legitimate by those in power. Not surprisingly, the social relations between teachers and their students are key to supporting students' identities and home cultural knowledge in her pedagogical approach.[118] Although she acknowledges school-based achievement as essential—"Students must achieve. No theory of pedagogy can escape this reality"—her main message is that it takes culturally competent teachers to produce culturally competent students.[119]

It is not surprising that culture surfaced as a central concern in scholarship about good teaching. For decades, the theories offered to explain why racial and ethnic minority students achieve at levels lower than their white counterparts have circled back to the cultural practices, values and orientations of minority communities, culminating, too vividly, in an uncritical reliance on theories of "cultural deprivation." Minority communities chafed at the implication that they were somehow "deficient" in relation to an arbitrary white, middle-class standard and that the public good would be served by assimilation processes that erased those values and practices. The problem, they argued, lay not in the attributes of poor children of color but rather in the oppressive systems of education to which they are subjected.

Over time, asset-based pedagogies have become more overtly political, challenging policies and practices that are regarded as unjust and undemocratic. A third approach, associated with literacy scholar Kris Gutiérrez, describes a collective third space that can integrate the literacy practices of the school as a formal institution and the literacy practices experienced in students' daily lives outside of school, most notably in their homes and communities.[120] By studying the tools and resources that students rely on in daily life, teachers can reconceptualize the classroom as a third space where cultural practices and prior knowledge are as valuable as disciplinary knowledge. This is more than using everyday knowledge as a scaffold for learning disciplinary knowledge, she argues. Rather, teachers orchestrating a collective third space in the classroom can instill a critical understanding of the world as it is and the world as it might be and of the physical and knowledge structures that distinguish these two worlds.

More recent discussions of the education of racial and ethnic minority populations—even the term "minority" is increasingly inappropriate, in light of the demographic changes of the past few decades—extend these efforts to view the cultures of children and youth as assets for teaching and learning. The current generation of scholars asserts a pressing need for pedagogical approaches that value the cultural practices of communities of color, in contrast to past practices that openly sought to subtract them from students' schooling.[121] "Culturally sustaining pedagogy" extends the insight that Shulman's representation of good teaching as rooted in pedagogical content knowledge was indifferent to culture in general and to the histories, experiences, and cultures of oppressed populations of students in particular.

Proponents of culturally sustaining pedagogy assume a political and moral imperative to maintain and amplify the cultural ways of being of communities of color in service to a more just society. They assert that a pluralist approach to the teaching and learning of culture in schools benefits *all* children but especially those whose linguistic traditions and cultural practices are at risk of erasure.[122] Placing the languages, literacies, and cultural practices of students of color at the center of the curriculum does, however, obscure attention to school subjects that do not map neatly onto them. Although proponents of culturally sustaining pedagogy acknowledge that the approach "strives to ensure that students gain full access to the practices associated with larger institutional and structural power as well as the tools to critique the processes of power," disciplinary knowledge gets little attention, especially when it is implicated in the reproduction of white middle-class norms that are seen as arbitrary.[123]

This is not the case in what Carol Lee refers to as "cultural modeling," a pedagogical framework for guiding students' learning of specific subject matter through channels of cultural knowledge with which they are already deeply familiar. Teaching literature to Chicago high school students, Lee and the teachers with whom she worked used everyday texts familiar to students, termed "cultural datasets," to support students' learning of disciplinary concepts and habits of mind found in "canonical" texts. For example, Chicago-born rapper Common's hip-hop song "I Used to Love H.E.R." uses the metaphor of a woman coming of age to represent the evolution of hip-hop as a musical genre. Discussions of this metaphor can prepare students for exploring the metaphor of blue eyes in Toni Morrison's novel *The Bluest Eye*.

Lee's cultural datasets both elicited students' prior cultural and personal knowledge and plumbed it for traces of core subject matter ideas, lifting these up for students' learning in language and through images with which they were already familiar. The approach, in effect, uses students' everyday knowledge and experiences as a bridge to less familiar features of disciplinary knowledge, including "the structure of the discipline, the modes of argumentation privileged, as well as habits of mind or dispositions entailed in doing the work of the discipline."[124]

Most of the examples we provide here consider culture as a source of prior knowledge and experience that can serve as a bridge to the learning of new, unfamiliar ideas and concepts. For some scholars, it is a political and moral imperative to place the ways of knowing of students' origin cultures on the same plane as "school knowledge" and to work to sustain these ways of knowing and literacies rather than treating them as misunderstandings that need to be remediated. This can be challenging to do when students' home knowledge is fundamentally at odds with the school knowledge that teachers and their disciplinary colleagues espouse, as we see in part II.

We do not seek to arbitrate among divergent forms of knowledge. Rather, we plan to lay out some teachers' efforts to bring such divergent forms of knowledge together, allowing students to identify connections between them, perhaps in the most unexpected of ways. Cultural knowledge and the social relations of the classroom have received more attention in the schooling of children and adolescents, where the links between home knowledge and school knowledge may be easier to see, but they are surely relevant to undergraduate education as well.

Convergent Teaching

We draw on all that we have summarized here to identify a set of teaching principles that undergird the image of college teaching that runs through the remainder of this book. Convergent teaching is the totality of what teachers think and do to support students' learning as they encounter and engage with new academic ideas in the context of their prior knowledge and experience. We use the term "convergent" primarily to convey a teacher's simultaneous and enveloping attention to subject matter, the learner, and the context or milieu in which learning takes place. "Convergent" also conveys joint attention to cognition, emotion, and identity as attributes of individual learners. Each component of this definition conveys something distinctive.

Our reference to "the totality of what teachers think and do" defines teaching as far more than what transpires in the time that instructors spend with their students in the classroom. It includes planning and preparation that precede the activities that transpire in the classroom, formal and informal assessment of what students have learned, and reflection on the commonplaces of teacher, student, curriculum, and context with attention to changes in each as teaching proceeds. The definition also acknowledges that the work of teaching is not always visible, as thinking cannot be observed directly, even as teachers' behaviors may be.

The phrase "support student learning" recognizes that teaching practice can take many forms, including lecturing, facilitating small-group discussion, tutoring during office hours and in hallways, monitoring and supplementing students' working through new ideas in laboratory and recitation sections, matching the content of asynchronous on-line courses to what students are likely to need, and so on. Moreover, learning, viewed as an intertwining of learners' cognitions, emotions, and identities, expands the notion of support beyond a narrow set of cognitive scaffolds to include attention to students' motivations, interests, and engagement, as well as to social and intrapersonal features of classrooms that can either strengthen or dampen these. The words "encounter" and "engage" expand further our vision of learning: it cannot be viewed simply as absorption of knowledge. Learning is a social activity involving the interaction of multiple minds, often asynchronously. What all this adds up to is that teaching, in the ideal, derives from (and responds to) students' learning as its primary concern. Clearly the social realities of the classroom and of students' lives pose challenges to linkages between them.

The phrase "new academic ideas" speaks to the primacy of the disciplines as "stuff" to be learned and, per our definition, to be taught. Finally, the phrase "context of prior knowledge and experience" refers to the role of students' prior knowledge in learning. Perhaps the best-known principle in educational psychology is that we understand new ideas by relating them to our existing knowledge and understandings.[125] As cognitive psychologist Dan Willingham puts it, "We understand new things in the context of things we already know, and most of what we know is concrete."[126] Convergent teaching treats students' extant academic, cultural, and personal knowledge as a critical starting point for and bridge to the learning of new subject matter. In this view, a critical teaching task is identifying and drawing out familiar, concrete examples from students' lives and analyzing them or comparing them with one another so as to reveal their "deep structure" or key abstract features, then bridging insights gained to discussion of structural features of new academic ideas. The approach allows the academically new and strange to resonate with the personal and familiar.

Putting these pieces together, convergent teaching requires continuous attention to core disciplinary concepts new to students, to what students already know and believe, and to a repertoire of instructional practices that can support students in moving from their existing knowledge to elaborated and abstract understandings that can be transferred, indeed with adaptation, into new contexts. With this definition of convergent teaching in mind, we proceed to part II, which offers our illustrations of good subject-matter teaching that can be a source of knowledge for under-graduate teaching improvement. Consistent with our definition, we use concrete examples of college teachers teaching disciplinary ideas, or ways of thinking, to their students to illustrate three abstract principles of practice at the heart of good college teaching.

PART II

CONVERGENT TEACHING

Having cast teaching as efforts to advance students' learning of subject matter, we now ask what good teaching of disciplinary knowledge looks like and how teachers can think their way through it.

We are fortunate that scholars and researchers in psychology, philosophy, sociocultural studies, and education, many associated with the learning sciences, have taken up the question of how such teaching proceeds. One key finding of their work is that learning and teaching unfold distinctively for students and teachers as they engage with diverse subjects of study across varying times and locales. Consider subject-matter knowledge. Processes for thinking about and learning mathematics, literature, science, political science, and other subjects differ because each discipline places learners on a specialized pathway of thought. Making one's way through the knowledge of any one field—via thinking, learning, or teaching— differs from doing so in others. Thus, thinking and learning in math differ greatly from thinking and learning in history, sociology, chemistry, and so on. The nature of teaching practice may vary across fields and subjects too. Add in differences in students' and teachers' identities and background knowledge, including their values and habits of mind, and variations too in teachers' willingness to attend to students' emotions in learning. Incorporate the power of time and place to shape what and who is taught, and we can begin to see why no one instance of learning will look quite like others.[1] Complex as it is, two features of undergraduate teaching stand out. It is intricate, meaning there is a lot of detail, in both depth and breadth. And it is contingent, meaning that what it looks and sounds like is sensitive to who learns and who teaches, what is learned and taught, when, and where.

In this section, we discuss convergent teaching as a framework for considering what we see as at the heart of good teaching. Convergent teaching speaks to teachers' thinking and acting in identifying, representing, and managing interactions between academic knowledge and the academic and personal knowledge that students bring from their lives to their learning. Three principles, each a platform for varying enactments of teaching practice, underpin convergent teaching.[2]

The first principle is targeting, which refers to carving out what's to be taught. Following this principle, an instructor identifies and specifies the disciplinary or field-based concepts, modes of thought, and other knowledge to be taught in a particular course, paying attention to what students need for related and advanced learning later in the course, in other courses, in the field, or in life.

The second principle is surfacing, through which a teacher unearths the prior knowledge students have that is relevant to their learning of new content. By drawing out what students know already—culturally, personally, and academically—the teacher may help create a bridge to understanding subject-matter concepts new to the students.

The third principle is navigating, by which a teacher orchestrates subject-matter concepts and students' prior knowledge so as to facilitate students' learning. The teacher steers instruction between what students know already (their prior knowledge) and what they need to learn (subject-matter concepts) by planning lessons, interacting with students about content, creating and discussing assignments, informally monitoring and assessing students' understandings of course content, revising earlier course plans, and reteaching using developing insights into what students need in order to progress in their thinking. To bring subject-matter concepts and students' prior knowledge together, instructors build lessons at their points of intersection—for example, by creating analogies, cases, and so on and by drawing on readings and other resources that capture key elements of both, blending them to help students enter new arenas of thought. This work involves intense planning about what to teach, when and in what sequence, what questions to pose to students, and how to organize student response, among other factors. It involves implementing plans and improvising around them amid an unpredictable range of classroom realities, such as students' emotional responses to content, teaching modes, and the social relations of classrooms. It involves taking stock regularly of how plans have materialized and whether and what students learn. It involves teachers caring about, and attending consistently to, the effects and effectiveness of their teaching, as mirrored in students' experiences.

In the next three chapters, we discuss these three principles and their constituent practices as instantiations of convergent teaching.[3] Though foregrounding teaching dynamics, we offer some glimpses of the institutional and social worlds that surround them, alongside consideration of teaching's more personal sides: the values, emotions, and commitments that may infiltrate teaching and that "being taught" can stir up.

In the following chapters, we introduce eight teachers whose thinking about teaching reflects these principles. Six of the eight teach undergraduates, four in community colleges and two in four-year institutions. Two do not fit this mold, including one who teaches in a graduate school and is one of the authors of this book, and one who volunteers to support middle school students' learning of algebra; we include them to emphasize defining features of the first two principles of convergent teaching, targeting and surfacing. The six featured instructors of undergraduates teach subjects that are foundational to advanced study, mostly in introductory, sometimes required, courses in the general education curriculum of undergraduate study (English composition, history, earth science, geography, philosophy). These six also had been exposed previously to principles of convergent teaching through participation in a year-long professional development program, MetroCITI, which aims to cultivate good teaching in urban, diversity-intensive colleges and universities.[4]

Taken together, the eight instructors vary in a number of ways: by race (one is Black, two are Hispanic, five are white); gender, age, career stage (beginning to advanced); job status (tenured and not); teaching field (e.g., social statistics, mathematics, earth science, history, English composition); and as already noted, institutional affiliation. Observing their teaching as we worked with all but one of these instructors, we saw them striving to support students' learning via instruction that responds and holds itself responsible to what students know, value, and aspire to while holding true, too, to their discipline's core tenets. Yet none of these instructors has perfected their practice. Each realizes that as they continue to encounter new students in a world of changing knowledge, they themselves have much yet to learn about how best to support others' learning.

Teaching in Support of Students' Learning

In combination, the three principles portray convergent teaching as rooted in four sources: teachers and the intellectual, cultural, and personal knowledge, values, and proclivities, and identities that they bring into classrooms; students and the breadth of accumulated prior academic, cultural, and personal learning, identities, goals, and values that they bring; subject matter as portions of disciplinary knowledge that teachers draw out of the larger fields in which they claim expert knowledge; and the large-scale social, cultural, political, and economic forces that shape them all.[5] These sources offer distinctive resources for learning and teaching and for the thinking that underlies both. Viewing each as interacting continually with the others, one can intuit how unlikely it is that students and their teachers will be fully alike in their views at any one moment in time. By the same token, it is not likely that any two disciplines (or parts thereof) will be fully alike in what they demand of scholars and students. Teaching and learning emerge from this dynamism.

Teaching's complexity and dynamism require teachers to use good judgment: to make the best possible choices about what to attend to and what to enact and desist from enacting amid shifting, unpredictable environments. Together, the three principles serve as guiding stars for instructors seeking to teach responsively and responsibly, balancing attention to them all. Yet these principles cannot be viewed as the "end all" or "be all" of good teaching, which calls for still more. Seeking to advance education's humanistic, civic, and democratic aims, other writers have sought to infuse egalitarianism into classroom teaching, recommending strategies for reducing bias and eliminating stereotyped thinking; inventing tools for enacting equity-minded teaching; guiding teachers in creating assignments that incite the interests and passions of diverse students; infusing civic consciousness and ethical reflection into content offerings; and cultivating students' cross-cultural competence.[6] Still others speak to college teachers' need to master even more basic practices: how to articulate clear and achievable course aims and expectations, manage class resources (including time) effectively, organize group work so as to align with teaching goals, provide students with clear and useable feedback, appeal to students' technological proclivities without losing sight of class aims, and so on.[7] Still yet others speak to the need to better systematize campus operations, for example, through improved information, organization, policy, and assessment, topics we take up in part III. And as we describe in chapter 1, an increasing number of writers speak to teachers', leaders', policy makers', and the public's need to embrace the implications of new and harsh economic realities, shifting societal demographics, and promises that technological innovation will change higher education for the better in the future.

Our emphasis on strategies for effective subject-matter teaching can get lost amid these larger agendas, which can elide attention to teaching's reason for being: to support students in their efforts to understand subject matter in depth and to bring it into their work, their lives, and the world at large. Although the practices we've just cited can help, none offer insight into how to take the all-important extra step of leading students right *into* and *through* subject matters to be learned—whether math, physics, philosophy, history, sociology, literature, or others. It is that extra step, *into subject matter and through it*, to which convergent teaching speaks.

To teach competently, professors must develop knowledge of and facility with basic practices—teaching's nuts and bolts. Teachers are not born knowing all this. And we strongly support efforts that aim to dissolve barriers while equalizing educational conditions and opportunities to learn. Though skeptical about overreaching institutional, technological, and policy reform, we believe that systems can be improved, even if incrementally. Important as these may be, we do not believe that they can go far enough on their own. What we would like to see in them is explicit attention to instruction that supports students, markedly diverse in their cultural and personal backgrounds, as they step into and engage subject-matter concepts and in ways that provide meaningful links to the knowledge they bring to class from their lives. Students' encounters with subject matter framed by knowledge from their lives are more likely to yield useable and transferrable learning than are encounters that distance academic content from who students are, what they value, know, and believe, and what they reach for.[8]

This view prominently shapes our conception of teaching as responsive to students' developed and developing cognitions and aspirations, their sense of self and possibility, of what they can come to know for themselves and their worlds through authentic engagement with disciplinary content. But how does one teach in this way? To address this question, we use research and theory applicable to teaching in a wide variety of educational institutions to formulate three principles of practice—targeting, surfacing, and navigating—that can foster students' learning and growth at the convergence of what subject matter can offer, what students and teachers alike bring to learning from their lives, and what larger social and cultural forces imprint on these efforts. Though convergence is only a portion of what counts as "good teaching," it is, with all three principles activated at once, complex. To portray its conceptual totality, we unroll it gradually, principle by principle.

We acknowledge that this step-wise portrayal, edited so as to project salient features of each principle, misses much of the buzz, sparkle, and mess of converging minds and lives, clashing and connecting in cacophonous classroom time—that is the reality of American higher education amid which convergent teaching typically comes to life. Further, we feature teachers in educational institutions that mirror the rich and complex cultural, racial, linguistic, and religious diversity of the United States in the twenty-first century. These teachers do not and cannot offer fully worked-out models of convergent teaching practice, yet we believe that all have taken significant steps toward laying out some of its foundations.

CHAPTER TWO

Targeting

Carving Out What's To Be Taught

A key task for an instructor is selecting the particular disciplinary concepts and modes of disciplinary thought to teach in a course, based on their likely contribution to students' further learning in that class and beyond. Thus, an instructor can initially ask which subject-matter concepts and ways of thinking are likely to carry his or her students further into the discipline or field at issue. Decisions about examples to use in explaining such concepts, media for conveying them, along with class readings, activities, projects, and instructional strategies follow from these initial choices.

How might college teachers identify such concepts? Core concepts can be likened to basic building blocks, prototypes, or miniatures, condensed depictions of a field's unique substantive concerns and distinctive knowledge structures and dynamics (think of William Blake's "microcosm" of "a World in a Grain of Sand").[1] In some disciplines, a core concept may be a germinating thought that influences, produces, or connects with other disciplinary thoughts. Areas of study may grow from and around it, extending the core idea, elaborating on variations, critiquing or arguing with its tenets, and so on.

The concept of a market, for example, is a foundational idea in the study of economics. A market is a structure in which parties enter into an exchange, sellers offering goods and services that buyers purchase with money. The concept of market has spurred multiple elaborations on its meanings and debates about the extent to which markets are "free," that is, unregulated by the government, or "efficient," that is, making available all of the relevant information that shapes the price of a good or service. Related concepts from the field of economics include scarcity—the notion that individually and collectively, our desire for certain resources inevitably exceeds the amount of those resources available—and supply and demand, a model in which price regulates the relationship between the quantity of goods and services demanded and supplied. Similarly, the concept of work is central to physics and the study of engineering. Put simply, work is the result of a force acting on an object to displace it. Work is closely related to other core physics concepts such as energy (the capacity for doing work) and power (the rate at which work is done).[2]

In college teaching, an instructor can use concepts central to her or his discipline or field as starting points for building a course—or for formulating a course syllabus as the map for a course. For example, the instructor might identify two or three core concepts for an introductory course, then settle on how to sequence those concepts across the semester (which concepts will precede which and which concepts will follow which, how or when the two will overlap, how much time exploring each may need, and why a particular sequencing makes sense for particular students' learning). In tackling any one core concept, that instructor might flesh out its meaning and structure in her or his mind and then consider how best to sequence and pace students' learning of component ideas and topics, given what students are likely to know already, where they are likely to gravitate in their thinking, and where they may be challenged. With the interior and exterior of a core concept mapped in this way, the instructor can then assemble readings, class activities, projects, and modes of instruction designed to help students grasp it.[3]

Course time is precious, of course, and as we saw in the prior chapter, there already are concerns about the limited time and effort that students devote to their studies. One objection to this approach is that the time devoted to the exposition of core concepts may reduce the amount of content that a course provides students. There's only so much time to go around, and curricular depth and breadth are almost always in tension within the confines of a single course. But because the approach brings students deeply into core disciplinary concepts linked to other nearby content, it promises to open up opportunities for students to enter that neighboring content in more meaningful ways, for example, in later coursework. One's prior learning in earlier coursework can provide learners with stepping stones into the new or it can illuminate ideas they encounter later that would otherwise feel strange to them. Tony Acevedo, a history instructor at Hudson County Community College whose teaching we take up in this chapter, refers to the teaching of core ideas as "teaching more by teaching less"—picking out those historical concepts and historical ways of thinking that merit sustained attention because they serve as building blocks for broader and more complex thinking in the discipline—even at the cost of reduced attention to other less central content.

We suggest that Tony's insight on core ideas in history as helping him "teach more by teaching less" applies to teaching in a number of other disciplines and fields as well but with this important qualification: the content focus, structure, texture, and very "syntax" of core ideas will vary, field to field, as will the other knowledge that grows around them.[4] Students seeking to understand the content and modes of thought of a particular field can use what they know about one or more of its core ideas as a "way in" to study of the field at large. To teach is to support such learning. In what follows we present several cases of such teaching. Although all the instructors activate all three of the principles herein featured, we focus on each principle sequentially.

Visualizing the Statistical "Middle": Aaron Pallas

We turn first to Aaron Pallas's teaching about the middle of a frequency distribution as a concept that is fundamental to the study of social statistics. Aaron, one of this book's authors, is a sociologist of education who began his professional career working as a statistician for the National Center for Education Statistics before transitioning to faculty positions in the College of Education at Michigan State University and Teachers College, Columbia University. Both institutions are large, renowned, elite graduate schools of education that prepare researchers and expert practitioners. Over a series of years during the 1990s, Aaron developed and taught a unit on basic descriptive and inferential statistics to doctoral students enrolled in a required college-wide research course, Educational Inquiry, at Michigan State University. Since then, Anna Neumann, the other author of this book, has used one lesson from this unit to explain the idea of a core concept in courses she teaches to doctoral and master's students at Teachers College about college learning and teaching. We've also jointly used it in delivering teaching improvement seminars to pre- and in-service clinical instructors at a New York medical school and law school and to participants in the MetroCITI professional development program. Unhappily, we do not have the capacity to link the teaching case and subsequent measures of student learning. This is true for all of the cases in this book, much as it is for most research on higher education teaching; this lack of a way to gauge the effects of the teaching case on student learning poses a unique challenge to efforts to develop a repository of effective teaching practices in the disciplines.

In the version of Aaron's teaching about the middle of a distribution that we recount here, the "students" are college instructors teaching undergraduate courses in history, sociology, physics, business, English, religion, and chemistry in diversity-intensive institutions; all were participants in MetroCITI in the 2015–16 academic year. The lesson, which is, in effect, a teaching-learning simulation, had to be compressed to ensure that Aaron could cover the key points within the time allotted, and occasionally he broke the "fourth wall" to explain his approach to participants.

The lesson hinges on the idea that the middle and spread of a distribution are foundational concepts on which students' learning of basic descriptive and inferential statistics depends. In the early elementary grades, students learn a formula for calculating a statistic that is supposed to represent the middle of a distribution: the average, or mean, formed by adding up all of the values, and dividing by the number of cases. That's knowledge that virtually every MetroCITI participant brings to the session, but it is strangely decoupled from conceptions of "middle" that Aaron sees as lying at the core of the study of social statistics.

As students typically present and understand it, the average—or mean—is a formula. Learning scientists might describe students' knowledge of this formula as procedural: to calculate the mean or average, one goes through a specific set of steps. And students can routinely transfer this set of procedures to new batches of data. But why is average, or mean, a measure of the middle of a distribution? And what is the middle, anyway? How may the concept of middle be visualized and understood as a property of a distribution of particular values rather than as a formula for calculating the average?

The lesson began with Aaron administering a survey with a single item to the ten MetroCITI participants: how many years ago did you complete your bachelor's degree? He noted that years can be counted, and that the distance between two and three years is the same as the distance between eight and nine years.[5] This differentiates years from an *ordinal* set of categories (e.g., strongly agree to strongly disagree, where we know that strongly agree represents a greater quantity of agreement than disagree but don't know the specific distance between the categories) and a *nominal* set of categories that have no intrinsic order (e.g., favorite flavors of ice cream such as vanilla, chocolate, or strawberry). He collected the surveys, and wrote the ten responses, one by one, on the whiteboard:

12	18
11	28
9	34
10	26
31	15

Obviously, he said, it would be very inefficient to describe the collection of the ten participants serially by saying, "Well, there's one 12, and there's one 11, there's one 9, one 10," and so on. Aaron didn't mention it explicitly at this point, but every student's value was listed on the board, and each could see his or her own contribution to the class data as a whole. He suggested ordering the values from lowest to highest and then broke the fourth wall to note that it might be possible to reduce the complexity of the data by putting the values into a table or a chart. He added that in an authentic teaching setting, like a statistics class, he would invite students to work in small groups to develop tabular and graphic representations of the class data.[6] Aaron provided students with a blank graph with post-BA years on the X axis (ranging from 0 to 40), and the frequency with which a particular value appeared in the class data on the Y axis and invited participants to draw the frequency distribution for the class. This particular distribution, he pointed out, was a bit peculiar, since there was no instance in which there was more than one person with a particular value.

Having developed the class distribution—which is different each time Aaron teaches the lesson depending on the number of class members and the specifics of their ages and personal circumstances—Aaron then turned to cultivating students' appreciation for its core features: its middle and spread and its emergent shape. Doing so required pausing the lesson for a brief warm-up exercise that, Aaron suspected, would inspire students to think in fresh ways about their own class's distribution, to which they would shortly return. For the warm-up, Aaron circulated a handout with graphs of several hypothetical distributions similar to the one they'd just created for their own class. He asked students to think aloud, together, and with him: what made the distributions different from one another? (Over the years, Aaron had designed the handout and a set of follow-up discussion questions to help students begin to think about the importance of the middle, spread, and shape of a distribution of data. He wanted to sensitize students to these three concepts prior to having them unearth them in their own class data, which would follow next.)

Returning to the distribution of number of years since each of the ten participants received their BA on the whiteboard, Aaron said, "What I'm going to invite you to do is think about ways to reduce the complexity of this information. Instead of having ten numbers to describe the distribution, we want to describe the class's response—the ten of your responses—to the survey question about years since you received your BA as concisely as possible—reduced to a single number that will represent the middle. What number would you choose? Or what numbers?" "You might decide," he added, "there is more than one way to do it. The issue is: what number or numbers might you choose as a single value to represent the middle of the distribution?"[7]

But before turning students loose to work on this task in small groups, Aaron imposed one constraint. "I've already said that I don't understand the word 'mean' or 'average,'" he said. "That's a term that doesn't make any sense to me. So you can't use those words. Or 'mode' or 'median' or 'range.' These are all terms you probably learned as early as fifth grade or earlier. But I don't want you to use those words." Aaron was firm. "What I want you to be thinking about is the *middle*. You've got the tools of the graphic representation. You've got the ten numbers. So this is the challenge: figure out how to represent the middle of this distribution with a single number and come up with a defensible argument for that number. So when I ask you, 'Why did you choose that number?' you can say, 'This is why we came up with this number, and why we think it's a representation of the middle of the distribution.'"

The students worked in small groups of three or four as Aaron walked around, listening to group conversations and from time to time asking, "Why?" or "What do you mean?" After about twenty minutes, he reconvened the class and asked each group to report on its deliberations. The discussion that followed lasted thirty minutes; here we spotlight a few interchanges.

One group laid out the class frequency distribution on a horizontal line from one end of a single sheet of paper to the other, then folded the sheet halfway between the smallest value of 9 and the highest value of 34. "That made a line in the middle, which was at twenty-one point five," the group's spokesperson, Joel, said.[8] "Yes," Aaron said, "that's a middle. It's basically just halfway between the smallest value and the highest value. But it doesn't take account of anybody else's information. It's based entirely on the lowest number and the highest number. It's not sensitive to anything in between. So it's only using two out of the ten of you. Only the nine and the thirty-four contribute to the representation of the middle." "The others of you"—he paused and smiled—"you're chopped liver!" As the group burst into laughter, he added that in this particular representation of middle, "the rest of you don't count."

A second group ordered the values from low to high, again from 9 to 34, and then, starting at each end, ticked off participants' post-BA year values one by one, eventually arriving at 15 and 18, the two values left after the others had been crossed off. "So the middle of that would be sixteen and a half," said its spokesperson, Sal. Aaron agreed that this was another way to think of the middle of the distribution. "You've got an equal number of people on either side. Five people whose values are smaller than the middle, and five people whose values are higher. And like you mentioned, you take the value of the position that is halfway between those two at center."

Another student, Whitney, listening carefully, spoke up. "I guess what I was grappling with—and we were talking about in our group—is like, which middle are we trying to find? Are we trying to find the middle of people? Or are we trying to find, simply, the middle of time ?" (that is, the middle year). It was a great question, Aaron declared. Whitney and her group were opening the door to the possibility that there might be more than one way to think about the middle of the distribution of years since the participants had earned their BA: the middle might represent the person—or in this case, persons—in the middle (as Sal and his group had pointed out), or it could refer to a middle value of years on which Whitney did not elaborate. Perhaps middle had to address them both somehow.

Another group had adopted this line of reasoning as well, going a bit further. "We devised a little fulcrum type of thing," said Jordan, "and then we put our numbers, our distribution, on that fulcrum. We picked a middle. Let's say the middle is twenty. And then we took differences from there, trying to do kind of a weighting on both sides. And just looked for when the numbers equaled each other on both sides of that middle fulcrum point." This is, indeed, one of the explanations that Aaron was looking for, as he often uses an imaginary see-saw, with the distribution positioned on it, as a heuristic and asks students to look for the point—the fulcrum—that lets the see-saw balance. Ellery, in another group, said, "We were going through a few different middles, and one of them was the same type of idea as that. Having the same number of years, balancing." "It's a great idea," Aaron said, since in this representation of the middle, "every person contributes to it. And every person's value matters." A shift in any one individual's value will shift the balance point. Working among themselves, the students had come to the insight that the idea of the middle not only entailed consideration of discrete participants or years but also called for a weighting and balancing between them and a recognition of the distances among them—the kind of thinking that children, taking up spots on a seesaw, might use intuitively as they work out how to position themselves on the board to make it balance.

Breaking the fourth wall again, Aaron explained that there is another way to visualize the middle that students frequently generate but that did not come up in the day's session. He asked students to add together the years since each participant had received their BA and then imagine putting the sum total of 194 years into a sack and then parceling each year, one year at a time to one person after another, going around the group this way several times until the bag's contents were divided up evenly among the ten participants. In this example, every person would get the same number of years, and that number would then represent the middle value. It's a different and visual way to consider the mechanics of calculating a mean or average, since, much like the formula, it involves adding up the total quantity across individuals (putting all in a sack) and dividing by the number of individuals (parceling the number of years out one at a time, person by person). But the formula on its own and without the seesaw or the "parceling out" imagery is decoupled from any understanding of why the resulting value (19.4 years, in this case) might be thought of as the middle of the distribution of years for the ten participants in the Metro-CITI session.

We offer this example to make the point that teaching which strives for students' deep conceptual grasp of a subject of study requires teachers who have located their field's core concepts, visualized them in depth, and considered the different forms they might take from different perspectives. Those teachers might then anticipate how their students are likely to come at those concepts and how they might respond to help students derive them authentically, as disciplinary experts do. We present examples of other teachers of other subjects doing this as well in other parts this volume. Our key point, for now, is that teaching for students' understanding requires a textured map of one's subject matter, one that highlights its constituent contents. The teacher must be deeply knowledgeable about the subject's core ideas and be willing and able to imagine them in different ways. The teacher must also be open to following students' thoughts toward novel (and potentially valid or useful) images of core ideas, even if these thoughts initially seem strange or misdirected.[9]

A teacher seeking to give students entrée to a field also will think ahead about pathways from any one core concept to other concepts nearby, especially those meriting students' learning, as well as about resources (such as examples from everyday life, popular culture, and the like) that can guide students' awareness of how and why they might move from here to there—in effect, what such movement stands to offer. For example, in his introductory research classes, Aaron typically paused to wonder how the thoughts about the middle that his students had come to could be leveraged for their learning of other statistical concepts, such as standard deviation and correlation coefficient, which are proximal. He also had thought this through in planning the class overall, appreciating that the concept of middle was a cornerstone to students' later learning of other concepts, such as null hypothesis significance testing.

One must ask how an instructor who has for years taught a given course through direct instruction might come to teach in this way, given the extensive effort it would take to transition to the new mode. Aaron describes how he did it this way:

> Anna and I were teaching this very conceptual, interpretive course on the nature of inquiry and education. But then the College of Education at Michigan State said, "By the way, we're changing our curriculum, and we want you to teach basic, descriptive, inferential statistics in the middle of the class." And it just felt really odd to all of a sudden be lecturing students that "here, this is the mean, this is the median, this is the mode."
>
> And at one point, I invited a colleague who was a mathematics educator who studied the mathematical learning of elementary schoolchildren to come observe me. She was kind enough to do that. And she was very gracious in pointing out to me that I had no idea what my students were actually learning. I just couldn't tell, because we were using a statistical software program. I think it might have been MiniTab, but it could have been anything, SPSS or whatever. And so students were in front of terminals. They were doing these things. But I couldn't tell what they knew. Yes, they had exams, but the exams were summative. I could tell after the fact what they had learned. But while they were engaging with material, I had no clue. And so I asked her for advice about how I might do it differently.

And she pointed me toward, believe it or not, third and fourth grade math curriculum materials where concepts like mean were being introduced. And it pointed me toward this different, more conceptual way of what was often, in those days, referred to as teaching for understanding.[10]

Of course, one can wonder too about the extent to which the idea of a core concept applies to disciplines and fields other than social statistics, as well as how instructors might go about using a core concept to frame (or reframe) a course, possibly one that an instructor has already taught several times but now seeks to redesign. We turn to Lauren Navarro, an assistant professor of English who teaches introductory writing at New York's LaGuardia Community College, for one example.[11]

Reclaiming Claims in English Composition: Lauren Navarro

With an enrollment approaching twenty thousand students in credit-bearing programs, LaGuardia Community College is the third-largest of the seven community colleges in the City University of New York system. About two-thirds of its students reside in the borough of Queens, and its students mirror the characteristics of New York City's most diverse borough. Nearly half of LaGuardia's students are Latino, and approximately 20% identify as Asian and an additional 20% as Black. One in nine students identifies as white. More than one-half of LaGuardia's students are foreign-born, but only 7% are international. Slightly more than one-half of the students are enrolled full time.[12]

In a typical term, Lauren Navarro teaches three sections of English composition, a required core course at LaGuardia, along with other courses such as Composition II: Writing through Literature, Food, Gender, and Culture in American Literature, Latinx Literature in the United States, and Cultural Identity in American Literature. Via her exposure in MetroCITI to core concepts as a way to think about structuring knowledge for teaching, Lauren turned to this idea in fall 2015 as a new way to extend her on-going refinement of the English composition course.

Some years back, Lauren had addressed a recurring concern in the course: learning to write requires that students write. It also requires that students have the opportunity to discuss their writing with the teacher and with each other. This is challenging to pull off when students of varying backgrounds are asked to write papers on topics that are fully of their choice—they write about different things, and their peer readers and the teacher too will often be unable to offer helpful feedback because they have trouble grasping the meaning sufficiently. Lauren speculated that having a large topic, or theme, in common—one that all students could write about, though in different ways, based on their unique backgrounds and prior experiences—could help address this problem.

Lauren had confronted this challenge by infusing her introductory composition course with additional readings on food and culture; in this way she hope to establish food and culture as a cross-cutting theme that would bind their writing assignments together. She had gone so far as to subtitle the course (which was formally English 101: Composition I) "Food, Culture, and the City." Students wrote on this theme, which Lauren further broke out into specific topics, all related to readings on food that she assigned through the semester; students used the readings on food to focus their writing and their discussions of writing. They simultaneously read about, thought through, and talked about issues pertaining to writing, the class's key substantive concern. Drawing on what they were learning about good writing, students produced essays on the assigned food topics; they also provided input to classmates' writing, spurring a class-wide process of cross-cultural learning about food that was coupled with writing improvement.

Lauren's goal of supporting her students in learning to write "an argument-based research paper" by "articulating a claim and positing a solution to a problem" remained central to the course, even as she added in the readings and writing assignments about food and culture. Feeling satisfied with her now well-established food and culture leitmotif for the course, Lauren readied herself to address her next course improvement goal: strengthening students' understanding and production of claims in argumentation. She would position "claim" as a core concept and reposition her teaching of other content around it, thus continuing to teach the many other topics that introductory composition courses address and continuing, too, to use the theme of food and culture to frame students' writing and other work in the course.

How did Lauren come to the view that the concept of a claim was central to the field of composition studies and the teaching of introductory writing? Instructors like Lauren may be influenced in their choice of core concepts by various sources: their graduate study (which informs their beliefs about their field's internal structure); their past teaching of the same or other courses, including their sense of what their students need; their reading of curricular guidelines; and their close adherence to the layout of textbooks. Prior to her participation in MetroCITI, Lauren had not reflected deeply on what a core concept could be for her class or how she might use one in framing the teaching of her course. Rather, she said, she had for years adhered to "received pedagogical knowledge and training" and had closely followed standard textbooks to teach the unit on claims and argumentation, usually in the ninth week of her college's fifteen-week semester. Thus in weeks one through eight, Lauren would address other writing topics as her textbooks directed.

What she had not tried to do, prior to her fall 2015 course revision, was to teach the earlier material in ways that would sensitize students to the concept of a claim, slowly preparing them for the core learning about claims that would come toward the end of the term. In prior versions of Lauren's course, the concept of a claim in argumentation was new to students when they encountered it for the first time in the ninth week of a semester; they did not clearly see links between what they had studied earlier in the term and the new lesson about claims.

Lauren had for some time been concerned that the three-week timeline for teaching claims late in the term was "rushed." Students would feel the usual end-of-semester pressures while struggling, predictably, with challenges in the overly condensed lesson: how to strive for balance between comprehensiveness and specificity in assessing and writing claims and thus avoiding vagueness or the inclusion of too much information. Students needed more time and more opportunities to practice and think through the complexity of claims in argumentation. The end-of-semester squeeze precluded longer-term attention to the course's key aim—teaching about claims in written argumentation.

Analyzing the course as she had previously taught it, Lauren asked, "If what we really want students to learn by the end of English 101 is how to write a solid argumentative research paper, why are we introducing them to this concept of the claim in argumentation at the tail end of the semester?" Lauren decided to experiment: she would complicate the standard sequence of content presentation, braiding lessons about claims with lessons about other features of writing through the full semester, in effect, teaching the concept of claim all along. Rather than waiting until the ninth week to focus on claims for the first time, Lauren introduced the subject in the second week, drawing attention to the logic of a claim. Around midterm, she turned to approaches for establishing a fact or proving a claim, as well as matters of causality and justification in producing and analyzing claims. With this foundation, in the ninth week, she introduced students to basic research methods—how to choose a topic, how to devise research questions, how to annotate, and how to identify what research techniques to use—as aspects of claim writing, and in the tenth week, she led the class in studying the topic of claims, evidence, and thesis. By the semester's end, she and her students had explored matters of value, fact, and policy as central to argumentation, going beyond their customary treatment. To accomplish all this, students engaged in a parallel study of food and culture, analyzing a wide-ranging set of readings— autobiographically inspired stories (e.g., Amy Tan's "Fish Cheeks"), news features (e.g., Michael Moss's "The Extraordinary Science of Addictive Junk Food"), and research-based analyses of public health issues (e.g., Jeffrey M. Smith's "Genetically Engineered Foods May Cause Rising Food Allergies"). Thus, throughout the semester, students used their developing thoughts about food to support their learning about writing, especially about claims and their uses in argumentation, a concept that now also spanned the entire semester.

The changes that Lauren instituted in her composition class—focusing on a core composition concept (claim in argumentation) and then rebuilding course content around it—involved multiple streams of coordinated thought. Lauren had to rethink writing assignments, ways of preparing students for them, her class's reading lists (on writing and on food), and her approaches to intertwining learning units on food and on various facets of writing. Under the new course design, she also found herself addressing new questions from students and helping them around stumbling blocks that she had not previously encountered. Thus, the course, as reframed, pushed her to think in new ways about claims, a topic she already knew well, while also getting her to consider how students were making sense of claims in the revised instructional format and allowing her to address features of content that they misunderstood, highlight their step-by-step achievements, and build on those.

Although we did not collect data on the quality of students' learning about writing in the class, we do have Lauren's own contemporaneous observations on this. By the end of the semester, she said, "Students were pros at identifying main claims, type of claims, picking out logical fallacies, homing in on holes in evidence and argumentation, and working together to achieve crisper, clearer, and more substantial claims." Lauren's "'relentless' focus on claims" (as one student described it) seemed, in her view, to help novice writers "find their voices" while enabling them to "question received wisdom" in ways many had not done before, certainly not in their writing. "Now, coming to the end," she mused, she saw something else as well. "I realize," she said, "that I was teaching myself the same lesson. As the project progressed, the way I thought about myself as an educator shifted. I felt a sense of authority over my own pedagogy that, I think, may have always been lurking underneath but that I was hitherto afraid to trust." Lauren's teaching about claims thus not only helped her students find their voices but helped her find her own.

In chapter 4, we meet another composition teacher, Allie Bach, who approaches the teaching of introductory composition in similar ways but with a different core concept: audience. Can core concepts usefully frame teaching in still other disciplines and fields? We consider this question next through Eryn Klosko's teaching of introductory earth science.

Homing in on the Scientific Method in Earth Science: Eryn Klosko

Eryn Klosko is a professor of geosciences and chair of the Department of Physical Sciences at Westchester Community College, located in Valhalla, in the New York metropolitan area. Affiliated with the State

University of New York (SUNY), Westchester serves approximately seven thousand full-time students and six thousand part-time students, more than half of whom identify as Black or Latino. Within her teaching responsibilities of four to five courses a term, some of which have lab sections, Eryn teaches an introduction to physical geology class, called Earth Science, to nonscience majors. This is the only science course that many of her students take. In the course, students study basic processes such as weathering, the development of glaciers, and plate tectonics as a theory for understanding natural phenomena such as volcanoes and earthquakes.

Eryn's teaching is anchored in the assumption that in order to understand natural phenomena, one must rely on the scientific method, thus "formulating testable ideas" about pertinent features of the natural world, observing, and "relying on evidence" to assess their veracity. Eryn has long adhered to the belief that students' study of geology and of the natural world should be informed by deep understanding of the scientific method as an arbiter of credibility. Building on this, she believes that members of the general public should use the scientific method to assess the subject-matter premises of public science policy. For Eryn, the scientific method is a core idea and also a core way of thinking in geology.

Eryn's views of the scientific method underpin her teaching. For example, in her past teaching of the earth science course, she devoted two class sessions early in the semester to teaching it as a model of scientific thought. With this basic lesson in place, she proceeded to move students methodically through the many topics that define introductory physical geology. Eryn assumed that educating students about the scientific method would encourage them to think scientifically through the rest of the course and sensitize them to how geologists construct and validate knowledge.

As is true of many introductory courses for nonmajors in the arts and sciences, Eryn's earth science course had evolved over the years into a broad and comprehensive survey course. But reflecting on the course after years of teaching it, Eryn was worried. Her students did not appear to be grasping the empirical basis of many important geology topics as they moved through the semester. "The students don't seem to understand that scientific ideas actually come from observations," she said. "They don't descend from the heavens." Eryn was realizing that what she had taught students about the scientific method in the early weeks of the term was not informing their thinking about geological phenomena that need to be understood through the method.

Eryn's participation in MetroCITI inspired her to reorganize her earth science course. She lengthened her opening unit on the scientific method and added opportunities for students to revisit it as a central element of the course as they worked through later units on geologic formations and events. Her aim, she said, was to reduce emphasis on her prior goal of broad content coverage while increasing attention to a new goal—having students rely on the scientific method to consider the credibility of ideas they encounter in science-informed texts and the popular media. Going forward, Eryn would cover less of the content of the field of geology; instead she would pick out those topics that she felt students would find important, as well as those that would deepen their understandings of how scientists think. This change, she explained, positioned the scientific method as the "essential thing that students get out of this entire class." "It doesn't really matter if they learn all these other little intricate details of earth science," she said, because if "they don't have a real sense of the scientific method, then the course fails them."

The changes that Eryn instituted—extending students' initial engagement with the scientific method, then narrowing the range of geologic topics covered so as to permit recursive consideration of the disciplined thought behind them—led her to echo the claim of Tony, the historian, that "teaching less," strategically and wisely, stands a better chance of helping students learn more about core concepts they can move into their academic and personal lives than does broad and scattershot coverage, which many are unlikely to revisit. The course changes that Eryn instituted, rooted in tough decisions about which knowledge to highlight and analyze and which to reduce or omit, demanded substantial effort: rethinking course aims and structure, formulating new discussion questions and activities, developing responses to new challenges in students' thinking, designing new assessments. But why did Eryn think that she needed to devote more attention to the scientific method? What had she heard and seen, in her students' talk and writing, that led her to launch a major reconstruction of her course? We return to this important question in our discussion of the principle of surfacing in the next chapter.

The cases of Aaron's Lauren's, and Eryn's teaching suggest that core concepts vary in their content focus, much as do the disciplines of which they are a part (e.g., the statistics class focuses on basic descriptive and inferential statistics, the composition class emphasizes writing, and the earth science class attends to geological phenomena; core ideas in these classes pertain to the discipline at issue). Core concepts also serve different purposes in their respective fields (in social statistics, the middle of a frequency distribution anchors the description of that distribution; in the composition class, a claim is an element of argumentation; in the geology class, the scientific method is an arbiter of trustworthiness in research). Finally, core concepts differ by field in their texture and in Joseph Schwab's words, their "syntactical structure," reflecting these features of the knowledge of their fields. Such differences reverberate through the undergraduate curriculum: the content and structure of thought, the very "feel" of a core idea—in philosophy, chemistry, psychology, history, mathematics, anthropology, and other fields—might vary across the disciplines.[13]

How, then, can teachers help students take up field-distinctive thinking, especially if the students' past schooling failed to provide them with adequate entrée to it? Historians, for example, have a distinctive way of thinking that has little to do with the memorization of historical facts such as names, events, and dates. Sam Wineburg has written extensively about how to think like a historian and the value of relying on primary sources. He notes that historians think about a document's author and its creation, situate the document in time and place, read the document closely, draw on background knowledge to understand it, look at what is left out or missing from the account it provides, and look across multiple sources to see points of agreement or disagreement.[14] How can novice students of history, previously unexposed to such modes of thought, be supported in taking them on, eventually learning to think in expert historical ways? We turn to Tony Acevedo for an example.

Learning to Think like Historians
in Western Civ: Tony Acevedo

Tony Acevedo, teaching an introductory course on the history of Western civilization at Hudson County Community College in New Jersey, used what he learned in MetroCITI in 2015–16 to put his students on the road to improved historical thinking. Hudson has more than ten thousand students, more than half of whom are Latino and only 10% of whom identify as white; many are the first in their family to attend college.

Tony, who typically teaches three to four sections of Western Civ each term, along with courses in US history, worried that many of his students did not read the history texts he assigned. Moreover, when they did, they became inundated with historical facts, losing sight of historical thinking and big ideas. Tony expressed concern that he was himself contributing to the problem through frequent use of multiple-choice quizzes that rewarded the recall of names, dates, and events rather than the generation and analysis of cross-cutting historical themes and concepts.[15] His History of Western Civilization II course had an ambitious agenda, exploring the impact of political, economic, and social revolutions that led up to nationalism, imperialism, and conflict in the twentieth century.

Drawing on the work of David Voelker, Tony developed a way to help his students learn some of the basic modes of thinking in which expert historians engage.[16] Each week, Tony would give students a quiz based on two claims pertaining to the historical topic his class was studying, such as "agriculture was the worst mistake in human history" or "Hitler and the Nazis were mostly to blame for the start of World War II."

Tony asked students to prepare for class by reading the assigned texts in ways that would position them to take two very different stances on each claim: a stance *for* the claim, and a stance *against* it. For both stances, students were to present accurate and specific evidence; their reasoning, for or against, was to be clear and sound. When students arrived in class, they faced the possibility of being asked by Tony to write two paragraphs: one arguing for and the other arguing against one of the claims.

To carry out this task, students could not simply memorize and repeat facts. Rather, they had to marshal historical evidence, analyze it, explore emergent historical ideas, and explain those ideas in ways that made sense. Facts were not irrelevant, of course, but they were to be treated as in service of building an argument. Rather than *looking up* the answer, students had to *come up* with their own answers, any number of which could be valid if they drew on historical examples and evidence. Tony described this new assignment, which replaced his frequent multiple-choice quizzes, as positioning students to think like historians. He found that more students read the assigned primary and secondary sources and that they read them more carefully. Examples of such primary sources included excerpts from Greek philosophers discussing women in ancient Athens and Sparta; a letter in which the Roman governor Pliny encounters Christianity for the first time; and women miners' and child laborers' accounts of working in nineteenth century mines in Britain during the Industrial Revolution.

Students liked the new assessments, finding them more interesting than the earlier multiple-choice approach. The format gave them more of a voice, and they came to understand the value of arguing soundly from multiple perspectives rather than only taking in information that reinforced what they already believe. Tony's students often wrote paragraphs that wove in content from prior weeks in the term, making larger connections across the course topics.

Tony's approach fundamentally transformed how many of his students learned history and strengthened their abilities to think historically. He planned to extend his approach by asking students to write *their own* "for and against" claims and to rely more heavily on primary source documents and less on the distanced treatments typically available in textbooks.

Tony exemplifies a teacher who seeks to advance his students' learning to think historically as he introduces core ideas in his introductory level course. For example, in MetroCITI sessions, Tony discussed his attraction to teaching the concept of nation, which he views as a core historical concept requiring learners to think in depth, as historians do—indeed about a limited bit of knowledge—as opposed to having them amass a breadth of disconnected facts on the topic without ever exploring its meaning. He attends closely to who his students are, what they know from their previous lives in school and from the world outside the classroom, and the distinctive challenges they present in class. But Tony keeps the study of history as a discipline in the foreground. He does not merely want to see students complete his course, with a grade and credit in hand; he wants them to know what it means to think about historical ideas, much as historians do, and to engage in such thinking themselves.

Much the same can be said about Eryn and her students, who learn about the scientific method and then use it the way geologists use it; about Lauren and her students, who come to understand evidence-backed claims and learn to produce them much as professional writers do; and about Aaron, who scaffolds class conversations to induce students to think and talk about core statistical ideas, thereby helping students voice statistical sensibilities that, prior to engaging in his class, they may not have known they had. It was not enough for these instructors to produce students who could cite "the right answers" to statistical problems without understanding the thinking that got them there, to follow writing procedures without understanding these procedures' connection to claims (including what counts as claims), to memorize scientific facts without understanding their origins, or to reproduce historical chronologies without grasping the nature of the events they represented. Feeling dissatisfied—worried, uncomfortable, annoyed—they "dug in," reconsidering what they would teach in classes that in some cases they had been teaching for years, all with the aim of bringing their students, ever more fully, into the circle of subject-matter expertise that they themselves had mastered and now sought to share.

CHAPTER THREE

Surfacing

Unearthing Students' Prior Knowledge to Foster Learning

Academic learning is sometimes described as students' efforts to internalize the knowledge of disciplines and fields like physics, history, mathematics, engineering, business, pharmacy, and others that colleges and universities offer via curricula developed and taught by faculty who are experts in these domains. Stopping there, however, yields an incomplete and mistaken view of what students' learning entails. Research on how people learn subject matter has shown that learning is a far more complex process—that there is more to it than taking in knowledge.[1] And because learning is complex, efforts to support it—such as those that focus on teaching—are as well. Instructors who think of their students' learning only as a process of knowledge internalization are likely to enact a foreshortened version of teaching.

What makes learning so complex? No one has said it better than Lee Shulman, who portrays learning as both "getting knowledge that is inside to move out and getting knowledge that is outside to move in."[2] "Basically," Shulman says, learning is the "interplay of [these] two challenging processes." The knowledge that's inside and that warrants coming out—often referred to as "prior knowledge"—may be academic or it may be cultural or personal. Learners may be in touch with it or they may not. Their prior knowledge may be so engrained in their minds, such a deep part of their beliefs and how they see and make sense of the world, that they won't be fully aware that they know it or that defensible alternatives exist. To advance students' learning of an academic idea that's new to them, teachers must support students in pulling out and acknowledging the knowledge rooted in their lives that bears on the new. This is what we mean by surfacing as a principle of convergent teaching.

Prior knowledge is powerful. When it lines up, even roughly, with a new subject matter concept, learners can use it to "get a leg up" on working through that new concept, drawing on ideas from daily life to leverage their learning. A teacher who is familiar with students' prior knowledge can help them to take advantage of their prior knowledge. However, several things can interfere with this. For example, students may be willing to bring out their prior knowledge, but their teachers may neglect to use it in teaching core disciplinary concepts; without the forging of connections between what students know and new academic concepts, students may learn superficially. Students may, for example, learn just enough of the new material that their teachers present to pass a test or a course but not deeply enough as to frame their future thoughts. Or they may learn procedures without deeply understanding why the procedures work as they do or the nature of the problem that the procedures seek to address. They may get to "right answers" (e.g., by calculating an average) but without understanding underlying knowledge landscapes and dynamics (i.e., visualizing average as a midpoint that balances a distribution of values).[3]

Another stumbling block can occur when learners' values, cultural views, spiritual beliefs, and hard-learned visions of "common sense" lead them to resist disciplinary ideas that are starkly inconsistent with their own. Student learning is difficult under such circumstances. Teaching is as well, requiring substantial reconsideration of core professional responsibilities and norms around what it means to teach responsibly, humanely, and with utmost respect. We acknowledge that addressing differences between students' prior knowledge and disciplinary knowledge is challenging under all circumstances and believe that many postsecondary instructors are ill prepared to address this task. We surmise that instructors who do figure out how to bridge such differences proceed largely on their own.

Teachers attuned to students' prior knowledge—both the kind that helps and the kind that slows or otherwise gets in the way of learning— attend as closely to what learners do with their prior knowledge as to what they do with the new concepts they are learning. They invoke practices for surfacing students' beliefs and understandings around content being learned just as energetically as they invoke practices for targeting and articulating the concepts to be learned, thus balancing their classroom practice between the first two principles of convergent teaching.

In this chapter, we present several examples of teachers working attentively to surface and use students' prior knowledge. In the first two, instructors use prior knowledge affirmatively to leverage students' learning of new subject matter. In the third, an instructor positions students to rethink prior beliefs that threaten to derail learning. Though teaching students in different kinds of educational institutions (middle school, a four-year institution, a community college), all communicate insights relevant to surfacing as the second principle of convergent teaching in undergraduate education.

Modeling "the T" to Understand Vectors in Algebra: Robert P. Moses

In a classic educational account, civil rights pioneer Robert P. Moses, who founded the Algebra Project, discusses his encounters with middle-school students learning mathematics in the magnet Open program at the Martin Luther King Jr. School in Cambridge, Massachusetts.[4] He was particularly concerned with the minority and working-class children in the program whose math skills were below grade level and who were internalizing the message that algebra was not for them. As the school community moved to commit to the idea that all seventh- and eighth-grade students should learn algebra, he struggled to reach students whose conception of number had not advanced beyond counting. Counting works fine for the arithmetic operation of addition, but for algebra, whose expressions apply the basic arithmetic operations of addition, subtraction, multiplication, division, and exponentiation to variables without a pre-specified value, knowing how to work with positive and negative numbers is an essential step. Moses surmised that some of his students were stuck in making the transition from arithmetic to algebra because they did not join questions about magnitude (e.g., "how many?") to questions about direction (e.g., "which way?").

Moses had the insight that students could use their knowledge about how to navigate the stations on Boston's subway system, the T, to reason about Cartesian coordinates and vectors, graphic representations of algebraic equations. The relative position of one station to another could be expressed as a displacement from a fixed starting point. Virtually every child in Cambridge was familiar with the T, and Moses took his students on a field trip, starting with the Central Square stop near the King School. Students rode the T inbound toward Boston and then rode outbound past their initial starting point, finally returning to Central Square.

Returning to the classroom, students constructed diagrams showing, for example, that Park Street Station was three stops inbound from Central Square, whereas Harvard Square was four stops outbound from Park Street Station. The diagrams conveyed both how many stops separated the subway stations and which way one had to travel to get from one to another. (Traveling two stops inbound from Central Square takes one to the Charles/Massachusetts General Hospital station, whereas two stops outbound lands one at the Porter station.) In talking about their trips and the diagrams they drew, the students chose their own benchmark stations as a point of reference, giving the benchmark station a value of 0. They learned that regardless of which station they chose as a benchmark, they derived the same numerical quantity in answering a question such as "In what direction and how many stops is Park Street Station from Central Square?"[5]

In this case, we saw Moses draw on the knowledge of the T and its stations that his students had constructed from their daily lives in Boston to help them understand signed distances, a concept fundamental to Cartesian coordinates and algebra, subject-matter gateways to study in advanced mathematics and scientific and technical careers. Using the T instructionally could work only because the King Open students in Cambridge shared a set of cultural practices about navigating the subway. (They knew more about it than some of their teachers, who were more likely to drive from place to place than take the T.) For a different population of students—say, rural youth in Pennsylvania—a teacher would need to look to different cultural practices and beliefs as forms of prior knowledge on which to build.

Robert Moses's approach worked because he had command of two important elements of teaching. First, he had deep understanding of the subject matter at issue, algebra, which made it possible for him to recognize the need to help students think through a core precursor to understanding and evaluating algebraic expressions (namely, that the distance between two points has both a magnitude and a direction). Second, Moses understood how knowledge of the T was deeply embedded in his students' everyday lives, and he believed in the power of "people talk" as a means of expressing ideas. We might infer that Moses's unearthing of what students knew already as a result of navigating their day-to-day lives helped him spot promising linkages between their personal knowledge and core features of the mathematics they were struggling to learn. In one sense, the T was a vehicle of daily life; in another, it represented a mathematical logic. Moses used both these facets of the T to help his young students learn some foundational mathematics.

Although Moses's approach of drawing from students' prior day-to-day knowledge worked well with middle-school children learning algebra, one might wonder about the extent to which the approach is applicable at the college level. How interested can college and university instructors get in their adult students' local prior knowledge, and how willing are those instructors to embed students' personal knowledge in their teaching of college-level subjects? To consider this question, we turn to the teaching of Scott Carlin, a geographer at Long Island University (LIU) Post who models one way to do this.

Situating Lives to Define Situated Prosperity in Human Geography: Scott Carlin

LIU Post is the largest campus of Long Island University, a private institution located in a suburb of New York City. Just under half of the institution's six thousand undergraduates attend full time. In 2016, LIU Post admitted 81% of its applicants; half of the enrollees identify as white, and about 20% identify either as Black or Latino. Slightly under one-half of the students who entered in 2010 to pursue a bachelor's degree had graduated in six years.[6]

Scott, an associate professor of geography in LIU Post's Department of Earth and Environmental Science, teaches courses on sustainability, earth science, and human geography. His introductory human geography class examines human development in the context of food and agriculture, urbanization, and social and economic geography. Seeking to anchor students' thinking conceptually amid this topical breadth, Scott, a 2014–15 MetroCITI fellow, selected the concept of prosperity, human geographers' representation of "what individuals are looking for in life," as core to his teaching of this course in fall 2014. He hoped that the course would "get students feeling like they have a sense of competency" when it came to varied images of prosperity for themselves and others.

Intrigued by the potential of students' prior knowledge to support their learning of the subject matters of human geography, Scott launched the fall 2014 version of his course by drawing out individual students' personal definitions of prosperity. He sought to use both what students knew and believed as they started his class (before exposure to much of the course's content), as well as what they could see and hear of one another's prior beliefs, to nudge them collectively toward nuanced research-based conceptions of prosperity.

As Scott experimented with approaches to drawing out his students' prior knowledge, he discerned that the native Long Islanders in his class were visualizing prosperity quite differently than his international students were. He pointed out the differences in class, showing students that these differences among them demonstrated a central feature of prosperity: as a concept and goal, prosperity varies for different populations, located in different places and times. For example, American students were more likely to view prosperity as an individual attribute, while foreign students expressed greater support for prosperity as a shared attribute. Further, he noted, although it has an aura of objectivity, the concept of prosperity is at least partly subjective, as it evokes values and sensibilities when individuals describe what it is. Pointing out to students how their personal definitions of prosperity differed depending on their geographic, socioeconomic, cultural, and political origins, Scott conveyed a challenging feature of the concept of prosperity that students might read about in their texts but that might not "hit home" until they saw it in their own and in their classmates' lives. He was then able to use features of students' lives to introduce a concept fundamental to his class.

Scott represents an instructor who has deep expertise in his subject matter, geography, who seeks to share with his class the cultural, social, and political situatedness, and thus meanings, of the term "prosperity." The concept of prosperity and its situated nature are central to Scott's pedagogical representations of human geography. It would have been easy enough for him to use lecture to define prosperity quickly and simply and then move on to other course topics. After all, he had plenty of theory and research to back up the assertions he could make. Scott learned that it was far more powerful to capture the concept of prosperity as it materialized in "live form" through students' talk in class and then to encourage students to see differences in representations of prosperity in their own and in each other's lives. Scott would return to images of prosperity through the remainder of the course, linking the concept of prosperity to other topics in the study of human geography.

Robert Moses and Scott Carlin use aspects of their students' prior knowledge to scaffold their understanding of core subject-matter concepts, a practice that infuses the strangeness of challenging new material in mathematics and human geography with the familiar. Select aspects of students' prior knowledge may, if well used, support their academic learning. However, prior knowledge also may pose teaching challenges, as when students surface ideas, including assumptions and logics, that clash with or elide disciplinary thought. Teaching in such instances may require respectful redirection of students' prior beliefs, including the posing of alternatives. To illustrate this point, we return to Eryn Klosko, teaching introductory earth science typically to nonmajor students at Westchester Community College in New York.

Distinguishing Empirical Evidence from Unfounded Belief in Earth Science: Eryn Klosko

Looking back on her thirteen years of teaching earth science, Eryn worried that some of her students were not grasping the distinctiveness of the scientific method and so weren't able to use it in adjudicating competing geologic theories. And as we observed in chapter 2, she believed that this limited their learning later in the course. On realizing this, Eryn decided to revamp her course, devoting more time to students' learning of the scientific method early in the term and then guiding their return to it through the full semester. While this change—a shift in emphasis and tightening of attention to the scientific method as the course's core idea—seemed like a step in the right direction, Eryn worried that it was not enough to secure students' understanding of the core tenets of the scientific method. What, she wondered, were students thinking that might deter them from connecting to the scientific perspective she sought to instill? More to the point, what prior knowledge and previously developed ways of knowing might be getting in the way of their use of the scientific method?

Eryn's hunch was that some of her students' thinking about science was being derailed by pseudoscientific ideas about the natural world, many of which were promulgated by a variety of popular media to which they were regularly exposed. For example, in a class of thirty-three students, there were at least five, perhaps more, who embraced pseudoscience or supernatural phenomena, taking in and believing much of what they saw on TV and questioning little of it.[7] To test her supposition, Eryn had her students fill out a questionnaire to take stock of their beliefs in magic, spirits, aliens, psychic powers, astrology, and other forms of pseudoscience. Eryn worried that while many of her students might correctly espouse the tenets of the scientific method on tests and in classwork, some would hold on to such beliefs in ways that could deter their learning of advanced geologic ideas, such as, for example, how scientists derive findings or negate false claims. She worried that her past teaching had not encouraged students to examine the scientific process in sufficient depth. Failure to pinpoint differences between science and pseudoscience could lead students to elevate popular (often compellingly rendered) pseudoscience over the scientific method in thinking through issues in their personal and civic lives.

Eryn began tackling this problem, laying out the differences between a natural, scientific system and one attuned to fantasy and the paranormal.

She then shared a scientific "checklist" emphasizing the features of the scientific method. She helped her students see that science (a) focuses on the natural world; (b) aims to explain the natural world; (c) uses testable ideas; (d) relies on evidence; (e) depends on the scientific community; (f) leads to ongoing research; and (g) benefits from scientific behavior. Eryn then gave her students a homework assignment that asked them to watch two short video clips from the Animal Planet TV series "Mermaids Revealed." She then asked students to use the features of the scientific checklist to write a brief essay on the clips, discussing if the footage was from a documentary reflective of serious journalism or a "mockumentary" that used the documentary format to lampoon a false belief. (The footage was, of course, from a mockumentary.)

Back in the classroom, students discussed the distinction between empirical evidence and unfounded belief. Eryn asked them what sort of evidence to prove the existence of mermaids would be most convincing. Through such discussions, during which students surfaced their deeply embedded beliefs (for example, in mermaids) and compared them to scientific ideas, as well as through discussions of how scientific ideas are derived (summarized on Eryn's checklist), students came to rethink some of their assumptions about the natural world. In doing so, they also deepened their understanding of the process of scientific thought.

Because Eryn regarded understanding of the scientific method, including the ability to distinguish science from pseudoscience, as central to students' lives and to mastery of earth science, she was willing to devote time not only to sharing her own knowledge of the scientific method but also to surfacing and supporting students' reflection on popular pseudoscientific beliefs they'd absorbed. That left less time for other course content, a sacrifice she was prepared to make. Were Eryn to forego attention to students' prior knowledge, her students might, indeed, memorize the tenets of the scientific method and even pass her tests and the course. But their attraction to unfounded belief might remain unmediated by more critical, science-based thought. Such flawed understandings might influence decisions that students would make in the future in connection with personal and family health, stewardship of the environment, and political leadership. This was something Eryn felt she could not risk.

Like Robert Moses and Scott Carlin, Eryn Klosko understood that students' prior knowledge can influence their learning of core ideas. But whereas Moses and Carlin unearthed student knowledge that aligned well with core subject-matter ideas, Klosko surfaced flawed beliefs that had the potential to deter students' learning. This required a different teaching approach, working through inconsistencies between students' prior knowledge and core disciplinary content. Eryn felt that she could move on to the course's broader survey of geology only after she'd established that base.

What alternatives do teachers have in addressing students' flawed prior knowledge in respectful ways? Although this topic deserves far closer examination than we can undertake here, we offer the following insight from our on-going work: students' prior knowledge may be substantively or logically consistent with new ideas and thus potentially helpful to them. But some prior knowledge may be flawed or incomplete and have the potential to derail students' learning. A student may be able to generate both forms of prior knowledge, but it's hard to know which form will be the first to surface—that is, which form is more accessible to and retrievable for students. Teaching, in this situation, may entail sorting through a classroom of different student responses reflecting prior knowledge that is both more and less useful to their learning.

One approach that a teacher can use to zoom in on prior knowledge that is usable for teaching and learning is to listen for and amplify student ideas and beliefs that promise to bridge to the subject-matter knowledge the class is studying, while minimizing attention to those that are less helpful. Another is to give students time and opportunities to surface positive alternatives on their own—for example, via extended whole-room conversation, focused group work that allows peer teaching, or opportunities to write out their thoughts reflectively. In such cases, it will have been beneficial for the teacher to prepare for class by imagining, in advance, the various forms of knowledge that students might raise and how she or he might respond to them if they materialize. We present a case of a philosophy teacher who uses such strategies in the second half of chapter 4.

We realize that approaches such as these will not always work, as when students' flawed beliefs are so deeply etched in their minds or their commitments to them so tight that alternatives, offered by teacher and peers alike, slide by. When such ideas threaten to harm students' learning of important substantive concepts, a teacher will likely need to address them head on—for example, by setting up comparisons to more desirable forms of thought, much as Eryn did with the checklist and mockumentary assignment that she created for the new iteration of her course. Teachers can, of course, also take their teaching out of the classroom, into face-to-face or virtual conversations with individual students that elicit the nature of students' prior knowledge.

Much like targeting, surfacing, our second principle of convergent teaching, demands a great deal from teachers: attentiveness, creativity, patience, and concern for the people in their classes whose learning they strive to support. But as the preceding cases of Eryn Klosko, Robert Moses, and Scott Carlin show, surfacing is hard to accomplish: no planning mechanism can predict the path or the time it will take to surface knowledge, useable for teaching, from students' lives; no script exists to guide this; no texts can serve as resources for its implementation. Although core disciplinary ideas can be targeted in advance, students' prior knowledge, for the most part, cannot be. It's largely unknown to teachers prior to students sharing it.

Teachers discern students' prior knowledge largely on the spot, in the heat of teaching; for support, they draw primarily on their own wisdom, common sense, and abilities to inquire, with care and respect, in the moment of talk with a student. Teachers can prepare by spending as much advance time as possible studying up on who their students are, what they likely know and value, what they reach for, and where and why they may stumble and struggle. They can pursue this inquiry ever more specifically as, through the course of a term, they grow in their understanding of who their students are, how and what they think, and how their thoughts both change and persist. With such knowledge in hand, teachers can shape representations of the core subject-matter concepts they've targeted to the specific students in front of them.

CHAPTER FOUR

Navigating

Orchestrating Subject-Matter Concepts and Students' Prior Knowledge

Acts of targeting and surfacing are key to convergent teaching. But what happens next? Having identified the subject-matter knowledge to be taught and relevant slices of students' prior knowledge, teachers can create opportunities for these two forms of knowledge to interact, as students weigh each in light of what the other offers. This is part of what we mean by navigating as the third principle of convergent teaching.

Ideally, a teacher can orchestrate a gradual build-up to this encounter between the known and the unknown. In Aaron's statistics class, students linked a new vision of the middle of a distribution (the balance point) to a highly familiar image, the seesaw, which they used to begin to think through the concept of the mean or average. Learners also can be primed to use new subject-matter concepts to change or somehow reorganize their prior knowledge. This can, of course, be quite challenging, as it may be for those of Eryn Klosko's students who are deeply attached to pseudoscientific thought. Addressed with care, teaching that proceeds in light of just the first two principles can, we suggest, stimulate learning. But often teachers must do more to promote and support students' learning at the point that prior knowledge and disciplinary knowledge interact.

Instructional navigation of this kind demands significant effort on the part of teachers—it calls for deep and flexible knowledge of the subject matters they teach and knowledge of their students, as well as a desire and will to inquire into how students think as their learning unfolds.

Navigating between two related but often differing forms of knowledge can be particularly intense, as instructors balance both sides—steering forward, guided by deeply mapped out subject-matter knowledge, but adjusting the route in light of how students respond, at times in surprising ways, to the new landscapes that come into view.

To illustrate what navigating, as the culminating aspect of convergent teaching, might look like in class, we first present the case of Allison (Allie) Bach, who crafted an intricate instructional design for teaching an introductory composition class at Hudson Community College. This is a story of navigation by design. We follow this with the case of a philosophy instructor, "Sofia," teaching at "Meritage University," also in the New York metro area. Sofia's teaching shows that even the most intentionally directed teaching demands wide-ranging improvisational response, constructed from much more than disciplinary expertise and knowledge about students' lives. It requires caring about and responding with care to who students are and what they feel as teaching and learning unfold.

Navigating by Design as Students Learn to Write: Allie Bach

Allie Bach, who has advanced from instructor of English in the English and ESL Division at Hudson to assistant professor of English, teaches approximately five courses per term, including several sections of English composition; she also teaches introduction to film and world literature to 1650, as well as an interdisciplinary course on culture and values.

When we first met Allie in fall 2014, she was struggling with a problem: her composition students, she said, did not purposely ignore or resist the writing concepts and practices she introduced in class but were so used to everyday writing, like emailing the boss or texting with friends, that they found academic writing, the focus of her class, difficult to replicate. Moreover, the writing that many of her students had learned in high school or in developmental classes—she cited the proverbial five-paragraph essay—differed too from the kind of writing she sought to teach.[1] Allie realized that what her students knew about writing already and how they enacted it outside class differed from the kind of writing she wanted them to understand and to produce. Based on her learning in MetroCITI, Allie decided to give the students in her fall 2014 composition class a different way to begin.

Drawing on insights from Linda S. Flower's research on cognition and rhetoric, Allie sought to restructure her students' learning of composition around a core writing concept: audience.[2] She viewed authors as writing to communicate with someone other than themselves. To make themselves understandable, they need to bear in mind their readers' expectations, needs, and topic awareness as they write. Further, as an expert in the teaching of writing, Allie knew that writers have options when it comes to wording, tone, images, sequencing of key points, topical focus, and the like. That semester, Allie did her best to help students learn how to match these standard elements of composition to the interests, linguistic proclivities, and background knowledge of the people who would read their texts.

Teaching the standard elements of composition was not new to Allie; this is what writing teachers do, and what she had done in the past. Teaching these elements, including the choices that authors (in this case, her students) have in deploying them, while also teaching how to make those choices in light of what readers need to know and think, would, however, be new for her. Allie would have to sharpen students' attention to audience, then hold their attention there through the full semester. She would then need to consider how to teach the standard elements of composition with the concept of audience in the foreground.

Though expecting her students to have a good understanding of the concept of audience from their daily conversations, including their texting and emailing (and who wouldn't, in an era of social media?), Allie suspected that many had not used that concept previously to frame their academic writing. Typically, students' first papers in her course included poorly structured narratives and insufficient explanation, or they lacked a topical focus, which meant a reader would not grasp the writer's key points. Many papers included specialized terms indiscernible to a reader without background knowledge of them; most did not include such background information. While more could be at play, the papers suggested that students, many of whom had something to say, had not thought enough about what their reader would need to grasp their messages.

To illustrate the challenge she regularly faced, Allie gave an example of a student, "very passionate about car shows," who, in his early writing for her composition class, described a recent argument with another car-show aficionado. Offering little background, the student had asserted that "Boshe, K&N and H&R made my car faster, giving extra horsepower, even saving my gas mileage." He then had noted that his "competitor," namely the person with whom he was arguing, preferred "Raceland, OBX, and Factory OEM." The student wrote then that the "competitor" had "won the raffle," and he followed by acknowledging that the event had changed "my beliefs in what I thought was perfect performance for my car."

Encountering the student's text, a reader who knows little about cars and car shows would likely be confused. What exactly is a car show? What kinds of cars were on display in the show that the student describes, and why? As "fans" of car shows, what did the student and his "competitor" hope to gain from attendance at this one in particular? What is a raffle in the context of a car show, and what might it mean to win or lose one? How does the "competitor" concept fit in? What is the meaning of the technical automotive terms that the student and his "competitor" use, and why do they matter?

Without such background knowledge built into the text, a reader gets lost, as did Allie. She could not grasp the content of the argument that the student, in his essay, said he had with his competitor; nor could she discern any larger point he may have been seeking to make. Was the student advocating for certain car parts or products? Or was he trying to make a point about car shows or raffles associated with them? Or was his aim, perhaps, to show how his thinking about something he thought he knew well could change, with car products simply serving as convenient examples? What point did the student wish to convey through the narrative?

Every semester, Allie faced the conundrum reflected in this example: how to help students share an insight drawn from their deep acquaintance with a topic central to their lives—an aspect of their well-etched prior knowledge—with readers less familiar with the subject. She came to realize that part of helping students learn to do this requires getting them to accept that to make yourself understood, you must (a) know what you're talking about, and (b) have a basic sense of who you are talking to. In brief, you have to know your audience. Making yourself understood also requires knowing the kind of talk—wording, tone, ordering of ideas, examples, evidence—that will help your audience get your point.

Allie was confident that in their daily lives, students understood a basic precept of human communication: to be understood, one must shape one's message so that others *get what you say*. That takes knowing those others and shaping what and how one talks to them in light of that. The challenge, of course, is to move this knowledge—and know-how—from students' daily interactions (spoken, texted, briefly emailed) to their academic writing. To do so, students would need to position themselves to pose, think through, and be guided by a number of questions. What kinds of arguments, examples, explanations, justifications, word choices, tone, and so on is my reader likely to expect, be open to accepting, and understand? And what kinds not? What can I provide to advance my reader's understanding of the point I want to make? To produce compelling arguments in writing, students would need to make good use of these and other elements of composition. They would have to understand them and use them effectively.

With this insight, Allie developed a plan: in fall 2014, she would teach her students to use the various elements of composition as she had in prior semesters. But rather than marching them linearly through that standard lineup as she had in the past, she would bind those elements of composition to the core concept of audience. She therefore committed herself to teaching each of the elements of composition, but this time *in relation to* the core concept of audience. As Allie saw it, audience is a powerful concept, driving the choices that expert writers make about which compositional element to use, how, when, and for what purpose. Allie would teach the concept of audience thoroughly early in the semester, first by linking it to students' everyday conceptions of audience, then by moving those conceptions from everyday use to academic writing. Through the rest of the semester, she would, as usual, roll out the elements of composition, but she would tie them back continually to the concept of audience. Her aim, she said, was to help her students "move from writing short, personal narratives," often "writer-based" in substance, form, and tone, toward producing well-crafted "reader-based" essays that were "longer, more complex," and that "incorporated outside sources." She would use the core concept of audience to shape a path along which students would learn her course's content.

Allie introduced the concept of audience in the third week of the fall 2014 term. She started class by asking students to list the various kinds of writing they had done throughout their lives—texts, emails, casual notes, book reports, business memos, letters of complaint, and so on. Allie then listed the responses on the blackboard for all to review together. Scanning the list, she asked the students how it was different to be writing an email to a friend as opposed to writing a complaint to Amazon for getting an order wrong. Students responded readily: different letters—about different things and to different people—include different kinds of information, they have different tones, and so on.

The stage now set, Allie pulled out a container containing several folded pieces of paper, each naming a different audience. Students organized themselves into groups, and a student from each group drew one. Students were to write a "group letter" convincing their designated audience to lend them $20. Thus, one group wrote to a younger brother, another group to a professor, and so on. Thus, each group composed a written request for the same thing ($20) but for a different audience. Allie had students read their group letters to the full class. She then asked the class to consider how the several group letters differed. How had each group shaped its text based on who group members were writing to? In the discussion that followed, Allie positioned students to formulate the very point she wanted them to grasp: how we write is shaped by our knowledge of who we are writing to, especially what we know about these persons. The concept of audience became a linchpin, hooking students' prior understanding of writing for an audience in daily life to their efforts now to learn what was involved in writing for an academic audience. With this connection firmly in place, Allie prepared to move her class forward toward still more complex views of audience, including use of various compositional elements for shaping readers' understanding.

In the next writing assignment, each student composed a letter to the college dean pointing out a campus problem of their choice, explaining it, and presenting their preferred solution along with appropriate justification. Continuing in the spirit of the earlier discussion, Allie encouraged students to think through their options in presenting their case to the dean. "What would the dean's expectations be?" she asked her class. "What kind of writing does he want to see in this letter? And what kinds of problems is he going to think are worth solving? How can you include evidence that will be persuasive to him? How can you show him that your solution is a viable, practical solution?"

Students brought their essays to class. However, in a departure from her past practice, Allie did not collect them. She had another task in mind. Working in pairs, students were to review each other's papers and provide their partners with feedback, but with a twist: the reviewer would read and comment on the partner's essay twice, each time assuming a different persona. In a first round, the reviewer would assume the perspective of the dean, who, Allie stipulated, would be inclined not to attend to the problem at issue. Generating as many objections as possible to the seriousness of the problem and/or the proposed solution, the reviewer would construct a "doubting list," in Allie's words, "noting every argument you can make against your partner's claims." Then in the second round, the reader would do this again, but this time from the perspective of "a student at the college who really wants this thing to take place" and "believes every claim that the letter writer makes." In this round, the reviewer would create a "believing list," providing evidence and examples to supplement those in the essay already. The reviewer also would recommend "clarifications" the writer could make that could help strengthen her or his argument.[3] After each student in the pair completed the two-round review independently, the two students shared their results with one another.

In this phase of her teaching, Allie had mobilized two aspects of students' prior knowledge of a particular campus problem (their sense of how college administrators think about that problem and of how college students conceptualize and experience it) to ready them to formulate a written request of the dean, their audience. Responding to one's writing partner's "doubting list" and "believing list" about the kind of argument that would work—or not work—with the dean deepened students' understanding of the concept of audience and also of how they might deploy selected elements of composition to address a particular reader. Excited by the thinking Allie heard her students trying out as they planned their essays and reviewed each other's work, she decided that henceforth, her assignments to the class would specify both what students were to write about and whom they were writing to. How would Allie's semester-long experiment roll out?

Late into the semester, Allie remained excited and hopeful about her revised approach to teaching writing. But she admitted to several challenges. Despite her efforts to position students to write authentically for a particular audience (e.g., the dean, a little brother, etc.), students knew that ultimately the paper's reader (and grader) would be the instructor. They also knew that little would come of their efforts. For example, the letters students wrote to the dean about problems that they and their peers experienced would have no impact at all, as they knew that Allie would not be taking them to college administrators. Allie wondered whether it might be possible to invent one or more real audiences for her students to attend to as they wrote as a way of infusing more authenticity into class assignments, perhaps through a class blog or a class literary journal.

Other challenges materialized through her first semester of teaching with the concept of audience. Allie quickly realized that not all students were equally familiar with the various audiences she might designate in assignments or with the genres of writing that particular audiences required. For example, in assigning the writing of an editorial, she learned that several students did not know what one was. Although willing to engage in extra teaching, Allie puzzled over how much time and effort to devote to covering such gaps in her students' knowledge, given her aim to keep the content of English composition and audience at the foreground of the course.

Another concern was that the concept of audience did not work well for all the writing topics she wanted to assign. For example, one assignment, to discuss a ritual of personal meaning, does not assume a clear audience. Would she retain the assignment, and if so, how might she locate it in the course, given the new focus? Further, the two-round peer feedback sessions that Allie worked into her class also yielded uneven results. Students varied in the quality of feedback they provided their partners, and she had to alter the review phase for students who did not wish to share particular essays with peers. How might she do this better?

Yet even as Allie encountered challenges, she imagined approaches to addressing them. What if, for some assignments, she asked students to specify their own audience? Doing so would position students to select audiences they already knew something about, thereby limiting her need to teach students about unfamiliar audiences, an issue at some distance from the course objectives. Allie also realized that students' newly gained knowledge of how to use audience in writing might not transfer to their writing in other classes, since her colleagues in other disciplines do not typically denote audience in their assignments. How, then, could she enable students to continue to use what they had learned about audience and further develop that knowledge in other classes that they took, now and in the future? And how might Allie share her own learning with colleagues, perhaps having them test and elaborate on it?

The preceding narrative portrays Allie's enactment of the principle of navigating. We see how she steered students' prior knowledge about audience toward learning what it means in the context of composition. The case presents an expert writing teacher's unique standpoint on the expertise she seeks to share with students, on her students' thinking about and acting on a specific aspect of that knowledge, on her options for further shaping their responses and actions she took to effect that shaping, and on the broader surround.[4] We offer four observations.

First, we see Allie navigating between a targeted core concept, audience, and her students' prior knowledge of that concept, much of which may be tacit. She sought to surface and activate that prior knowledge so that students could use it to improve their academic writing, the broad goal of her introductory English composition course.

Second, we observe the consequences of her organizing a course around a core concept, audience, not just in the class sessions specifically devoted to that concept but also in the course sessions that followed. Use of the core concept obliged her to reconstruct the course, leading her to align other course topics with the concept of audience and to trim and revise other course content. In doing so, she changed, too, how students engaged with those course topics.

Third, we note that rather than relying on lecture, Allie designed class activities, including discussions, to elicit students' prior knowledge of the concept of audience and to orchestrate its encounter with audience as a concern in academic writing. Her students' learning about audience emerged from how they thought their way through these activities, with Allie offering guidance and suggesting ways forward as the students articulated their insights and came up against challenges.

And finally, we note that for Allie, teaching is not limited to the time she spends in the classroom. Outside class, Allie plans, reflects on, and revises the myriad decisions that she makes toward advancing her students' learning of English composition.

The way Allie brings navigating to life, is strategic, calculated, watchful, and fully responsive to her views of students' needs. It self-corrects. It evolves. It's open to change as insights emerge through phases of planning, implementation, and retrospection. It is fully designed but cultivated, slowly, as well.

Improvising as Students Awaken to Philosophical Inquiry: "Sofia"

The case of Allie's teaching illustrates how key features of convergent teaching can come together when the third principle of convergent teaching, navigating, is activated in an introductory composition course. Yet we must acknowledge that the picture we've drawn so far is not complete. For one thing, in placing college teachers' thinking and action in the foreground, we have downplayed the contexts in which this teaching occurred, save for brief descriptions of teachers' campuses and the students in their classrooms. This means that to this point, we have disregarded the power of institutional contexts—for example, teaching resources, promotion and tenure policies, institutional imperatives, along with broader state and federal policies, economic forces, and cultural norms and practices that collectively shape how the three principles of convergent teaching can be enacted. We discuss such contexts and ways to use them to promote convergent teaching in chapters 5 and 6.

But before making the leap to institutional and organizational contexts, we must address another question. As teachers give students access to the disciplinary knowledge that they (and possibly their colleagues) have targeted for their classes and as they surface students' prior knowledge, navigating between them, *what's going on with the students*? In particular, what might being steered between the poles of familiar, personal knowledge and unfamiliar, academic knowledge feel like? And how, then, can a teacher address students' emotions, identities, and substantive knowledge, all at once? This question highlights the personal meaning that subject-matter learning can have for students, sometimes opening new and exciting vistas for them but at other times bringing painful issues to light that, if mishandled, can dampen students' desires to learn.[5] That it takes into account questions of emotion and personal meaning makes convergent teaching a powerfully moral undertaking. In the following case of Adina, a student in a first-year introduction to philosophy class taught by Sofia, her teacher, at Meritage University, Sofia faithfully works through the three principles, attentive to Adina's learning of a core philosophical concept while heeding closely what Adina feels, who she is and what she values, and who she seeks to be.[6]

Meritage is a diverse, private urban university serving about eighty-five hundred students, 60% of them undergraduates. Virtually all are commuters. Undergraduate programs span liberal arts and preprofessional areas. A majority of students aspire to careers in the health professions. About two-thirds of undergraduates are students of color. Most students rely on financial aid. Most of the undergraduates in Sofia's introductory philosophy class were first-generation college students; many were immigrants or children of immigrants.

What follows is an account of what happened as Sofia led the class through the early portion of René Descartes' *Meditations on First Philosophy*, a text assigned in many introductory philosophy classes. It was the second week of the spring semester, and students had just returned from winter break. Most of what follows here comes from a thirty-minute class segment.

Early in *Meditations,* Descartes subjects his most basic beliefs to doubt. "Do I exist?" he queries. "Might I be asleep—dreaming? Could I be part of another being's dream? Does the world I see, hear, smell, and touch truly exist? Or am I deceived? Could this world be an illusion—the handiwork of an 'evil genius' who uses us for his ends?"[7] Appreciating doubting of this sort is central to understanding Descartes' *Meditations*. Sofia had previously shared what she thought could happen in class as she introduced Descartes' doubt. Some students would relish it, she predicted. Others would question Descartes' common sense and possibly his sanity. Some would debate him. Others would struggle. Some could shut down. Sofia, a tenured associate professor, had taught this class, including Descartes' writings, many times over the twenty years she's served on the Meritage faculty.

When Sofia first introduced Descartes and his question—"Am I asleep? Is this all a dream?"—students volunteered a surprising thought: this sounds a lot like the movie *The Matrix*. The class erupted into talk, with students who knew the movie well filling in those less familiar with it. Sofia let that conversation play out a bit.

In *The Matrix*, a computer hacker named Neo learns that what he thinks is the "real world" is actually an illusion created by a complex computer program. That vast computer system feeds off the energy produced by human beings who are kept immobile in a dream state in pods. Much like Descartes' *Meditations*, *The Matrix* raises the question of whether human beings are trapped in illusion, unable to rely on their senses alone to discern what is real.

Two days later, Sofia opened the discussion by asking students about Cartesian doubt: what is it? "We see it in math. We see it in science," said Sofia. "So, what kind of special doubt does he express in *Meditation One*?" The students hesitated. Some offered words they recalled from the assigned reading. "Senses," a student off to the side answered. Sofia replied, "It has to do with the senses." Another student wondered out loud: "The senses—they're deceived. Sense deception?" "That's part of Cartesian doubt, right?" said Sofia. "It's one of the things he doubts." "He doubts his whole existence," a third student quietly interjected. Sofia confirmed that observation as well: "He does start doubting his own existence." But she added, "What's his method, though?" In a hushed voice, a student answered, "It's like breaking down, like, to the fundamentals and then building up on, you know, what he finds is real." "Right," Sofia replied.

Taking a comment here and there, she wove students' words into a picture of what Descartes is up to in early *Meditations*. "He takes our most basic beliefs," she explained, "and calls those basic beliefs into question so that other beliefs—built on those basic beliefs—also are called into question. He wants to find the most fundamental beliefs that we can't possibly doubt." Sofia paused, then asked again, "So, which are those basic beliefs that he calls into question?" "The senses?" a student offered tentatively. "Right," Sofia replied. "Here's a belief, for example—that I believe my senses are reliable. But Descartes, in his doubting says, 'No, my senses sometimes aren't!'"

Continuing back and forth, Sofia asked students to name other beliefs that Descartes subjects to doubt. She then looked these over. Cartesian doubt, she began, "is a theoretical form of doubt in which our basic beliefs are called into question so that—," and then a student interrupted with "To clear away uncertain beliefs to find certain ones?" Sofia picked the thread back up. "All such beliefs are questioned," she continued. "I can only know I am here in class today if I can know for certain that I am not dreaming, that I am not in the matrix. But I can't know for certain that I am not dreaming. So therefore, I can't really know for certain I am here in class."

Sofia then switched gears. "In *Meditation* Two," she noted, Descartes "looks around. 'Well, is there anything that I can't doubt?' And that," Sofia explained, "is exactly it." She then proceeded to lay out, for the first time, the point that she hoped her students would get: "The mere fact that he is wondering about—his own existence—proves he is existing." Sofia paused. "So." She looked at her class, "What do you think?"

Here, then, is what we see. In the opening moments of class, Sofia drew out what scholars of human cognition would call her students' prior knowledge—in this case, about what Descartes is thinking—that although our world feels real, it may be just a dream.[8] With about a dozen students in class, Sofia was dealing with at least a dozen bits of "prior knowledge." She anchored the class's work in an image drawn from popular culture—the movie *The Matrix*—that students explained to each other. In other words, she used a bit of popular culture to draw together the prior knowledge that each student brought to class and discussed Cartesian doubt in their terms.

Here and there, Sofia "marked" a student's comment that could be useful later. She repeated it, or she asked the student to say it again, or she wrote it on the board. She thereby lifted it gently above other comments without interrupting the flow of classroom talk. Sofia also let her students struggle with ideas, like doubt, that were central to the lesson. Rather than answering her own questions, she waited for a student to offer a reply. When a given student responded, she asked that student for more or created an opening for another student to build on an idea. She also let students interrupt her and finish her sentences. Sofia thereby pulled students into the view of doubt that, initially, she'd outlined in the barest of ways.

Sofia also capitalized on the fact that *The Matrix* resonated with her students regardless of differences in the full range of prior knowledge—academic, cultural, personal—that they brought to class. In this way, the movie offered a useful starting point for launching discussion of the philosophical ideas in *Meditations*.

This, then, is how Sofia, as teacher, worked with her students' prior knowledge: she brought it to the surface. She consolidated its varying forms that arose from her students' highly varied backgrounds, via a cultural artifact, the movie, *The Matrix*. She nudged it forward.

Two points bear comment. First, in keeping with the first principle of convergent teaching, Sofia had targeted doubt—in this case, Cartesian doubt—as a core concept for her students' learning. However, she did not begin class by presenting her expert understanding of this concept. Instead she positioned students to lead the way. Descartes doubts his senses, one student pointed out. He doubts his whole existence, added another. Sofia spotlighted helpful comments, weaving them into a summary drawn from students' own words about Descartes' ideas. Students, at this point, "got" Descartes' message. But they hadn't yet imagined its implications. They had not yet thought through the questions that Cartesian doubt instigates about whether we really can trust our senses. Can we believe that we are fully conscious of our worlds, ourselves, our lives? Although they could repeat what they'd read in Descartes, they weren't yet struggling with whether they believed that Descartes' questions are warranted.

Moreover, in this early class conversation, Sofia did not push her students to struggle with doubt, the targeted core concept. Instead she pushed them to surface images of doubt with which they were personally familiar. *The Matrix*, a movie that resonates with Descartes' questions about existence, popped up, and students spontaneously discussed it, drawing on what they knew, explaining its plot and central idea to classmates who knew little about it. Sofia let students talk about existential doubt in *The Matrix*. She stood by, listening closely, taking note, drawing out students' views, using their words to create a collective image of the movie's representation of doubt. We therefore see the second principle, the surfacing of students' prior knowledge, in amplified form; it's the first piece of convergent teaching to take strong root in Sofia's classroom. Though briefly introduced, the first principle, with its focus on doubt as Descartes means it, had not yet settled deeply into the class's talk. As enacted in this class, convergent teaching starts largely in the middle, with attention to an idea with which students are familiar. It then tacks back and forth between students' personal understandings of doubt, and doubt recast as a philosophical construct that Sofia, much earlier, had targeted for her class's learning.[9]

Second, Sofia worked with students' prior knowledge—unique to each student—but she did so indirectly, channeling it first through a more widely shared popular culture text. As we note in chapter 3, one way for a teacher to approach students' prior knowledge is to regard it as something to be drawn out and examined and as something that the teacher, if need be, ought to correct or revise or, better yet, position students to correct. This approach rests on the idea that prior knowledge is *of an individual* (the student), overlooking its origins in the communities that have shaped what students know. It also casts the teacher's role primarily as one of adjusting a student's prior beliefs so that they match those of the academic expert, the teacher, whose beliefs in turn have been shaped by her disciplinary or professional community. There are other ways for teachers to approach learners' prior knowledge—less as a process whereby the teacher corrects students' initially voiced ideas than as one in which the teacher searches through a vast number of students' offerings, identifies useable forms, and then voices and brings them together.

But even this view is problematic if it assumes that all students in a class share in prior knowledge arising from life in a community of origin (a culture, a neighborhood, a region). It is highly unlikely that any college class—except perhaps the most local, remote, and homogenous—will, these days, reflect such uniformity in prior experience and thought. Consider Sofia's class, populated by students of diverse ethnicities, races, national origins, and no doubt, gender and sexual identities, religions, and linguistic backgrounds. It's unlikely that "correction," as an instructional practice, could be made to apply to them all, if even to any single one. One must then ask, how can a teacher navigate the many different forms of prior knowledge likely to be present in her class, steering a diverse community of students, each espousing differing prior knowledge, toward learning a targeted core concept?

To address just such a pedagogical conundrum, Sofia filtered students' varying contributions through an artifact derived not from their ethnic or other local cultures but rather from the broader popular culture that college students of highly diverse backgrounds share. That artifact is, of course, the movie, *The Matrix*, familiar at the time of the class we have been describing to many college students, regardless of background. Many of the students in Sofia's class were familiar with *The Matrix*, and thus, despite their differences, were able to draw on it as a starting point for thinking about Descartes' *Meditations*. One more thing helps, namely, that classroom-based peer cultures, if activated effectively, can work fast. As we might expect, some of the students in Sofia's class had not seen *The Matrix*. Those who were familiar with it were able to quickly explain it those who weren't.

Through this stream of discourse, students started to link, however tentatively at first, the movie's key question of whether we really exist to Descartes' *Meditations*, including the more complex question that his text broaches of how we can come to address this question.[10] We suggest that more may be at play: surrounded by their peers who are talking about doubt, students may begin to feel their own questions surfacing alongside some anxiety about the applicability of this idea to their own lives. Some may start to think, in some depth, about what they feel.

Let's return to that moment when Sofia's students realized that the big question in *Meditations* runs awfully close to the big question in *The Matrix*. Both lead us to ask, "Are we real? Is our world an illusion?" Curious about what her students would make of all this talk about doubt, Sofia had just asked, "What do you think?" Sitting amid her peers, Adina spoke up. "He makes sense," Adina said, "but it is just not working for me." "What do you mean, 'It's not working'?" Sofia asked her. "I know personally I wouldn't . . . ," Adina replied, her voice dropping. "It's like . . . you've been knowing all this stuff since, like, forever. And then, like, you're gonna doubt it. Like, I can't follow along with him because I don't believe in that personally—" "Yeah," Sofia interjected quietly. Adina continued: "—so I just can't. You believe in something for so long. It's hard—" Sofia picked up on this observation, noting, "It's hard for you to call these basic beliefs into question." Adina interrupted. "Exactly." Sofia replied, "So you are saying, like, 'Yeah, so it's all well and good. He is out there in the woods doubting these things—'" "Exactly," Adina replied, barely audible. "—but, like, it makes sense," Sofia continued, "but you're not going to get up and go out on the street and really wonder whether you're dreaming or not." "Exactly." Adina's voice was now clear.

Echoing Adina, Marcos, a student off in the corner, spoke up. "When you believe a certain thing for years," Marcos said, "you don't just jump on another idea right away. It's hard to accept it." Marcos, like Adina before him, was pointing out that Descartes' kind of doubt was rubbing hard against what they knew and had come to believe in their personal lives. That was their prior knowledge talking. Sofia quickly responded, "Now he doesn't want us to believe that those beliefs we hold to deeply don't exist. He doesn't want us to believe that we actually are dreaming." "But maybe," she added, "just admitting the possibility that it could all be a dream . . ." "I know," Sofia continued, "it's not a pleasant thought." "It's not comfortable," Adina replied. And Sofia responded, "It's not a comfortable thought, right? And Descartes says as much himself; he's not really comfortable with this. I mean, picture yourself—alone—wondering about all this stuff." Then turning back, Sofia added, "He's with *you*, Adina."

Through this conversation Sofia pointed out to Adina, Marcos, and others in class that just as they struggled with doubt, so did Descartes. She read out loud a passage in which Descartes explains that he feels as though he's "suddenly fallen into a deep whirlpool. He is so tossed about." He can't "touch bottom," nor can he "swim up to the top." Sofia looked up from the text. "What do you hold on to?" she asked, "if you're admitting the possibility that these long-held beliefs are all false? What, then, is there to hold on to?"

Student talk filled the room. Sofia listened, responding to one or another voice, occasionally hearing an idea that gently she repeated so that others could hear it but without shutting others down. She corrected still others whose thoughts seemed about to lead them astray. "I've got it," Adina now firmly chimed in. "It's, like, your beliefs are what makes us, us." "You, *you!*" Sofia exclaimed. "Exactly," Adina replied. "When you doubt that your beliefs—" "—you are doubting yourself in a way," Sofia inserted. "—and then," Adina noted, picking up, "when you are trying to make believe that our beliefs are not there, it's like . . . you're not really—" She stopped abruptly. "It's just so *weird*. I'm still not on board with this. But it makes sense."

Adina and her peers were struggling, much as Descartes struggled early in *Meditations*. Sofia wanted her students to know just how closely their experiences echoed those of Descartes. He battles the swirling whirlpool of confusion that threatens to pull him under, she explained. "If only he can find something—at least something that he can hold on to, at least for a little while, that would help just a bit." Then, without skipping a beat, Sofia, speaking as Descartes, laid out his most startling insight: "The mere fact," she said, "that I am wondering about it, that I can hold on to."

"So that is the thing," Sofia continued, "but then he says, 'Here is the rock. Here's my foundation. I know I exist because I am a thinking thing. And I know that I think, I imagine things, I deny things. I have this consciousness of my thinking, imagining, and denying. I have this awareness. I have a mind.' So, okay." Sofia slowed down: "So that is his rock."

Sofia spent the rest of class that day reiterating key points from early *Meditations* as students brought them up. They gave voice to Descartes' claims about doubts, about the fallibility of the human senses, about what he—and we—can know about existence. In doing so, they tackled dreams and illusions, how emotionally hard doubting can be, how easy it is to be deceived by one's senses. Sofia led her students deeper and deeper into Descartes.

Students began citing Descartes' own articulation of these issues. They began conversing with the text, with Descartes. They saw Descartes's struggle with his doubt. It sounded like their own. More and more, they addressed his thoughts from the vantage point of their own. They explored how he feels and, subsequently, how he thinks, what he comes to know and to claim—namely, that he thinks and thus that he exists, as, in fact, do they. References to *The Matrix* dissipated.

Listening to the class, we learn that when students' deeply held prior knowledge is at odds with a new subject-matter idea, previously targeted by a teacher for a class's learning, students may struggle. They may question, resist, fight, act out. They may retreat into past protective views, refusing to follow the path toward understanding the concept—in this case, doubt—that their teacher has laid out, much as Adina seemed about to do. They may argue, vigorously, if they see no connection between their lives and the new knowledge a teacher presents, especially when they sense a clash between them. Alternatively, they may defer to what they see as their teacher's ideas or that of their text, but only while in class or when carrying out academic work. In different ways, they may draw a bright line between their academic learning and personal lives, walling one off from the other.

What all this suggests is that navigating requires far more than steering between the ideas of a field of study and those represented in students' prior knowledge. Navigating also calls on a teacher to help students work through their emotions, to resolve what may seem, to them, to be irreconcilable differences between what a text would have them take in and what they are drawn to believe based on what they see, hear, and otherwise take as "real" in their daily lives. Helping in this way required Sofia to follow Adina, pursue her concerns, voice and revoice them as real and true, and support her search for alternatives, for ways through.

The good news is that higher education has teachers like Sofia, who follow their students' substantive thinking and emotional responses. Usually on their own, these teachers have figured out ways to connect, work with, and support students like Adina, who may fear the collisions they see coming between academic and personal knowledge. Sofia handled this first by showing Adina that she was not alone: Sofia pointed out that Descartes struggles in his text much as Adina was in her learning of his philosophy. Descartes, then, is *with* Adina, much as Sofia said. And importantly, so was Sofia, who followed Adina and then amplified her earliest insights, creating a space for Adina to declare, in her own voice, that "our beliefs are what makes us, us," and thus that to have a belief is, in fact, to be, to exist—much as now she asserted she did. Much as Descartes found that he, too, did.

As the class neared the end of discussion, Adina again spoke up. "I have a story," she declared. "In high school, I took physics. And our teacher was, like, when you touch something, like you are feeling it, but you are not really touching it. There's still space in between—" The class again exploded into talk. "Did you know that?" one student asked another. Describing the incredulity she'd felt in physics class that day, Adina recalled, "I was looking at him like he had ten heads!" Sofia jumped in, saying, "There's still space in between—you have the sensation." "You feel it," explained Adina, "but you're not really touching it." The ricochet of student voices drowned out Adina's and Sofia's voices. "Wait," a student said incredulously, "you mean you're touching, but there's still—" "Isn't there, like, a rule of halves or something?" another student asked, "like half of half of half. You can only go half the distance of something, and then another half, and then another half." "Like, I'm not really touching this pen right now?" another wondered out loud. Raising his voice, another student asked, "Is that a theory, or is that proven?" "No," Adina replied firmly, "that's for real." And with comments swirling around her, she added, "It is kind of like doubting yourself." Yet one more classmate persisted, saying "So I don't feel, like, the chair?" "No," another responded, as a rush of voices filled up the room. Sofia jumped back in again. "This is a different way of thinking about the chair, right? You have a sensation of touching the chair you sit in. But the nature of the chair is different from what our senses experience." "Good story, Adina!" another student exclaimed.

As this final episode suggests, Adina had continued to think about the first idea, derived from Descartes' discussion of doubt, that Sofia had introduced in class: that sensation without thought is not a trustworthy guide to knowledge about the world. But now Adina seemed less troubled by this notion, offering as an example a different piece of prior knowledge than that which had haunted her earlier: that in a high school physics class she'd learned that what we experience as our hand touching an object, in fact, is charged atomic particles, in our hand *and* in that object, that resist occupying the same exact space. We do not really touch that object. The senses deceive, much as Descartes proclaimed.[11] But that we doubt in such ways—that we question and otherwise think through the validity of what our senses proffer as real—cannot be questioned. As Sofia explained to her students, "I know that I think, imagine things, deny things. I have this consciousness of my thinking, imagining, and denying. I have this awareness. I have a mind." The workings of our minds and our awareness of them lend support to the belief that we exist.

We now must ask what this case implies for teaching students like Adina, along with the many others whose learning Sofia seeks to propel, and for teaching students like the ones that the other instructors presented in this section of the book support in a variety of educational spaces. Drawing on the several cases of undergraduate teaching—by Lauren Navarro, Eryn Klosko, Tony Acevedo, Scott Carlin, Allie Bach, and "Sofia"— and of teaching in other sites—by Robert P. Moses and Aaron Pallas— we observe the following. First, targeting, surfacing, and navigating matter in teaching that seeks to support students' subject-matter learning, a critical aim of higher education. Second, students' experiences of digging out and scrutinizing their prior knowledge in light of the new and possibly strange academic concepts that teachers set before them can be highly emotional, even wrenching, demanding of teachers an abundance of patience, respect, and care—an attunement to learners' emotions as much as to their cognitions, for the two are entwined. And third, the principle of navigating, through its attention to students' learning and its emotional overtones, may, in the long run, influence how students know themselves and the powers of their minds.

In supporting classroom learning through this wide-angle lens on what convergent teaching entails, instructors stand a chance of helping students to create themselves and to know themselves as learners. Undergraduate teaching in this view is far more than a job or career-building endeavor. It is more than a practice, and it requires much more than the enactment of policy. It is a moral endeavor and personal vocation. It is a way to live one's life.

We do not, however, believe that convergent teaching is the last word on good teaching practice. Rather, it captures a portion of what's available for use now—by teachers, leaders, policy makers, and others—to reconsider undergraduate teaching as lying at the heart of American higher education. As a deliberative process, reconsideration prompts the question of what is to be done. Addressing this question goes beyond teaching to the larger social, cultural and institutional contexts that shape college teaching in general and convergent teaching in particular. We discuss these powerful matters in the next part of the book.

PART III

POLICIES AND PRACTICES

Alejandra Garcia is a freeway flyer.[1] She spends three hours each day driving from one campus to the next, arriving just in time to teach her undergraduate courses in English composition and writing. This semester, she is teaching two classes at Interboro Community College, two more at Greenvale State's downtown campus, and one at Mulberry Hill, a small, private suburban institution. When she finished her PhD in English, she aspired to a full-time faculty position. But jobs in her field are tight, and for the past eight years, she's eked out a living as an adjunct, supplementing her teaching with freelance editing work.

Alejandra's situation is precarious. At each institution, she is appointed on a semester-by-semester basis, with no guarantee of continued employment. If enrollments are projected to fall, she may not be renewed, and on more than one occasion, she has been notified of her teaching assignment less than one week before the start of the term. The schools for which she works need her, she's concluded, but they don't really respect her, or the hundreds of other adjuncts in their employ. Mulberry Hill provides access to an office for the English department adjuncts, but neither Interboro nor Greenvale State has office space for adjuncts, let alone access to computers or telephones. As a result, Alejandra holds office hours in coffee shops near campus, her personal laptop computer and a sheaf of papers to grade beside her cup of tea. Although she enjoys her students, the institutions that employ her don't pay her for academic advising, and she frequently finds herself apologizing as she runs to her car to get to her next class.

None of the three departments in which she works invites her to department meetings, and truth be told, she probably couldn't attend them anyway, as they are frequently held at times during which she's teaching at one of the other campuses. Though she's met the chairs and administrative staff of each department, she scarcely knows the regular faculty, most of whom are not teaching the lower-division courses in which she specializes. Even the other adjuncts in the departments are, at most, casual acquaintances.

Alejandra's performance as a teacher is based primarily on end-of-term evaluations filled out by her students. She's viewed as lively and friendly, a professor who takes an interest in her students, even though most don't try to meet with her out of class. The positive evaluations give her a warm glow, and no student has ever gone to her department chair or the dean with a complaint about her teaching. Still, she wonders if she's doing a good job, and how she might improve her teaching. But only one of the institutions for which she teaches offers professional development activities for adjunct faculty, and the face-to-face sessions conflict with her teaching responsibilities at one of the other campuses.

═════

We opened this book with the case of Chris Felton, a tenure-track assistant professor at Roseville, a liberal arts college. We provide a bookend with Alejandra Garcia, a contingent faculty member teaching at three institutions simultaneously. Together, college teachers such as Chris and Alejandra are teaching most of the undergraduate courses in the United States. And, as is true for the vast majority of the 1.5 million faculty they represent, Chris and Alejandra strive to teach the best they can amid ambiguous and conflicting expectations, and intermittent and nonspecific support from their colleagues, their institutions, and their fields.

Things can get better; institutions can clarify and solidify their expectations and supports, and individual faculty can take greater control of their teaching practices. College teachers can forge stronger links between their highly developed subject-matter knowledge and approaches to teaching what they know. Their colleagues and institutions can do far more to support them in doing so.[2] The message of this third and final part is that we can build on what we know about convergent teaching to enable college teachers like Chris Felton and Alejandra Garcia and their students to succeed in the classroom.

In part I of this book, we documented the social, political, and economic contexts of undergraduate education in the United States that have diverted attention away from college teaching. We opened with a (and perhaps the) fundamental contradiction of US higher education— declining public confidence coupled with rising demand. This paradox has propelled policy proposals and initiatives that bear on many facets of higher education. Cost, debt, and affordability; access, particularly for those previously disenfranchised from the higher education enterprise; rebundling and unbundling the curriculum to better prepare students for the careers on which they will embark; and new technologies that promise to pinpoint what students need to know and to deliver instruction at scale to more students at lower cost are all on the policy table, or at least the sideboard adjacent to it.

What's missing in this discourse is attention to Chris Felton, Alejandra Garcia, and their peers, the college instructors who are central to undergraduate education. There is no vision of what good college teaching looks like or how to support it. In chapter 1, and then throughout part II of the book, we developed the concept of convergent teaching. We defined convergent teaching as the totality of what teachers think and do to support students' learning as they encounter and engage with new academic ideas in the context of their prior knowledge and experience. Convergent teaching, as a core strand of a more encompassing "good teaching," entails the teacher's attention, simultaneously, to subject matter, learner, and context. We emphasized three principles of convergent teaching: targeting, the identification of the disciplinary and other content that is to be taught in a particular course; surfacing, the unearthing of students' prior knowledge and experiences that may be relevant to their learning of course content; and navigating, the steering of instruction between what students know and subject-matter ideas with students' learning and growth in mind.

In this final section of the book, we review existing policies and practices to support convergent teaching and offer recommendations for both novel and traditional approaches for doing so. Our final two chapters distinguish two streams of analysis. In chapter 5, we consider campus-based policies and practices to support convergent teaching. This includes an array of strategies for promoting good college teaching generally, as there are relatively few existing approaches that are closely aligned with our more focused conception of convergent teaching. Our stance is that policies and practices that are directed at recognizing, supporting, and rewarding good teaching are important foundations for supporting convergent teaching in particular.

In Chapter 6, we address policies and practices focused more directly on cultivating convergent teaching. These veer toward larger issues of organizational and systemic change and pose a different set of implementation challenges. Chapter 6 also includes a set of recommendations for what individual faculty can do to support their own development as practitioners of convergent teaching.

In some cases, the location of a particular initiative in chapter 5 or Chapter 6 is arbitrary. The lines are not that finely drawn, as convergent teaching depends heavily on a variety of forms of teaching knowledge and practice. But we wish to emphasize that neither set stands alone. Successfully implementing the kinds of policies and practices we review and suggest in chapter 5 will require the large-scale organizational changes of chapter 6. Conversely, organizational and systemic changes, in the form of reframing, mandates, incentives, capacity building, and persuasion, must work through the kinds of policies and practices described in Chapter 5. Together, these chapters offer a path forward for supporting convergent teaching in US undergraduate education.

Undergraduate teaching improvement should involve all levels of the higher education system, including policy actors at all levels—government policy makers, system and institutional heads, deans and chairs of academic departments, decision-making bodies of disciplinary associations, philanthropic leaders, and the faculty themselves. These actors can contribute to teaching and learning improvement in varied ways: government, system, and institutional leaders can restructure campus decision-making and reward systems and, in some cases, move the faculty's attention to teaching, inciting them to ever-higher learning goals for their students and revising priorities among teaching, research, and service. Philanthropies and disciplinary associations can mobilize resources for multi-institutional efforts, which would constitute an important correction to the largely local (campus-based) focus of much prior teaching improvement; the broader view promises to crack open insular processes and promote cross-campus sharing of good ideas. Academic leaders like deans and department chairs and the faculty themselves can infuse expectations for good teaching into faculty mentoring programs, course assessment procedures, promotion and tenure criteria, and other academic support and evaluative systems.

Harking back to our discussion of convergent teaching, we assert that it is the faculty and only the faculty who can bring its three principles to life. Only the faculty, as specialists in their fields, can imagine and experiment with new ways to target, carve out, and sculpt disciplinary knowledge and subjects so as to respond effectively to features of students' prior knowledge that promise to advance their learning. Faculty are central to all approaches to teaching improvement.

CHAPTER FIVE

Campus-Level Supports for Convergent Teaching

In the following two chapters, we make a single critical recommendation: that we act swiftly and strategically to heighten the quality of teaching for all undergraduate students in the United States. The American K–12 education system took up this banner long ago. It is now time for US postsecondary education to do so, drawing both on new ideas and on good ideas already in hand but mainly in the province of specialists.

In this chapter, we review the history of teaching improvement initiatives in American higher education and the current policies and practices that either support or ignore undergraduate teaching. We begin with an overview of efforts to reform college teaching and learning over the past several decades, showing how professional development and the reward and recognition of good college teaching are institutional imperatives and demonstrating that the work of undergraduate teaching improvement has to take place mainly through campus systems and on individual campuses. We then discuss three broad initiatives: the readying of the institution for improving teaching, the professional development of college instructors, and institutional policies and practices to support and reward good college teaching.[1] Our discussion across these three initiatives covers a broad range of topics, including approaches for taking stock of campus structures, processes, and cultures bearing on undergraduate teaching and its improvement; planning and coordinating design and implementation of new teaching improvement initiatives, such as professional development programming for convergent teaching; and evaluating and rewarding good college teaching, especially in the context of appointment, reappointment, promotion, and tenure.

A History of Initiatives to Improve Teaching: What Do We Know?

Sociologist Steven Brint has summarized efforts to reform college teaching and learning, focusing on the three decades between 1980 and 2010.[2] Such efforts emerged in response to the expansion and diversification of higher education's institutions and its students and also as a way to demonstrate accountability to the public and its tax and tuition dollars, ever scarcer in eras of financial stress and declining government funding. Brint identifies two major initiatives, the first addressing professional development as a route to teaching improvement and the second emphasizing the assessment of student learning outcomes.

To improve college teaching, liberal philanthropies such as the Carnegie Foundation for the Advancement of Teaching and advocacy organizations such as the Association of American Colleges and Universities developed initiatives that melded traditional conceptions of progressive pedagogy such as active learning and an emphasis on teaching for understanding with a view of teaching as a form of scholarship. The scholarship of teaching and learning became an organizing framework for institutionally based teaching and learning centers and provided them with momentum to expand. The goal throughout was formative: let's see what we can do to improve teaching. A summative assessment of whether students were in fact learning more as their teachers took on the scholarship of teaching and learning was beyond the scope of this first movement.

The second movement, assessment of student learning outcomes, drew on a heightened sense of public accountability for the performance of colleges and universities. States, along with the associations that represent state-level higher education systems, worked abreast of philanthropy and advocacy organizations, framing their efforts around the measurement of the outcomes of a college education. At the state level, institutional funding was often tied to an institution's "performance," but performance funding generally emphasized outcomes such as retention and graduation rates rather than direct measures of student learning.

Acting in parallel, regional accrediting organizations veered toward models of "outcomes-based accreditation," demanding that institutions specify a set of institution-level student outcomes, measure these directly, and demonstrate that information about student outcomes feeds back into a cycle of continuous quality improvement. This movement got a shot in the arm from the 2006 report of the Secretary of Education's Commission on the Future of Higher Education, titled *A Test of Leadership: Charting the Future of US Higher Education*, commonly known as the Spellings Commission report. The Spellings Commission recommended that institutions of higher education measure student learning via assessments such as the Collegiate Learning Assessment (CLA) and fold learning outcomes data into a consumer-friendly database that could be used by stakeholders to hold institutions accountable for their performance.

If the earlier efforts of philanthropies and advocacy organizations such as Carnegie and the Association of American Colleges and Universities were heavily formative in nature, those of the outcomes movement were both formative and summative: the guiding thought was let's measure student outcomes and assume that the invisible hand of the market will oblige institutions to change their practices to yield better outcomes. The first movement worked with college faculty on day-to-day teaching issues, whereas the second focused more heavily on institutional and system-level performance with an eye to still broader constituencies. Whether or not the policies and practices driven by the outcomes movement would change what teachers did in the classroom was not a focal concern.

The lessons derived from Brint's review of higher education improvement efforts are grim. He finds scant evidence that either the philanthropic and advocacy reforms to improve college teaching practice via professional development or the expansion of efforts to measure student learning outcomes have had practical consequences for what happens in undergraduate classrooms. The primary culprit, he suggests, is a culture that supports students, faculty, and administrators in maintaining low academic standards in the college classroom. Beyond this dynamic—which was identified as early as 1932 and has been voiced in many different ways over the years—the social organization of higher education and weak technologies for assessment have proven significant barriers to improving teaching.[3]

Although many institutions and faculty will attest to the importance of student engagement and active learning in the classroom, promoting active learning in more than superficial ways requires sustained and intense professional development. Relatively few faculty have been exposed to the kind of intense professional development that we suspect is needed for lasting changes in classroom practice. To date, many efforts to promote college teaching have been pitched too broadly, reaching many faculty in a relatively shallow or symbolic way. Alternatively, some are "artisanal," in Brint's terms, cultivating improved practice in small communities of self-selected college teachers spanning multiple campuses but offering few mechanisms by which to disseminate improved knowledge of teaching practice to others. Neither approach can propel large-scale institutional changes in the quality of undergraduate teaching.

The current student success movement, organized around timely degree completion for undergraduate students, has its roots in the outcomes assessments Brint describes. But attempts to measure student learning outcomes are mired in abstraction, as institution-level measures such as the CLA are far removed from what specific faculty on any particular campus are doing in their classes. This seems almost inevitable, given the fact that most undergraduate courses are about some specific disciplinary content that may not be easily captured by broader critical thinking assessments. One might ask, for example, how a campus-level average score on the CLA can influence what a particular instructor does to teach the concept of war in a modern European history class populated by recent immigrants from various countries. The technical challenges of linking student learning assessments to particular classrooms, faculty, and subjects are vast, and the current generation of such assessments is neither cheap nor simple to administer at scale.

This, then, is the backdrop for our discussion of readying institutions for teaching improvement, professional development, and institutional reward and recognition systems.

Readying Institutions for Teaching Improvement

A comprehensive institution-level approach to undergraduate teaching improvement begins with an assessment of an institution's history, values, aspirations, and mission, all important elements of an institution's culture. Institutional stakeholders must look at the alignment between these features of institutional culture and the institution's current policies and practices, whether codified or not, identifying both congruences and discontinuities. As we and others have noted, there is often a sharp disjuncture between rhetoric and reality. Institutions may proclaim a commitment to high-quality undergraduate teaching and view it as central to the campus's ways of life, even to the point of building assessments of teaching quality into faculty performance reviews. But the evaluation procedures as enacted and the associated evidence may be shallow and perfunctory.

Organizational theorists describe this gap as reflecting a distinction between ostensive and performative organizational routines. An ostensive organizational routine provides a structure for what is supposed to happen, whereas a performative organizational routine is what happens when particular organizational members enact the routine at a particular time and place.[4] A faculty handbook may, for example, specify how teaching is to be considered in the process of reappointment, promotion, or tenure, detailing a set of ostensive routines for collecting and evaluating data on teaching performance that convey a deep valuing of teaching as a part of faculty work. But when the tenured faculty of the chemistry department at a comprehensive college meet to discuss an assistant professor's bid for tenure, they may spend five minutes looking at course evaluations toward the end of their two-hour meeting, a performative routine at great distance from what the faculty handbook structure specifies.

How comfortable are college faculty with this dissonance? Some might be discomfited enough to try to resolve it by inventing new routines that give more attention to teaching quality in departmental deliberations about promotion and tenure. Still others might decide openly that other strands of faculty work are more important than teaching for personnel decisions. While it's impossible and probably undesirable to resolve all such dissonances—some researchers suggest that they may serve productive functions[5]—surfacing those bearing on undergraduate teaching and discussing which ones warrant attention is critical, as that will reveal both sites of resistance and opportunities for organizational change.

Is an institution inevitably caught between long-term commitments to its historic vision of good teaching and a desire to increase its prestige through greater research productivity?[6] Are the faculty receiving mixed messages about the relative importance of research, teaching, and service to the campus mission? Are efforts to redirect faculty attention to convergent teaching and student learning outcomes likely to challenge a collegial campus culture in which faculty see themselves as independent professionals?[7] The institutional stocktaking for which we call can reveal these and many other challenges.

Any institutional self-study must also take account of the balance between full-time and contingent faculty. As we noted earlier, non-tenure-track faculty, both full time and part time, shoulder an increasing responsibility for undergraduate instruction on most campuses. We and others have speculated that this trend reflects institutional efforts to reduce costs and increase curricular flexibility. But it creates tensions that undermine undergraduate teaching improvement. There are no direct costs associated with ignoring contingent faculty as part of an institution's teaching force. But professional development, which is only effective when it is sustained, *does* have direct costs. And, put baldly, it is ridiculous for an institution's policies and practices to imply that the institution will help its permanent faculty to improve their teaching practices but that it expects the contingent faculty to just get better on their own.

The array of policy instruments available to campus leaders—mandates, incentives, capacity building, changing power and authority relations, and persuasion—are less powerful when directed at faculty whose ties to the institution are more fragile than the "permanent" faculty assured of some measure of job security and stability. Persuasion works best when there are durable, trusting relationships between the persuader and the target of the persuasion. That's rarely the case for contingent faculty, who typically are hired within academic departments that do not have the authority (or resources!) to set institutional policies regarding faculty professional development.

Similarly, mandates work best when they are enforceable and perceived as fair. Mandates involving professional development for contingent faculty who have many demands on their time may need to be accompanied by payments for the cost of that time.[8] Increasing the costs of maintaining a cadre of contingent faculty of course flies in the face of the logic of cost-cutting that gave rise to adjunct, part-time, and other contingent faculty in the first place. There is no easy workaround for this problem, in our view. Capacity building—providing an institution with resources for long-term investment in capacity—can support other policy instruments, such as mandates, incentives, and changing power and authority relations, but it is also expensive, requiring long-term funding streams and a willingness to acknowledge that change will not be immediate. Incentives can be effective, but they are designed to allow individuals to opt out and must be perceived as valuable by the targeted individuals, which can be costly.

Our advice regarding improving the capacity of contingent faculty to teach undergraduates at the campus level has two components. First, campuses must work much harder at incorporating contingent faculty into the academic life of the institution, treating them as full members of the faculty. They must provide them with the physical and material resources they need to do their jobs in a way they can be proud of and recognize them as professionals entitled to a measure of respect with regard to notifications about teaching assignments and participation in academic unit life, among many other matters. It's a version of the academic golden rule: treat contingent faculty as you would like to be treated yourself. Yes, there are direct costs associated with treating contingent faculty as full institutional members, but the long-term payoff in the building of mutually trusting relationships between contingent faculty and the institution can enhance the power of institutional policies and practices that support undergraduate teaching improvement to reach them.[9]

Second, institutions must recognize that any serious effort to improve undergraduate teaching at the campus level must include contingent faculty in a serious way. This almost surely will require increasing the budgets for programs and policies that support undergraduate teaching improvement. A back-of-the-envelope calculation is that incorporating contingent faculty into the same programs as full-time, tenure-track faculty could double the budgeted outlays.[10] This is a serious commitment of resources, especially since many existing initiatives, such as campus teaching centers, are underbudgeted. Acknowledge these costs, we argue, and find the resources to build them into the institution's ongoing operating budget.[11]

Though a commitment to undergraduate teaching improvement must be diffused throughout a campus, with many administrators and faculty on board, we recommend that the campus chief academic officer designate a particular person to be responsible for oversight of the design, implementation, and assessment of undergraduate teaching improvement at the campus level. This responsibility should be accompanied by the requisite authority and resources to advance undergraduate teaching quality. The designated campus leader needs to be knowledgeable about convergent teaching and teaching improvement, including the procedures in place or under development in other institutions, and have a deep understanding of the local culture. Those enacting this role will be cheerleaders, ambassadors, brokers, and managers, taking every opportunity to champion the importance of undergraduate teaching both within the campus community and beyond it. This leadership role also calls for forging new initiatives with various campus units, both academic and otherwise, and marshaling the resources necessary to support both existing structures, such as a campus teaching and learning center, and novel ones that promise to elevate and reward good college teaching.

No one approach to undergraduate teaching improvement will suffice. Campus leaders responsible for undergraduate teaching improvement should ensure that their initiatives address both professional development and the formulation and reformulation of institutional policies related to teaching in general and convergent teaching in particular. Such policies may bear on faculty members' work and careers, on academic units, and on central administrative processes. Some changes might be realized quickly, whereas others may be longer-term efforts to build capacity. In cases in which faculty are able to arrange consultations with a campus teaching center, they may be able to pursue changes in their teaching practice largely in isolation. In other cases, institutions undertake large-scale programs, such as the Science Education Initiative, in which large introductory courses may be the target for redesign and improvement and so the academic department as a whole may be the appropriate target for teaching improvement. In still other instances, campus-level policies and resources oriented toward rewards and recognition, which are most likely to stimulate sustained change, are established. A diversified approach is essential.

To illuminate the range of possibilities, and opportunities for coordinating them, we next discuss the professional development of faculty for undergraduate teaching, which we follow with an account of institutional processes that can be used for evaluating and rewarding college teaching. The division is arbitrary, as the two are articulated.

Professional Development for Undergraduate Teachers

In virtually every field of endeavor, practice and experience count. No one expects novices to be experts, and gaining expertise requires sustained practice and reflection. Professions differ in how they induct novices and in how they support the acquisition of the full range of knowledge, skills, and "know-how" associated with mature practice. In the law, novices pursue a three-year postbaccalaureate curriculum, often intern over the summer in law offices, sit for the bar exam, and then work for law firms as associates. Students of medicine complete four years of preclinical coursework and clinical rotations before entering a multiyear internship and residency program that precedes solo or group practice. In contrast, the occupation of classroom teaching is hazier on induction, but its ambiguity illuminates our point.

Students enrolled in undergraduate and graduate K–12 teacher preparation programs must demonstrate subject-matter knowledge and enroll in courses on methods of teaching. Their coursework is frequently supplemented by their participation in one or more sustained student teaching placements. Once provisionally or fully certified by the state, novice teachers are then hired by school districts. For newly certified teachers, the handoff from a campus-based preparation program to a school district can be abrupt, and they may be unclear about who is responsible for supporting them over the first few years of their careers. Is it the preparation program from which they emerged or their new employers?

What is striking about these examples is that in each case—law, medicine, and K–12 teaching—there is a formal transition from the professional preparation experience (occurring in graduate or undergraduate programs in colleges and universities) and what we'll call "real practice." There is no formal, structured induction process for college teachers that parallels any of those we've just described. Even the embattled K–12 domain, unsettled as it is on teacher induction, recognizes a need to do something. But as of this time, no one takes systematic responsibility for preparing college teachers—neither the graduate schools from which they emerge nor the institutions that hire them to teach. In higher education, the gap between graduate school and future college teaching is immense, with no bridge in sight.

Building on the arguments of higher education scholars and leaders such as Derek Bok, William Bowen, and Michael McPherson, we argue that the professionalization of the college teaching force ought to begin with the systematic preparation of graduate students who will populate the ranks of college instructors.[12] Graduate schools are well positioned to provide a foundation for teaching practice that novice college instructors can carry forward into their teaching careers, and we recommend that they take on this responsibility.

Although many universities sponsor college teaching preparation programs, the participants typically select themselves into them, and overall participation levels are sporadic. This is not surprising, and there are many possible explanations. In some institutions and disciplines, there may be nagging suspicions about doctoral students who place equal or greater value on teaching than on research: "Will they be serious scholars?" some of their research mentors might ask. For many faculty, scholarship is about the discovery of new knowledge, and the doctoral dissertation is both its central representation and the culminating experience of doctoral study. Expertise may be held to reside in disciplinary specialization. In this view, scholarship may be understood as a zero-sum proposition: if research and teaching are complementary and time and attention are fixed, any attention to teaching comes at the expense of research.

This proposition is demonstrably false. The most well-known efforts to undermine it originate in the work of Ernest Boyer, whose model of scholarship includes the scholarship of discovery, the scholarship of integration, the scholarship of application or engagement, and the scholarship of teaching and learning.[13] Our own work on the early post-tenure careers of faculty in research universities shows that scholars can enact a commitment to the subject matter they are passionate about via their research, their teaching, and/or their efforts to apply knowledge within and beyond the walls of the academy.[14] Moreover, meaningful and creative scholarly learning can arise from all three of these activities so central to the faculty career.[15] It may still be necessary to persuade faculty and graduate students that this is true and to head off the peculiar stigma attached to teaching and to preparing for a teaching career.

We therefore call for all doctoral programs in all fields of study that lead to college teaching careers to be infused with college teaching preparation. We acknowledge that not all doctoral students will become teaching faculty and that the mismatch between the production of doctorates in particular fields of study and the supply of full-time faculty positions in those fields is of grave concern to some professional associations.[16]

We believe that there is a powerful argument for having all doctoral students participate in seminars or other settings devoted to the teaching and learning of the core ideas in their discipline. Scholars at every career stage can benefit from systematic identification of and reflection on core ideas in their field, including their own critiques and extensions of those ideas, and thought as to how they might convey those ideas to others through their writing, their teaching, and other modes of communication. Central to this is a kind of cognitive curation in which individuals consider why a particular idea is so central and why it generates other concepts, questions, and methods within an area of specialization, a broader field of study, or an expansive global landscape. It's at least conceivable that learning to teach, especially via the principles of convergent teaching, could deepen all doctoral students' understandings of their fields, regardless of whether they foresee themselves pursuing academic careers.

Equally, we recognize that new faculty often teach students with backgrounds that vary greatly from their own and that they will do so in institutions that are very different from the undergraduate institutions that they attended. Thus new faculty who strive to access their students' prior knowledge in the spirit of convergent teaching may be challenged in so doing. Part of learning to teach, while in a doctoral program or possibly in mentored externships, is learning to identify, access, and address diverse learners' prior knowledge, bringing it to bear on core disciplinary ideas. Creating programs that give doctoral students access to the tenets of convergent teaching and providing them with opportunities to gain competence in putting those tenets into practice in mentored settings would be a huge and complex undertaking. Yet we view it as crucial if we think that all teachers of all of America's undergraduates should be oriented toward improving their teaching.

We are not by far the first to suggest that doctoral students and early career faculty be supported in learning to teach. In what follows we discuss several notable precedents.

Preparing Future Faculty (PFF) Programs and Graduate Certificates in College Teaching

Our recommendation, echoing those of others, that higher education take greater responsibility for readying college teachers for the classroom, is not new. Over the past twenty-five years, dozens of doctoral degree-granting institutions have partnered with more than three hundred other two- and four-year colleges and universities to help doctoral students aspiring to faculty careers to prepare for them. The PFF program was conceived in 1993 by the Council of Graduate Schools and the Association of American Colleges and Universities and received support from the Pew Charitable Trusts, the National Science Foundation, and the Atlantic Philanthropies. Although direct financial support ended long ago, PFF invited doctoral-granting institutions to develop programming that would address some of the features of faculty life, including looking for an academic job and understanding the diverse faculty responsibilities of teaching, research, and service.

Many campus-based PFF programs persist today, exposing graduate students to the full scope of faculty roles and responsibilities and providing oversight by multiple mentors as aspiring faculty develop their research, teaching, and service portfolios.[17] Most PFF programs are organized as partnerships or clusters of institutions and/or academic departments.

Many institutions that have sponsored PFF programs now offer six- to fifteen-credit graduate certificate programs in college teaching. The features of these certificate programs vary substantially across institutions but typically highlight centralized coursework in college teaching, either embedded in a graduate program in higher education or freestanding within the graduate school. This coursework is often complemented by discipline-specific teaching seminars offered by academic departments and a supervised practicum in college teaching. Frequently, these offerings are offered at no cost to enrolled doctoral students. Participating students often develop detailed statements of their teaching philosophy and a teaching portfolio, which they embed in websites they develop as part of preparing for faculty careers. In spite of their titles, most teaching certificate programs extend beyond teaching preparation, orienting students to the academic job search, the nature of tenure and academic freedom, academic governance processes in American higher education, and approaches to balancing one's roles and responsibilities both within and outside of academia.

The Graduate Certificate in College and University Faculty Preparation at Howard University is typical of these programs. The Howard program is fifteen credit hours, spread across two required core courses, two elective courses, and an experiential teaching opportunity. The two core courses are titled Faculty Roles and Responsibilities and Effective Technologies in Teaching and Learning. Elective courses, frequently offered in an on-line format, address diversity in the classroom, inquiry-based learning, and training to become a research mentor, among other topics. The experiential teaching opportunity can take the form of a teaching assistantship carried out at Howard, a teaching internship under the supervision of a professor at one of a dozen four-year partner institutions, or a project of at least a semester in length that uses research methods to develop and implement teaching practices designed to improve student learning. To complete the certificate, candidates create an e-portfolio with a statement of their teaching philosophy, design sample assignments with stated learning goals and objectives, develop strategies for evaluating student learning, and engage in other self-reflections on their teaching practice.[18]

Another example is Duke University's Certificate in College Teaching, which allows for a combination of Duke Graduate School courses on the features of college teaching and departmental pedagogy courses in fields such as African and African American studies, biology, English, environmental science, mathematics, philosophy, and political science. Our assessment of such courses and similarly-framed courses at other institutions is that they appear to situate foundational knowledge about teaching practice (e.g., writing usable syllabi and learning objectives, incorporating new classroom technologies, using group work, etc.) within the teaching of a particular discipline.[19] They do not, as best we can tell from available data, address the challenges of identifying, framing, and teaching the core concepts of the sponsoring department's discipline. Nor do these teaching preparation courses appear to systematically address students' prior knowledge, approaches to surfacing it, or strategies for bringing it to bear on students' subject-matter learning.

There are exceptions, of course. We note specifically the statistics education concentration in the Department of Educational Psychology at the University of Minnesota, pioneered by Professor Emerita Joan Garfield and her colleagues, who have written extensively on the teaching and learning of statistics in the spirit of pedagogical content knowledge.[20] It's possible, too that we are making too much of the syllabi available on line as guides to what transpires in these departmental teaching preparation courses, as a syllabus cannot convey the full range and depth of conversations that ensue in class.

We view the range of offerings provided by the programs described in this section to be extraordinarily valuable to aspiring college faculty, and we applaud efforts especially to emphasize subject-matter teaching. We recommend, however, that programs' current offerings be further broadened to build in attention to facets of convergent teaching not currently being addressed (e.g., sensitizing faculty to the full range of learners' prior knowledge and its uses in teaching).

The Campus Teaching Center

Regardless of whether novice college instructors participate in teaching preparation programs while they are in graduate school, there's little question that new faculty need support in their first jobs. In fact, faculty at every career stage can benefit from teaching support, though what's appropriate may differ depending on where they are in their careers. Campus-based teaching and learning centers are a common vehicle for delivering professional development services to faculty at different career stages and in various fields. Hundreds of institutions across the country host such centers under varied titles. Most are affiliated with the Professional and Organizational Development Network in Higher Education, commonly known as the POD Network.

The POD Network's self-studies, coupled with a few case studies of particular campus teaching and learning centers, have demonstrated the variation across institutions in center resources and missions.[21] Some operate on a shoestring, with tiny budgets, limited space, and sparse staff support, whereas others are well resourced and central to their institution's functioning. This variability makes it difficult to summarize desirable configurations of staffing and support, as these are tied to key features of the institution, such as the centrality of teaching to the institution's mission, the size of its student body and faculty, and its financial health.

Teaching center directors report three primary program goals: to create or sustain a culture of teaching excellence, to advance new initiatives in teaching and learning, and to respond to and support individual faculty members who seek professional development.[22] But they also indicate that the primary service they provide is new faculty development/orientation, which is a broad and variegated activity.[23] The typical array of services center directors report include providing consultations for individual instructors about their classroom teaching, offering institution-wide orientations and workshops about teaching and technology in the classroom, conferring teaching improvement grants and awards on individuals and departments, and serving as a repository for resources and publications about curriculum development and teaching practice.[24]

Given the array of requests that institutions make of campus teaching centers, they can struggle to find a niche that enables them to sustain a focus on teaching. Center activities often bleed into other domains, such as educational technology support, leadership development, mentoring, and institutional assessment.[25] Some teaching centers, for example, administer course evaluation systems on behalf of their institutions. Others have sought to shed that responsibility, fearing that administering evaluations that feed into high-stakes personnel decisions might undermine their image as faculty support units.[26] Developing relationships with institutional administrators that permit centers to expand their services in particular directions or that enable them to decline requests that are not clearly aligned with the center's mission can take up significant staff time, thought, and energy.

Surveys indicate that more than three-quarters of POD center directors report to a provost or associate/assistant vice provost. In general, lodging teaching centers in the units of the chief academic officer of an institution is desirable, as it places the centers near the academic core of the institution and facilitates formal lines of authority and budgets. All too often, though, centers are not recipients of a stable and adequate internal stream of funding, obliging center directors to be entrepreneurial and to raise funds to support their efforts. Relatively few teaching centers use a fee-for-service model, perhaps because the disincentives are too great for departments to make investments from thin department budgets. An unintended consequence of this strategy is that the teaching improvement initiatives offered by teaching centers are more likely to reach individual faculty across the institution than a concentration of faculty within a single academic department. This pattern makes it more difficult to leverage department-level change.

Because a large institution will likely have a larger and more complex teaching center than a smaller institution, it is difficult to characterize a typical staffing configuration. On average, a center has a director, one or two associate or assistant directors, and three or four academic, professional, and/or consulting staff, but there is a great deal of variability around staffing levels.[27] The presence of a full-time center director with an administrative appointment promotes stability in a center's goals and programmatic initiatives.[28] As is true for most academic units, the salaries and benefits paid to center staff constitute the majority of teaching center costs.

Conversely, center programming budgets are generally small, with half of all center directors reporting an annual programming budget of less than $50,000, some of which doubtless is devoted to activities that address not just teaching improvement but also other center priorities.[29] A few are much larger; the Center for Research on Learning and Teaching at the University of Michigan is able to award approximately $300,000 annually in grants to approximately one hundred faculty for teaching improvement projects.[30] An award of approximately $3,000—or some other incentive with significant value—can facilitate faculty investment and participation in teaching improvement initiatives.[31] We suspect that many teaching centers are not funded at a level that enables them to achieve their goals to support instruction and student learning.[32] If the campus teaching center is to be the institutional hub for teaching improvement, it requires a level of staffing and programming that will allow it to reach the desired number of faculty with an intensity that can sustain changes in teaching practice.

Few institutions have the slack resources to be able to write blank checks to academic support units, though. The case for more support for campus teaching centers may hinge on the ability of centers to provide better evidence of impact on instructional practices and student success. This is the message of the American Council on Education's collaboration with Strada Education Network. Their 2017 report on assuring high-quality postsecondary pedagogy describes three initiatives that aim to supply information regarding the relationships among faculty professional development, the use of evidence-based instructional practices, and student outcomes.

Their rationale for intensive evaluation and assessment of faculty development programs is straightforward. "Faculty developers would never suggest a faculty member give a high grade to a student because the student read the chapter and claimed they learned from the material," write the authors. "Faculty developers are very effective in designing assessment strategies so that faculty can demonstrate students know or can do something before a grade is awarded." "Why," they ask, "should the efforts of faculty developers be any different?"[33] Even more bluntly, historians Lendol Calder and Tracy Steffes ask, "Is this really the best we can do, asking the public to take our word for it?"[34]

If campus teaching centers are to strike a bargain with their institutional overseers for an increase in resources in exchange for better evidence of impact, some of the new funding will need to be devoted to building individual centers' capacity for self-evaluation. Surveys of POD center directors indicate that they have limited capacity to assess their centers' efforts, lacking the requisite training, time, and resources. Few gather direct data on teaching practice or on student learning outcomes.[35] Even the evaluation plan for the University of Michigan Center for Research on Learning and Teaching, the nation's oldest and arguably best-supported teaching center, circumscribes the domain of evaluation outcomes, inferring changes in teaching practice from instructors' intentions and actual changes in attitudes and pedagogical knowledge, and skirting attention to student learning outcomes.[36] This should not come as a surprise; measuring changes in teaching practice and in student learning is difficult, costly, and time consuming. This is especially true for measures of students' subject-matter learning.

The Tracer Project

Although it is presumed that there are linkages between teaching and learning that make faculty professional development desirable, is there actually persuasive evidence that the kind of professional development offered by campus teaching centers can change faculty teaching practices and yield better student learning outcomes? The answer is a qualified yes. One of the most celebrated studies in the faculty professional development literature is the Tracer Project, conducted by researchers at Washington State University, a large public land-grant institution, and Carleton College, a small, elite private liberal arts college.[37] The project sought to demonstrate that when faculty participate in professional development activities focused on teaching and learning, their teaching practices change and, in turn, student learning improves. Each institution had its own portfolio of faculty development activities, and a surprisingly high propor-

tion of the full-time and contingent faculty in both institutions participated in one form of professional development or another.

The Tracer Project benefited from efforts at both Washington State and
Carleton to assess student performance via direct samples of student work.
Both institutions required students to present writing portfolios in order
to graduate. Washington State had instituted both a writing across the
curriculum initiative and a critical thinking project, developing a rubric
that faculty raters used to assess elements of critical thinking in students'
written responses to course assignments. Carleton adapted this rubric to
fit its writing program and a quantitative inquiry, reasoning, and knowledge initiative to enhance students' quantitative reasoning. At both sites,
learning to design assignments aligned to the rubrics and participating
in student portfolio rating sessions were critical faculty development
activities.

The book reporting the findings of the Tracer Project provides extensive evidence from Washington State University and Carleton faculty reports of what they learned from the faculty development initiatives in
which they participated, especially how learning to rate student portfolios
subsequently informed their own teaching practice. The process of rating
portfolios made students' work, along with the faculty teaching practices
inspiring it, more public, allowing individual faculty to compare their assignments to those of other faculty and to compare the quality of the
critical thinking reflected in their own students' work to the quality of the
thinking in other classes at their institution.

Rating a large number of student portfolios and discussing them with
other faculty enabled faculty portfolio raters to hone a sense of what was
possible, and many faculty raters found that they could design new course
assignments that were more successful at eliciting evidence of critical
thinking than their previous versions and that they could raise their expectations for students' work. The authors show how these benefits spread
throughout the two institutions, shaped by their distinctive structures and
cultures. "There is nothing generic about this work," they contend, and we
agree wholeheartedly.[38]

The Tracer Project serves as a "proof of concept" in establishing links
between faculty development, faculty learning and teaching practice, and

college student academic performance within institutions. As we've noted, in most institutions, the nonrandom selection of faculty into faculty development programs and the lack of common assessments across courses and disciplines greatly complicate efforts to infer causal relationships between faculty development and student learning. The use of a common rubric for looking across student work samples at Washington State and Carleton addressed the latter problem, although there were clear tradeoffs in adopting such an approach.

The shared attention to critical thinking precluded an examination of faculty development effects on students' grasp of disciplinary knowledge, which is at the heart of our argument in this book. Assessing students' disciplinary knowledge would require rubrics tailored to the features of the relevant discipline. It is striking to us that the book chronicling the Tracer Project features a comparison of students' critical thinking in the writing they produced in an upper-level Washington State University entomology course both before and after the course was guided by the critical thinking rubric. The student gains with respect to critical thinking after faculty development were substantial—indeed a positive finding. However, the evidence did not address the impact of faculty development on students' learning of the subject matter of entomology itself.

Also challenging as a research design issue is the possibility that the rating of students' critical thinking was influenced not only by instructors' adoption of instructional practices designed to elicit critical thinking but also by the use of a new set of assessments. After exposure to faculty development, the faculty created new prompts for the student writing that faculty rated according to the critical thinking rubric. It is possible that the new assessments simply were more successful in eliciting evidence of critical reasoning rather than that there were changes in what students learned in their classes after faculty participated in professional development. Two variables changing at once—exposure to professional development, and assessment prompts—make it difficult to isolate the effect of faculty development. Even so, it is encouraging to see an association between faculty participation in professional development activities and the average critical thinking performance that raters assign to samples of student work.

Assessing Campus Teaching Centers

How can campus teaching centers demonstrate to the campus community, and most pointedly to the administrators who set their budgets, that they are making a difference? The best examples to date have relied on an explicit theory of action and traced the flow of resources through program activities, changes in faculty orientations and behaviors, and ultimately student achievement. Toward this end, we strongly endorse the development of logic models to guide campus-based teaching center evaluations.

Logic models are tools used to characterize the features of programs (e.g., a faculty teaching improvement program), including their duration, participants, and goals and objectives. They typically specify the intended inputs of a program, the program's suite of activities, its intended reach (i.e., the volume of participants), and short-term, medium-term, and long-term outcomes.[39] For teaching development programs, for example, short-term outcomes might include changes in participating instructors' attitudes, motivations, aspirations, knowledge, and skills. Medium-term outcomes might involve changes in teaching practice, while long-term outcomes might be changes in their students' learning.

Logic models for the evaluation of teaching improvement initiatives have many virtues, but we focus on two here. First, they facilitate visualizations of and hence conversations about the linkages among the elements of the model and the mechanisms that connect activities to outcomes. Is it plausible, for example, that a given array of resources can support a program's planned activities? And is there good reason to think that the array of activities will yield the desired changes in teaching practice and, downstream, students' learning? Second, logic models draw attention to the elements that must be measured in order for one to evaluate the functioning of a particular program. If a program is intended to increase faculty use of evidence-based teaching practices, for example, how would one gauge program success? What specific data might an evaluator gather to demonstrate the level of use of these evidence-based teaching practices?

The American Council on Education, in consultation with the POD Network, has developed a matrix that can be used to assess a particular campus center's standing in relation to a set of standards regarding organizational structure, a center's physical location, resource allocation and infrastructure, and programs and services, each of which has four or five criteria.[40] A center can be rated "developing," "partially developed," or "fully developed" in relation to the standards and the criteria that make them up. For example, one of the criteria for programs and services is reach, the extent to which the center reaches the instructional faculty of the institution. The rubric for this standard describes "developing" as "depending upon campus mission and size, less than 10% of instructional faculty, including those with contingent appointments or graduate students; unevenly distributed across appointment type and department/college." In contrast, "partially developed" is described as reaching between 10% and 20% of instructional faculty, and "fully developed" as a minimum of 20% of instructional faculty, with the additional proviso that the campus center reaches departments at the program level and attracts teams.[41]

We view teaching centers and the several related projects we have described here as helping prepare early career faculty while also providing support to those in more advanced stages of their careers. These centers and programs exemplify the full range of teaching improvement resources and opportunities that can be offered to faculty and that can serve as a base as well for faculty to learn practices consistent with convergent teaching.

Other Campus-Based Models

Although teaching centers can offer resources that engage faculty in innovative practices to support student learning, in this section, two other campus-based models striving for similar goals merit our attention: the Association of College and University Educators (ACUE) Course in Effective Teaching Practices and the Science Education Initiative (SEI).

One approach to offering college faculty access to faculty professional development is to contract with a professional development provider who has invested in developing a set of durable and tested tools that can be applied broadly across different types of postsecondary institutions. This is the niche that ACUE seeks to fill.

ACUE, founded as a limited liability company in 2014, embarked on a whirlwind effort to convene experts to develop a framework for effective college teaching practice. Drawing on research on practice, the framework articulates five elements: designing an effective course and class, establishing a productive learning environment, using active learning techniques, promoting higher order thinking, and developing assessment tools to inform instruction and encourage learning. Each element is further differentiated into topic-specific online learning modules, such as "planning effective class discussions," "using concept maps and other visualization tools," and "checking for student understanding."

Together, the twenty-five modules form the basis for ACUE's Course in Effective Teaching Practices, delivered to cohorts of faculty on a particular campus that has contracted with ACUE, typically through a strategic multiyear collaboration designed around measurable learning goals for faculty and students. The course, delivered on line with local facilitation, asks faculty to complete about one module a week, following a unique sequence developed for each partner institution. Modules include demonstration videos, expert interviews, instructor resources, formative assessments, and supporting citations to relevant research. Participants are expected to analyze video clips of both exemplary and less-than-exemplary practice, participate in facilitated, online cohort discussions, and reflect on how they can change their practice in response to these examples. Each module concludes with a requirement for faculty to implement a new technique from among a choice of recommended practices applicable to face-to-face or online instruction.

Faculty must also write reflections on the experience of implementing each new technique in their class. These reflections are expected to indicate why the faculty member chose the technique, provide evidence of student behavior to demonstrate what went well and what challenges were encountered, and explain what the participant will do to refine or adapt their use of the technique in the future. Reflections are shared with other participants in their local cohort and scored remotely by ACUE using a rubric that also provides feedback on the reflection. This learning design is intended to bolster faculty members' knowledge and implementation of the practices recommended in each module. The learning management system through which ACUE's courses are delivered gathers and provides data to the partner institution regarding levels of individual faculty engagement, learning, and implementation.

ACUE succeeded in forging a collaboration with the American Council on Education to offer professional development via a certification program. The Certificate in Effective College Instruction that ACUE awards faculty who complete the course is endorsed by the American Council on Education and recognized by its College Credit Recommendation Service as a form of workplace learning equivalent to three graduate-level academic credits. The ACUE model is scalable, and as of early 2019, 104 institutions had partnered with ACUE across thirty states, including twenty-six private institutions participating through a coalition created by the Council of Independent Colleges with a $1.2 million grant from the Strada Education Network.[42]

As is true for most teaching improvement initiatives, direct evidence of impact on student outcomes is elusive. ACUE is pursuing a six-level evaluation framework that the organization hopes can provide evidence of better faculty engagement, faculty learning, faculty implementation, student engagement, student outcomes, and institutional outcomes.[43] Changes in student and institutional outcomes are the most challenging to measure and may not be observed immediately, but there already is evidence of positive impact on faculty engagement, faculty learning, faculty implementation, and student engagement.

The individual student outcomes that ACUE proposes to track include course enrollment and completion and grades/GPA, outcomes that are chosen in consultation with partner institutions and may vary across sites. The institutional outcomes to be measured are student retention and graduation rates. These outcomes are consistent with the goal of connecting effective college teaching to student success, but they are at some remove from demonstrating that the students taught by faculty participants in ACUE's effective teaching program have increased their knowledge in and understanding of the subject matter of those classes, which has been a central concern of ours. We acknowledge that this is a very stringent standard, as a campus cohort of faculty participants may draw from many different fields of study, most of which do not have ways of providing stable assessments of student learning that could measure the impact of exposure to the ACUE course.

We view the ACUE Course on Effective Teaching Practices to be a promising approach for preparing college faculty to use pedagogical practices that may engage students and increase their academic success. ACUE's Effective Practice Framework emphasizes various forms of pedagogical knowledge, but by design it does not address practices for learning any particular subject matter, as the conception of convergent teaching presented in part II calls for. ACUE finesses this by featuring college faculty from various fields in the on-line videos of the course using the effective practice principles in real classes and then asking course participants to implement these principles in their own (subject-matter) classes, which is then followed up with subsequent reflection, cohort discussion, and facilitator feedback. This does have the capacity to bring subject matter into view, albeit peripherally, as faculty are exposed to examples and feedback that cross disciplinary lines. And even if subject matter is not in the foreground, our theme in this chapter is that a variety of pedagogical practices are necessary to support convergent teaching.

Subject matter is much more central to our second example of new efforts to improve college teaching. One of the best-known recent initiatives is the SEI, founded by physicist Carl Wieman.[44] Wieman has recently recounted the history of the SEI, an effort to improve the teaching of science at the University of Colorado and the University of British Columbia over roughly a decade.[45] He oversaw a competitive grants program to six science departments in each institution, awarding approximately $1 million per department over a five- or six-year period (around $5 million at University of Colorado and $10 million at University of British Columbia).

Wieman recognized that the formal faculty incentive system in each institution was the primary barrier to change. He believed that a competitive grants program with department-level awards of a sizeable amount could transform science teaching. The department was the key unit of change, as courses are lodged in departments. The change mechanism was what he referred to as science education specialists: postdoctoral fellows with disciplinary knowledge and teaching expertise who were hired by, and embedded in, the academic departments. Working with these specialists, faculty could examine what students should be learning in a particular course, what they were actually learning, and what kinds of research-based instructional practices could promote the desired learning. Although implementation of the SEI was uneven across departments, Wieman found evidence that hundreds of thousands of credit hours in science classes each year were taught differently—that is, using practices drawn from the learning sciences—due to the initiative.

Wieman's book is full of insights, some specific to the SEI and others more broadly applicable to teaching improvement efforts. Although the initial focus was on transforming courses, he came to understand that transforming faculty was more appropriate; some faculty would vigorously resist curricular and instructional change, seeing it as a threat to their professional identities. Thus, it made more sense for the project to recruit faculty who were receptive to innovation. Wieman also concluded that he had underestimated the importance of direct incentives to faculty for engaging in course transformation, such as course releases, extra teaching assistants, or partial support for a research assistant. The incentives, he mused, needed to be substantial enough that the threat of losing them would spur compliance with the initiative's goals.

Finally, Wieman saw the overall quality of management and organization within the institution and its departments as the primary determinant of whether the SEI was well implemented in a department. Change was unlikely to occur unless actors at every institutional level—system heads and policy leaders, college presidents and senior administrators, and department chairs and individual faculty—came to understand good undergraduate teaching as subject-matter driven, student-knowledge driven, and research- and assessment driven. Some departmental cultures, especially those that downplayed collective activity, reduced the likelihood of success. Conversely, some department chairs took strategic action to support the SEI, such as reassuring junior faculty that poor course evaluations in an early iteration of a transformed course would not be held against them.

Wieman remains optimistic, as do we, about the potential of research-based teaching improvement initiatives such as the SEI to improve undergraduate teaching in the sciences and other fields. There is indication, however, of obstacles even beyond the significant learning curve faculty face in establishing learning goals, documenting student thinking, developing instructional materials, and assessing their impact. The sustainability of course transformation at the department level in the absence of substantial external incentives is an unknown, and in several of the funded departments at the University of Colorado and the University of British Columbia, fewer than 50% of the faculty participated in the initiative. Moreover, even the well-funded SEI was poorly aligned with campus-level policies and practices regarding faculty promotion and tenure and the level of central support for academic departments.

The SEI spotlights the importance of braiding teaching improvement at the individual instructor level with teaching improvement at the department level and of gaining the support of top institutional leaders. These lessons, though derived from science classrooms, may be applicable to other disciplines and fields of study. We appreciate the centrality of subject matter and learning sciences research to the SEI, as it resonates with our conception of convergent teaching.

Having described a number of campus-level supports for convergent teaching, we turn to discussion of still broader institutional processes for evaluating and rewarding good college teaching. Though they address teaching understood broadly, these processes also promise to support convergent teaching.

Institutional Processes for Evaluating and Rewarding College Teaching

As we have noted, institutions can learn a great deal from contrasting their formal policies and procedures with what happens when these policies and practices are enacted in day-to-day campus life. Nowhere is this clearer than in institutional processes for evaluating college teaching, most notably in reappointment, promotion, and tenure processes. Reality rarely mirrors ideals, though we do believe that careful crafting and evaluation of administrative policies can bring them closer together. Thus far in our argument, we have not drawn any connections between institutional policies for recognizing and rewarding good teaching and college teachers' instructional practices in the classroom. In this section, we discuss campus policies for evaluating and rewarding teaching as a route to improving teaching.

The field of higher education can learn a great deal from the history of K–12 teacher evaluation. In the K–12 sector, as in higher education, there is a fundamental distinction between formative and summative evaluation. Formative evaluation of instructors is primarily intended to improve their teaching practice. The general theory of action is that a formative evaluation process surfaces features of an instructor's performance and creates a context for the instructor to reflect on that performance and to change his or her instructional practices in response to the reflection. This cycle is most likely to occur when the evidence of teaching performance is salient to the instructor, perceived as legitimate, and provides a road map for possible actions.

Conversely, the primary purpose of summative evaluation in K–12 educational organizations is selection and certification—the identification of those instructors whose performance meets a minimum threshold of adequacy and of those who fall below that threshold and who therefore should be let go. In higher education, we see summative evaluation in action in high-stakes personnel decisions such as reappointment, promotion, and tenure, in the case of those faculty who are on the tenure track, or in the decision to rehire a contingent faculty member or not. Such decisions can be highly charged, as individuals' livelihoods depend on whether a summative evaluation procedure results in continued employment or termination (a harsh term that is scarcely softened by those policy analysts who refer to it as "deselection").

Summative evaluation is an administrative decision that in and of itself is not intended to have a direct effect on an instructor's practice— although some believe that the threat of termination is a powerful motive to change one's practice. Rather, summative evaluation amounts to an evaluator gauging evidence regarding performance against some threshold or standard and determining if the performance is "above the bar." In the context of reappointment, promotion, and tenure, such judgments often revolve around evidence pertaining to a faculty member's accomplishments in research, teaching and advising, and public and institutional service. Faculty committees and administrators typically make successive judgments based on institutional criteria appropriate for the locus and stage of review.

The fundamental challenge in evaluating college teaching is the tension between formative and summative evaluation. The purposes of each are quite distinct. Formative evaluation is devoted to the improvement of teaching practice and relies on sources of evidence that can enable instructors to reflect on and alter what they do in the classroom; it is often spread over time, allowing faculty, especially those in a probationary period, to improve their practice via periodic feedback. Formative evaluation therefore has a very different rhythm from summative evaluation, which is keyed to personnel decisions such as reappointment, promotion, and tenure that may occur on a fixed timeline. Summative evaluation of teaching informs personnel decisions about whether a faculty member has demonstrated a level of competence consistent with academic unit and institutional criteria, which often are an amalgam of judgments about the three primary domains of faculty work: research, teaching, and service. It is possible that specific forms of evidence for an individual's teaching performance may serve both formative and summative ends. But what's useful for one kind of evaluation need not be useful for the other. A familiar metaphor is that in formative evaluation, the institution serves as a coach, while in summative evaluation it serves as a cop.

We next discuss ways whereby institutions can incorporate evidence about faculty teaching performance into reappointment, promotion, and tenure processes in the context of both formative and summative evaluation.[46] It's axiomatic that change in faculty teaching performance hinges on individuals' motivation, knowledge, and opportunity. We strongly recommend that the evaluation of faculty teaching embedded in reappointment, promotion, and tenure processes build in these features. We also maintain that good evidence for both summative and formative evaluations consists of durable and valid artifacts of teaching practice and performance, which we describe shortly.

We begin, though, by outlining a process ubiquitous in higher education that, deployed uncritically, poses a serious threat to the validity of claims about teaching quality: students' ratings of instruction. Student ratings yield data that are almost universally used in formative and summative teaching evaluation processes, especially evaluations associated with reappointment, promotion, and tenure reviews. But these cannot be understood as proxies for student learning, and they ought not overshadow other measures of teaching practice or of what students have learned from a college instructor.

We are not arguing for the elimination of student ratings, as they may reveal students' experiences of a class that are worth attending to, and students' voices are important. How students experience the classroom, for example, can influence their openness to learning, and there are aspects of classroom life for which students are good informants. But relying on student ratings to the exclusion of other sources of evidence can yield erroneous conclusions about the quality of an instructor's teaching, including how much students are learning.

Following the discussion of student ratings of instruction, we lay out three processes well suited to developing durable and valid artifacts of college teaching practice: peer observation, teaching portfolios, and faculty self-evaluation. At the moment, these are only loosely tied to student learning outcomes; we draw on the K–12 education research literature to examine challenges in making this connection. We close with a discussion of instrumental and symbolic rewards that shape institutional cultures supportive of good college teaching and propagate good teaching practice.

Reducing Reliance on Student Ratings of Instruction

The vast majority of US institutions of higher education ask their students to rate their classes at the end of the term, often via a battery of Likert-scale items addressing features of the course and its instruction. Such rating instruments also feature questions about students' background and the nature of the course, as well as open-ended items that allow students to write comments about the positive and negative features of the course. The specific questions, mode of administration, and criteria by which courses are to be evaluated are, for the most part, individually negotiated between an institution's administration and faculty, and these differ substantially from one college to another. Thousands and thousands of hours of faculty and administrator time go into designing and implementing these ratings, which are often the primary source of evidence about teaching quality in high-stakes reappointment, promotion, and tenure decisions.

We worry that much of this effort is misplaced, stemming from a lack of clarity about the intended goals of evaluating college teaching and how best go about it. Are we interested in how students experience teaching, or in the extent and quality of student learning, or possibly both? Do we seek formative data that instructors can use to improve their instruction as their careers progress, or do we need data for a summative, predictably scheduled decision, or both? Of what value are student ratings of instruction to these varied purposes? We devote substantial time to discussing them not because we believe that they are essential to the evaluation and support of college teaching but because they are not going away.[47]

Here, we argue strongly against the use of student ratings of teaching as a primary tool for teaching improvement. We present three vignettes to undergird our claim that student ratings of teaching provide only limited insight into faculty teaching practice or, more baldly, faculty contributions to students' learning of the subject matter of a course. What's at issue is what meaning(s) can be extracted from such ratings. One important question is whether the ratings measure what they purport to measure or something else entirely.

Years ago, we were amused to learn that colleagues invited students to their homes for the final class of the term and distributed the course evaluation bubble sheets to them along with milk and cookies.[48] It was a slight variant on what a colleague working at the New York City Board of Education once referred disparagingly to as a "cookie evaluation" of a professional development seminar: "How was the seminar? Did you like the cookies?"

It was no surprise, then, to learn of a study that documented that the provision of chocolate cookies actually influenced student course evaluations.[49] A team of researchers at the medical school at the University of Münster in Germany taught a course in emergency medicine to undergraduate medical students. Students were randomly assigned to small groups taught by the same two instructors, half of which had available an ample supply of chocolate cookies and half of which did not. Students completed a course evaluation after the two-hour course session, which addressed acute coronary syndrome. A manipulation check suggested that the cookies were a substantial treat and treatment: on average, students in the cookie groups ate 3.6 cookies, or about 2.5 ounces of cookies, during the session.

There was clear evidence that students in the cookie group rated the course more positively than those in the control group. The overall effect size was estimated to be .51, a moderate effect. Shockingly—at least to us— the participants in the cookie group rated the teacher *and* the course material significantly more positively than did the participants in the control group. Because the authors are physicians, they speculated that the results were due to the physical and psychological effects of consuming chocolate.[50] But they, as do we, interpreted the findings as alarming, in that factors unrelated to the quality of postsecondary teaching clearly influenced student ratings of the course and the instructor.

There is much more evidence of this phenomenon. About fifteen years ago, two psychology professors at Weber State University conducted a study of age and gender effects on college students' ratings of teacher expressiveness—for example, their warmth and enthusiasm.[51] Although their study was limited to six sections of a single class in a single institution, the results demonstrate one way in which student ratings can go awry. The researchers asked about 350 undergraduates enrolled in an introductory psychology course to watch a thirty-five-minute presentation on stages of relationship building. The slides portrayed a computer-generated genderless stick figure, the audio script for which was read by an individual whose voice, the researchers concluded, did not suggest a specific age or gender.

Following the presentation, the students were asked to rate the instructor using a form resembling the one commonly in use at the institution. In particular, the participants rated the instructor's expressiveness, including whether the instructor spoke enthusiastically about the subject, made the student feel that she or he would be accepted and included, used voice tone to identify important concepts, and appeared interested in the subject.

Because the researchers were psychologists, there is, of course, more to the study. They randomly distributed four different versions of the teacher rating form to the students. One described the (stick figure) professor as a male under the age of 35, another as a female under the age of 35, a third as a male over the age of 55, and a fourth as a female over the age of 55. The researchers sought to create the impression of a particular age and gender for the ambiguous instructor, to see if students would rate the instructor's behaviors differently if they thought the instructor was male rather than female or younger rather than older.

The results were decisive. Although students in general did not rate the computer-generated stick figure accompanied by a genderless voice very positively, they rated instructors' expressiveness significantly more favorably when they thought their instructor was male rather than female. This was not true for all of the attributes on the student rating form, but it didn't really need to be to demonstrate evidence of bias. The paper reporting the study entered the compendium of evidence supporting the claim that ratings of faculty teaching practice can be biased against women.

The suspicion that student ratings of their instructors might be influenced by extraneous factors was not new. In 1973, a team of medical educators tested the hypothesis that students—in this case, advanced practitioners seeking to learn from a lecturer—could be enticed by the social context to believe that they had learned important subject matter.[52] They hired a professional actor, dubbed him the distinguished "Dr. Fox," and had him deliver a lecture entitled "Mathematical Game Theory as Applied to Physician Education." Although the lecture drew on a paper published in *Scientific American* more than a decade before, the researchers described the lecture's content as "irrelevant, conflicting, and meaningless." They coached their hired actor, who of course had no substantive expertise, to speak authoritatively and with humor as he responded to questions with statements that were internally contradictory, littered with made-up words and ideas, and replete with red herrings—in short, nonsense.[53] Would their audience of learners, they wondered, be seduced by the lecturer's style into believing that they had learned something meaningful?

Across three small audiences of professional medical educators—who by virtue of their own training and experience might be expected to be good arbiters of teaching and learning—the results were clear. The audience members overwhelmingly indicated that the material the instructor presented was interesting and stimulated their thinking, that he presented the material in a well-organized way, and that he used enough examples to clarify the material. The study showed that even professionals can be seduced to mistake style for substance. And if professionals are vulnerable, what of the typical undergraduate student? Should we not worry that student ratings of instructors might be overly sensitive to instructor behaviors that have nothing to do with the subject being taught or with what and how much students learn?

Juxtaposed with these idiosyncratic studies and more than a few others like them is a large body of research on student ratings of instruction that argues that the ratings are reliable, valid, and free of bias from factors that are unrelated to teaching effectiveness. Some of this research has been conducted within schools by institutional researchers, whereas some has been undertaken by purveyors of ratings instruments to demonstrate the desirable technical properties of those instruments. In the various studies and meta-analyses that have been assembled to support these claims, there's persuasive evidence that student ratings of instruction are internally consistent, in the sense that instructors who are rated more positively on one feature of their practice are likely to be rated more positively on others as well.

At the level of the instructor, average student ratings are relatively stable over time; an instructor whose average ratings are more favorable than others at one point in time is likely to be rated more favorably at other times as well. And across multiple courses and course sections, there are generally very small associations between the average rating that students assign to an instructor and the instructor's personal attributes, such as gender, race/ethnicity, age, and full-time or part-time employment status.[54]

The two camps—those who argue that student ratings of instruction are biased against particular groups of instructors, especially women, and those who argue via large-scale datasets that they are not—are largely talking past one another. There's a lack of recognition that the large studies and statistical patterns are more or less irrelevant to whether individual faculty perceive their evaluations are legitimate. In the long run, there may well be little evidence that student evaluations are systematically biased against individuals based on their social characteristics. But the first time a female instructor receives a negative comment on her appearance or demeanor—as so many have—the research literature becomes irrelevant. A concrete case of bias is much more salient in shaping perceptions and subsequent actions: faculty who sense bias in student evaluations are unlikely to use them for improving their teaching.

Virtually all college teachers have either experienced an evaluation they feel is biased or know someone who has. There is a constant stream of examples, and social media allow them to be retold and amplified very efficiently. As we were writing this section, a Canadian biology professor tweeted, "Two married colleagues each brought their son to a lecture because daycare closed last-minute. This was mentioned in both of their student evaluations. Try to guess which prof was called 'unprofessional' and which was described as 'a great parent.'"[55] This tweet went viral (at least by academic standards). The incident captures an important point: regardless of the claims researchers make about the virtues of data derived through student ratings of instruction and regardless of the size of the literature backing their claims, instructors' deep reservations about ratings are powerful enough to call into question their usefulness for teaching improvement, even if the more basic claims to their validity were solid. Instructors' deep beliefs, rooted in personal experiences of biased ratings or the vicarious experiences of others, can lead them to discount the validity and hence utility of student ratings of instruction.

Though faculty may judge student ratings to be susceptible to various forms of bias, some researchers may deem such beliefs to be "myths" that are unfounded yet widely circulated. A group of Israeli researchers surveyed more than two thousand faculty in Israeli institutions of higher education, asking if they subscribed to the belief that student ratings are biased.[56] Do the measures employed in student ratings lack reliability and validity? Are students competent raters? Is there potential for abuse via negative comments and ratings? Are the ratings primarily a popularity contest? Are student ratings influenced by irrelevant factors?

Nearly three-quarters of the respondents believed that students use their ratings in a vindictive manner. Roughly half held to the belief that student ratings are driven down by low-achieving students, that they are not reliable or valid, that students are too immature to rate faculty instruction, that evaluations mostly measure instructor charisma, and that courses with low grades get lower ratings. Though the authors argue that it's irrational for faculty to pay more attention to their "experiential and intuitive notions" than to "published conclusions based on large-sample statistics," they recognize that personal experience matters. Senior faculty in the study were more likely to subscribe to the "myths" about biased ratings than less-experienced college teachers. This may be because of "repeated exposure to relatively rare, yet prominent, instances of biases," the authors concluded.[57]

In sum, student ratings of instruction may be of limited value to faculty teaching improvement. Students may rely on extraneous attributes of their instructors in rating them, and faculty, believing this to be widespread, are therefore likely to discount such ratings as a source of feedback on their instructional practices, regardless of large-sample research. This is not always the case, but it happens with some regularity. The availability of social media allows reports of bias to diffuse throughout the professoriate. Researchers drawing on large bodies of data, as in the Israeli study, may refer to beliefs about bias as myths, but faculty beliefs that biases are real will lead them to dismiss student ratings as a resource for changing their teaching practices.

Although they are sometimes referred to as student evaluations of teaching because we interpret them in relation to tacit or explicit standards of "good" or "bad," Stephen Benton and William Cashin suggest that the term student ratings is more appropriate. The evaluation of college teaching, they argue, is an institutional process that ideally draws on multiple sources of evidence, often including student ratings of their experiences in the classroom.[58] What students are able to do is report their *perceptions* of what transpired in the classroom and their *opinions* about the value of the course and the instructor. That is but one piece of a far larger puzzle.[59]

What features of instruction should students be invited to rate? Not everything, surely. Even ardent supporters of student ratings of instruction carve out territory that they think is beyond the scope of student expertise. Students may have opinions about virtually all features of the course, but their experiential base is bounded. Hence, Benton and Cashin note that "there are important aspects of teaching that students are not competent to rate (e.g., subject-matter knowledge, course design, curriculum development, commitment to teaching, goals and content of the course, quality of student evaluation, support of department's accreditation and program review requirements.)"[60]

Perhaps most importantly, student ratings of instruction should not be understood as evidence of student learning. That is, there is little direct evidence that the students enrolled in classes that receive more positive ratings learn more in these classes than do the students in classes garnering less positive ratings.[61] We won't belabor the argument here, but the technical challenges in making such a claim are formidable. They hinge on a common metric for learning that takes account of the knowledge students have prior to enrolling in a course and their knowledge after exposure to the course, across a large sample of sections of the same course and courses in different fields. The technical demands of good research on the link between student ratings and student learning are substantial.

The best evidence of the correlation between student ratings of instruction and instructors' contributions to student learning comes from the K–12 schooling arena. Measures of Effective Teaching, a large-scale three-year study funded by the Gates Foundation, gathered data on samples of mathematics and English language arts teachers in grades four through eight (as well as high school teachers of introductory algebra, English, and biology) in six large school districts. Teacher effects on student learning were derived from complex statistical models known as value-added models that used state achievement tests in English and mathematics as well as alternative assessments in mathematics and reading.

Student ratings stemmed from a survey instrument developed by Harvard Professor Ronald Ferguson's Tripod Project that asks students to assess the "7 Cs"—the extent to which teachers care, captivate, challenge, confer, clarify, manage the classroom, and consolidate. At the level of the classroom teacher, the average value-added score (representing a teacher's effect on learning) and the average composite score on the Tripod student survey had a small correlation of about .10 in both English and in math.[62] Although the metaphor of a Venn diagram is not precise, student ratings yield only a small overlap with respect to whether students learn more in one class versus another, even in the relatively controlled world of self-contained elementary and middle school classrooms with content standards and standardized assessments. Student ratings of instruction are but weak indicators of students' learning.

In spite of the hazy nature of student ratings of instruction, we expect them to persist. But they need not be relied on so heavily by colleges and universities as evidence of teaching quality. Although there are occasional feints away from widespread administration of student surveys of courses and instruction, there are powerful forces that sustain them. As we noted in our opening chapter, the social compact between students and the colleges and universities they attend is in flux, and the metaphor of student as consumer has become prevalent. Students expect to be able to rate their classes and teachers, just as they rate products and vendors on Amazon, restaurants on Yelp, and drivers for Uber and Lyft. Such ratings are now the backbone of a web of formal and informal accountability in many spheres of life. We know that institutions of higher education are highly responsive to the ratings they receive; it would be inconsistent for them to disavow numerical ratings that they can generate themselves at relatively low cost.[63]

What is most important, we believe, is to minimize the role of student ratings of instruction in high-stakes personnel reviews. Instead, institutions of higher education can and should forge policies and practices that generate new ways to assess teaching quality. As an example, in May 2018, the faculty senate of the University of Oregon passed an initiative that directs faculty personnel committees, department heads, and university administrators to refrain from using numerical ratings from student course evaluations in promotion and tenure reviews and merit compensation reviews. Nor, according to this resolution, are they to use signed written comments from student course evaluations. Instead, the university is to rely on a suite of data consistent with a framework entitled Continuous Improvement and Evaluation of Teaching System.

Elements include a web-based anonymous and nonnumerical midterm student experience survey, an end-of-term nonnumerical student experience survey, an end-of-term instructor reflection survey, and a peer review framework relying on instruments that units are expected to customize to the university's teaching evaluation framework and unit procedures.

At about the same time, the University of Southern California made a similar decision.[64] Provost Michael Quick did not abolish student ratings of teaching, but going forward, these ratings will not be used in the high-stakes personnel decisions of reappointment, promotion, and tenure. The university continues to revise its student ratings instruments, removing what Ginger Clark, assistant vice provost for academic and faculty affairs and director of the university's Center for Excellence in Teaching, refers to as "popularity contest" items, such as "How would you rate this professor?" or "How would you rate this course?" Instead, items focused more specifically on the course's teaching and assessment practices and students' self-reports of their own learning in the course will supplant them. Faculty members will need to show that they reflect on their ratings and revise their teaching practices in response to them, but this is more in the realm of teaching evaluations being used for formative teaching improvement than for summative, high-stakes decisions. It remains to be seen what will replace the student ratings, but the university does have protocols for evaluating course design via syllabus review and a classroom teaching observation protocol that is keyed to its definition of excellence in teaching.

Student ratings will persist, but we are encouraged by these recent moves to reduce their salience in high-stakes personnel decisions. Increasingly, institutions are recognizing the importance of using a more diverse array of indicators of teaching performance that can support both the formative and summative aspects of the evaluation of faculty teaching. There already are good alternatives to student ratings of instruction that can serve the dual goals of formative and summative evaluation. In the next section, we turn to these other durable artifacts of teaching performance that can complement and, where appropriate, supersede student ratings of instruction.

Other Durable Artifacts of Teaching Practice and Performance

We use the term "durable artifacts of teaching practice and performance" to characterize the measures we believe are most useful for formative and summative evaluation, including evaluations of teaching used for reappointment, promotion and tenure decisions. An artifact is a humanly constructed, concrete object representing some meaningful abstraction. An artifact is durable when it is stable, recorded, and accessible to others; such artifacts can be collected, archived, and reviewed over time, facilitating production of evidence for claims about change in a professor's teaching practice or in their thinking in and about teaching. The media for durable artifacts can be written statements or reports, course syllabi and assignments, audio or video recordings of the classroom, or samples of student work, to name a few that are common in teacher evaluation.

Here, we discuss three durable artifacts of teaching practice: peer observation, teaching portfolios, and faculty self-evaluations. Although these do not go so far as to assess the extent to which a college teacher influences student learning, well-constructed versions of these are able to do something that student ratings of instruction cannot: reveal how teaching unfolds over time (e.g., through repeated course observations) and represent instructors' thinking and planning about what transpires in their classrooms, whether in the name of convergent teaching or forms that are far broader. We turn to peer observation first.

Peer observation protocols hold great promise as a source of evidence that can support both formative and summative purposes. Briefly, peer observation involves a cycle of interaction between an instructor and one or more observers of the instructor's classroom practice. A common cycle typically begins with the observer reviewing the course purpose, syllabi, and materials and conducting a preobservation conference with the instructor to discuss the instructor's plans for the class session. The observer then witnesses the class session, takes structured notes on both faculty and student talk and action, and writes up the notes of the session in narrative form. The cycle concludes with a timely postobservation conference to discuss the account of the class and possible action steps.[65]

Many institutions specify when and how often peer observation of teaching should occur. It is not uncommon for institutional policies to specify an annual observation in the probationary period. For example, guidelines at Appalachian State University, part of the University of North Carolina system, call for academic departments to undertake observations in two courses per year of all probationary faculty, full- and part-time non-tenure-track faculty, and teaching assistants.[66] Increasingly, peer observation is also a component of post-tenure review. The University of Oregon, for example, requires peer review of at least one course every other year for tenured associate professors. Post-tenure review in general, of teaching in particular, is framed as formative, not primarily summative; it is assumed that the vast majority of tenured faculty are meeting their professional responsibilities in a satisfactory way but that everyone can improve. "The primary function of post-tenure review is faculty development," Oregon's documents state. "Post-tenure review is not a process to reevaluate the award of tenure."[67]

There is no one best way to organize a peer observation system, but it is most important that it be discussed and agreed on by the faculty and institutional administrators who have a stake in it. If the procedures, standards and criteria are transparent, it is likely that the faculty who are to be observed will view the peer observation process as fair.

Observations can be guided by structured protocols, although we guard against two extremes: formulaic checklists that emphasize the frequency of teaching behaviors and a blank page that does not direct the observer's attention to anything in particular.[68] Our orientation to convergent teaching leads us to recommend attention to the selection of course content and the salience and centrality of the topics covered in a class session, the ability of the instructor to surface the prior knowledge and experience of students that is relevant to the new concepts to be learned, and how the instructor navigates the space between students' prior knowledge and the new subject matter to be learned. There are, of course, many other features of good pedagogical practice that are worthy of attention as well, and many existing peer observation protocols are designed to capture these.

Whether pursued for formative or summative purposes, peer observation of teaching will be most useful if the observations are reliable and valid. Few faculty develop the desired observation skills without training, and institutions may consider investing in training faculty observers and compensating them for the substantial time needed to carry out a high-quality observation cycle. In the largest study of the training of raters of K–12 teaching practice, the investigators of the Measures of Effective Teaching project found that even after seventeen to twenty-five hours of training, nearly one-quarter (23%) of raters were disqualified from rating for the project due to the volume of discrepancies between their ratings and those of experts.[69] The observation protocols in the study were highly detailed and were studied in the context of the Gates Foundation's interest in reforming teacher evaluation systems through rewards and sanctions associated with quantified ratings of teacher performance. Even if colleges and universities are loathe to impose scores with this level of precision, peer observations will be of most value for teaching improvement if the teachers being observed believe that the raters have been well trained.

Teaching portfolios are our second durable artifact. An excellent model for teaching portfolios was developed at the University of Nebraska–Lincoln.[70] A critical insight from its approach is that peer review is far more than peer observation. Rather, peer review, in the form of course portfolios, makes teaching visible in a way that is more expansive than the more limited and episodic visits of individual faculty to their colleagues' classrooms. A portfolio simultaneously exposes a college teacher's thoughts and practices to many other colleagues and allows for the possibility that these colleagues might comment on the portfolio and engage with a particular college teacher in productive ways. The course portfolio is thus a durable artifact that helps to support a *community of teaching practice* or faculty learning community, both made up of individuals who share a commitment to improved teaching practice, interact with one another around their shared purpose, and create concrete and durable representations of teaching practice, such as a common vocabulary; tools, symbols, and concepts; and printed and virtual documents.[71]

One could, for example, imagine putting a teaching portfolio on line and making it visible to others. Making teaching visible in a culture that generally has viewed it as a private matter is brave and can spur teachers to think deeply about what they are up to and how they might improve their practice. But simply placing materials on line in a gallery format is a one-sided approach, in that it does not by itself demand or encourage a response from a critical and sympathetic community of like-minded teachers. Hence, a gallery might not pay off in terms of engagement around teaching philosophy and practice in the way that a course portfolio can.

The University of Nebraska–Lincoln model uses a *course* portfolio, not a teaching portfolio; that is, it treats a specific course—the *target course*—as a unit of analysis, not the entire set of courses that a faculty member might teaching.[72] There are two different types of course portfolios, each with a differing purpose. The benchmark portfolio offers a snapshot of a course. It includes memos and associated artifacts covering the course's context and design and the instructor's direct and indirect goals for student learning and development; the specific teaching methods, course materials, and assignments used in the course and a description of how these allow the instructor to assess students' academic progress and learning; and the presentation and analysis of documentary evidence of student learning in the form of the work that students produce during the class. It is not an archive of the course but rather a mechanism that the teacher uses to reflect on the relationship between course goals and student learning.

Conversely, the inquiry portfolio is a focused effort to inquire into one's teaching practice, again in the context of a specific course, but often longitudinally.[73] In developing an inquiry portfolio, a college teacher picks a single issue and then prepares a series of three memos, the first of which states the teaching problem to be investigated and why it is important or significant, the second of which generates one or more hypotheses about the possible impact of some change in existing teaching practice and a design for testing those hypotheses, and the third of which analyzes data gathered through the design in order to gauge whether the changes in practice yielded the desired results in student learning. As in the benchmark portfolio, the collection, presentation and analysis of samples of student work produced in the class is central to the third memo and indeed to the portfolio development process overall.

Because benchmark and inquiry course portfolios are durable representations of college teachers' reflections on their teaching practice, they can be reviewed by others internal to an institution as well as beyond it.

In some respects, the course portfolio resembles the kinds of scholarly products that are typically sent to external reviewers for reappointment, promotion, and tenure. They are self-documenting and allow reviewers to offer both formative and summative evaluations of the teaching practice that they reflect. Course portfolios also can be the focus of discussions in faculty learning communities on a campus.

As a rough guide, the authors of this model suggest that preparation of a portfolio will take roughly fifty hours of a college teacher's time over the course of an academic year (the usual duration of a benchmark portfolio project from start to completion). The intensity of this commitment, in their view, justifies some compensation, which at University of Nebraska–Lincoln took the form of a $1,000 stipend for completing a benchmark course portfolio. Other forms of compensation, such as course releases, work-study student support, or graduate research assistants, also are possible. Still, the direct costs of this kind of incentive for voluntary participants can add up if many faculty take up the opportunity. An annual cohort of twenty-five faculty preparing benchmark course portfolios would mean $25,000 in stipends.[74]

There is another model of a teaching portfolio that warrants mention, in our view, although it is less directly connected to institutional evaluations of teaching. In the early 2000s, researchers at the Carnegie Foundation for the Advancement of Teaching began thinking about how technology could facilitate the creation of durable records of teaching practice.[75] They realized that videos of classroom practice, coupled with lesson plans, commentaries, and other artifacts, could be arrayed in the form of a gallery or an exhibition. Videos of classroom practice allow for the analysis of a finer level of granularity of teaching, and a sequence of videos tracing an instructional unit can demonstrate some of the nonlinearities of teaching practice that lesson plans, being tidy representations of the sequence of a course, can obscure.

As one might surmise from this description, galleries and exhibitions of teaching practice may have a particular pedagogical value in the context of teacher preparation programs at both the K–12 and postsecondary levels, although most digital exhibitions of classroom teaching are at this point associated with K–12 teacher preparation programs. A class of aspiring teachers can watch a series of web-based videos, and just as with a gallery of paintings, each might see something different, leading them to construct an interpretation that draws on their prior knowledge, including familiarity with the classroom context, the learners, and the subject matter being taught.[76]

The main challenge in using digital exhibitions as a way of making teaching practice public is that the producers of the teaching practice may be decoupled from those who are given the opportunity to review and comment on it. Put differently, when digital exhibitions are used in teacher preparation programs, there may be nothing that links the teacher whose practice is captured in the gallery to those who view it, as would be true in a faculty learning community or other community of college teaching practice. This problem is not insurmountable, but if the goal is to provide formative feedback to the novice and more experienced instructors brave enough to expose their practice to public scrutiny, there has to be a mechanism by which to do so. Certainly, digital tools allow observers of digital records of practice such as classroom videos to comment on and annotate those records. Layers of annotations create the possibility of rich conversations developing between observers and the teacher about teaching practice, benefiting both experienced and aspiring instructors.

Our final durable artifact is the self-evaluation, in which college teachers conceptualize their teaching practices, describe and evaluate their various features, and propose their links to student learning. The reappointment, promotion, and tenure policies at most institutions allow candidates to summarize their scholarly accomplishments. But there is much more lore about how to write a narrative statement emphasizing research than one that focuses on teaching.

Individual faculty are, of course, best positioned to comment on their goals, aspirations, and philosophies of teaching. But statements of philosophy of teaching, although increasingly common, often are sterile, merging student course evaluation data with vague commitments to particular pedagogical practices. It's a rare teaching statement that does not allude to "active learning," but what exactly does that mean in practice, and why is it important?[77] The use of educational technology such as clickers in the classroom may be de rigueur, but how specifically does it contribute to student learning? Instead of relying on these tropes, teaching narratives could draw on the principles of convergent teaching and outline how instructors decide what to teach in light of their understandings of the field, how they get to know what their students think about what they will and do teach them, and how they help students interact with seemingly new and strange ideas and ways of thinking.

Although reflection on practice is an intrinsic good, the payoff is even greater when instructors' reflections are brought into conversation within a community of peers. Thus, an instructor's colleagues should discuss, debate, and interrogate statements of teaching philosophy, clarifying ambiguities, seeking concrete examples, and solidifying an orientation on the part of the teacher toward growth and development in her or his teaching in response to feedback. As is true for virtually all features of scholarly work, quality improves in response to peer review. Statements of teaching philosophy are no exception. They can be an important durable artifact of teaching accomplishment, but they should not be filed away into a dossier without having had the benefit of feedback from colleagues.

We have argued that student ratings of instruction are of limited value for both formative and summative evaluations of college teaching performance. In contrast, durable artifacts such as peer observation, teaching portfolios, and faculty self-evaluation can serve as sources of insight into the quality of teaching and ways to make it better. These specific artifacts do not exhaust all of the possibilities, but they are fairly easy to generate once a campus commits to a diversified set of evaluative measures. What prompts such a commitment? We turn next to the ways in which institutional culture can support teaching excellence and convergent teaching.

Institutional Culture Supporting Teaching Excellence

Previously, we noted the importance of building institutional cultures that value teaching and observed that there are many ways to do so. One important strategy is to orient institutional processes, especially those pertaining to academic affairs, toward the faculty career. These should not begin with reappointment, promotion, or tenure decisions or even with the multiyear efforts that faculty put into preparing for them. Rather, they should be encoded into all phases of the faculty recruitment cycle, beginning with the framing of position descriptions that foreground teaching expertise and requests for durable artifacts of teaching performance as part of the job application process. Increasingly, institutions and academic departments are asking candidates for faculty positions to demonstrate their pedagogical practices in a sample teaching lesson that parallels the more familiar research talk. When framed thoughtfully, a sample teaching lesson can simultaneously provide evidence of a candidate's promise as a teacher and convey to both job candidates and to the college community the importance of teaching quality.

But the attention to and evaluation of teaching in hiring and other personnel processes is just one approach to building a culture that values undergraduate teaching quality. Institutions should recognize and reward excellent teaching, symbolically elevating the value of teaching to faculty work and to the institution's mission. For example, titles are an important source of status both within and beyond the institution, and many institutions have used titles (e.g., chairs for teaching excellence, named professorships) and resources that accompany them to elevate and inspire teaching improvement.

Teaching Awards

Numerous examples of the power of such recognitions and rewards exist. The University of Michigan annually awards five Arthur F. Thurnau professorships to tenured faculty who have made outstanding contributions to undergraduate education. Supported by the Thurnau Charitable Trust, the awardees receive a $20,000 grant to support their teaching and carry the title for the remainder of their careers at the university.[78] Similarly, the University of Virginia sponsors an alumni association distinguished professor award that is made annually to a member of the faculty with ten or more years of service. The award carries a $10,000 stipend (and a lifetime membership in the alumni association). Importantly, recipients of the University of Virginia award are expected to share their teaching expertise with colleagues and students in the three years following receipt of the award. One mechanism for doing so is working with the university's teaching resource center to lead teaching workshops, mentor faculty colleagues on teaching issues, or organize a reading group of faculty and teaching assistants on college teaching.[79]

Michigan and Virginia are large, well-resourced institutions, but there are promising examples of teaching excellence awards at institutions of all types. Seminole State College's foundation administers approximately twenty endowed teaching chairs intended to reward faculty for their contributions to teaching and learning. At Seminole State, an endowed teaching chair is fully funded and ready to be awarded when the endowment for the chair has reached $100,000.[80] Miami Dade College, the largest community college in the United States, annually awards approximately five endowed teaching chairs through its foundation. Recipients receive an annual stipend of $7,500 for three years to support their teaching.[81] Illinois Central College offers the Dr. Thomas K. Thomas Endowed Teaching Chair, which annually recognizes faculty with a stipend of up to $3,500 or the equivalent in release time to support the recipient's plans to improve instruction.[82]

Since endowed professorships are frequently used to recruit and retain faculty renowned for their research, institutional development initiatives are often oriented toward fully-funded endowed professorships. At many institutions, such professorships require a multimillion dollar commitment. Endowed teaching chairs need not be that costly and thus are good candidates for development efforts. Whereas many donors are gratified that their gifts can support student access, the sheer number of students who may be touched by a faculty member is far greater than the number who are likely to benefit from direct scholarship support. We recommend strategic fund-raising efforts to support endowed teaching professorships and believe that alumni and corporate foundations are among the most promising prospective donors.

Whether or not they are endowed, we encourage institutions with a tenure system to consider dedicating a certain number of tenure-track faculty positions to undergraduate teaching, treating excellent teaching of undergraduates as a central feature of faculty accomplishment. But it would be unwise to sequester these faculty as having the sole, or even primary, responsibility for teaching undergraduate students. Rather, those who are recruited and selected specifically on the basis of their teaching prowess can model good teaching, work on its improvement, and help others understand what good teaching looks like. Appointing and rewarding faculty primarily on the basis of their teaching accomplishments might go against the grain in institutions whose reputations rise or fall on the research productivity of their faculty, but it really is a matter of priorities. Colleges and universities that take undergraduate teaching and student learning seriously should invest in the faculty who can enact that part of the institutional mission via sustained faculty appointments.

Culture is a powerful vehicle for institutional change. In discussing the use of titles, recognitions, and other faculty rewards, we have barely scratched the surface of approaches to shaping campus cultures toward support of teaching. We ask institutional leaders to highlight everyday practices and special events that contribute to an institution's conception of good teaching. And if few such practices and events exist already, we suggest taking the time to invent them.

Toward Improvement: What We Can Do

Organized efforts to improve the teaching practices of college faculty take many forms, and our review in this chapter illuminates a small fraction of these. Rather than promote specific ways of designing any particular initiative, we offer the following recommendations.

First, we encourage campuses to engage in systematic self-study to understand alignments and frictions among institutional aspirations, mission, and culture and the salience of undergraduate teaching and its improvement. All campuses can develop ways to support teaching improvement and to recognize and reward good teaching in institutional personnel policies.

Second, we recommend that the campus chief academic officer designate a particular person as responsible for oversight of undergraduate teaching improvement and endow that individual with the authority and resources to advance undergraduate teaching quality.

Third, the colleges and universities that are preparing the next generation of college teachers should expand their programming to ensure that all doctoral students have opportunities to learn to teach and to put that learning into practice.

Fourth, we call on institutions to strengthen their investments in campus teaching and learning centers, while holding these centers accountable, in attainable ways, for demonstrating that they have impact on faculty orientations and attitudes, faculty teaching practices, and student learning outcomes. Institutions should devote resources to improving the measurement of these desired outcomes and also provide support for developing the capacity to carry out useful evaluations.

Fifth, we recommend that colleges and universities use their personnel policies to support and sustain high-quality teaching. Institutions can dedicate tenure-track and other long-term contract positions to faculty who demonstrate teaching excellence and build an appreciation for undergraduate teaching quality into the faculty recruitment cycle. The personnel policies guiding faculty reappointment, promotion, and tenure can be calibrated to support and recognize good college teaching, most notably by moving away from student ratings of teaching and toward the creation, display, and interpretation of durable artifacts of teaching practice such as peer observation and interactive faculty self-evaluations.

Finally, institutions can raise the profile of undergraduate teaching and its centrality to a campus mission in a variety of ways, including by conferring titles and awards carrying resources that support the illumination and dissemination of good teaching practice. Institutional leaders also can use symbols and local culture to lift up teaching as a valued feature of the campus's identity.

CHAPTER SIX

Supporting Convergent Teaching beyond the Campus

While it's important to build the college and university structures and processes that support convergent teaching and good teaching broadly, as we discuss in chapter 5, we believe that it is equally important to garner support from sources other than colleges themselves. With this aim in mind, we consider, first, the efforts of disciplinary movements in the United States and in Europe to strengthen undergraduate teaching, focusing especially on initiatives known as tuning, measures of college learning, and discipline-based educational research (DBER). We follow then with discussion of some of the risks to these and other improvement efforts, that is, what could (and indeed, often does) go wrong, despite the best intentions to improve teaching. We believe that illuminating real and potential structural obstacles built into higher education in the United States, as unpleasant as they may be to contemplate, is an essential step in designing effective teaching improvement efforts. We can't be blind to what could get in the way. We close the chapter and the book with advice to faculty whose expert ideas, creativity, and energy are—and, we think, always will be—at the heart of both teaching and teaching improvement efforts.

Disciplinary Knowledge Movements

In this section, we examine the work of disciplinary associations and other collections of disciplinary scholars to advance undergraduate teaching in particular disciplines: the tuning process and the measures of collegiate learning initiative. These are merely illustrative, as there are many more movements and projects in present-day and the recent past.

Tuning

What has come to be known as the tuning process has its roots in efforts to rationalize higher education in Europe. As one might expect, education systems differ across national boundaries in Europe, just as they differ across states in the United States. The variability in institutional structures, degrees, and curricula made mobility across institutions located in different European countries quite difficult. No one was quite sure what was equivalent to what: would passing a particular course taken in an Italian university represent mastery of the same content as passing such a course in France? What came to be known as the Bologna Process, a set of agreements signed by national ministers of education in Europe at the University of Bologna in 1999, set in motion efforts to define educational qualifications in terms of what students know and can do and to develop the European Credit Transfer and Accumulation System. Participation in the Bologna Process is voluntary, and countries have embraced it with varying levels of commitment.

Shortly after the signing of the Bologna agreements, many European scholars embarked on the tuning process. The idea of alignment and independence conveyed by tuning is important, as there were serious concerns that centralizing higher education policies and practices might compromise strongly held traditions of institutional and faculty independence. As a process, tuning is intended to identify commonalities and shared understandings of what students should know and be able to do in different subject areas and majors. But it is also intended to allow for patterned differences grounded in the unique circumstances of countries and particular institutions of higher education. Importantly, it is faculty who lead the tuning process, defining the core of scholarly disciplines, mapping curricular and career trajectories, and developing tools for the assessment of student learning. Internationally, tuning is led by an international higher education and research center called the Tuning Academy, which originated in tuning projects situated at the University of Deusto (Spain) and the University of Groningen (The Netherlands).[1]

The US version of tuning began in 2009, with the launch of Tuning USA, a pilot project sponsored by the Lumina Foundation. Tuning USA supported efforts in Utah, Indiana, and Minnesota to bring faculty, administrators, and students from various types of postsecondary institutions together to discuss expectations for what students should learn in the disciplines and hence to support equivalences across institutions and assessment and accountability practices. Utah focused on history and physics; Minnesota on biology and graphic arts; and Indiana on chemistry, education, and history. Not long after, Texas joined, focusing on mathematics, biology, chemistry, business, computer science, and engineering specialties. Lumina then funded the Midwest Higher Education Compact to oversee the tuning of the fields of psychology and marketing in Illinois, Indiana, and Missouri, the first cross-state tuning effort in the U.S.[2]

Of particular interest in the United States is the American Historical Association's (AHA) engagement with the tuning process, as the AHA is the largest professional organization of historians, with more than twelve thousand members. With the support of the Lumina Foundation, the AHA embarked on a tuning process in 2011, led by faculty in the AHA's Teaching Division and drawing on more than 150 faculty participants from a diverse set of institutions across the country during the project's 2012 and 2015 waves. The AHA tuning process resulted in statements of the history disciplinary core in 2013 and 2016. This core describes the discipline and its core concepts and specifies a set of core competencies and learning outcomes at various levels of specificity. For example, the 2016 version of the history disciplinary core states that history students can (1) build historical knowledge; (2) develop historical methods; (3) recognize the provisional nature of knowledge, the disciplinary preference for complexity, and the comfort with ambiguity that history requires; (4) apply the range of skills it takes to decode the historical record because of its incomplete, complex, and contradictory nature; (5) create historical arguments and narratives; and (6) use historical perspective as central to active citizenship.[3]

This may still seem rather abstract, and it's true that the tuning process (as well as its successor, the Degree Qualifications Profile) speaks to what students should know or be able to do upon the completion of a major at a particular degree level (e.g., a bachelor's degree). However, the process does not provide guidance on what concepts or specific disciplinary ideas might or could be targeted in a particular class, even a lower-division undergraduate first course in a particular field of study. Despite the absence of such guidance, we suspect that tuning projects *can* help faculty discern the disciplinary concepts they wish students to learn in a course. Ironically, this is because the outcomes of a tuning process—statements of what students should know and be able to do—are somewhat abstract and not overly detailed and specific. The tuning process expects that there will be local adaptations grounded in geographic, cultural, and other specifics that will shape what is to be taught and learned and why. Thus, faculty can use statements about disciplinary knowledge, skills, and competencies to orient their course design and lesson planning, which are inherently local enterprises embedded in particular institutions that serve particular populations of students.

The tuning process and its sibling, the Degree Qualifications Profile, are primarily designed to facilitate institutional processes by providing common metrics and meanings for academic degrees. We've argued that tuning can be used by individual faculty to guide their efforts to implement convergent teaching, especially the principle of targeting. But we must acknowledge that although they may think otherwise, faculty are not wholly autonomous. Rather, they are embedded in academic units that offer sequences of courses adding up to a major program of study or contributing to other programs of study. How tightly or loosely the courses one teaches are linked to other courses in a unit's curriculum and the means whereby such courses are made to relate to one another may shape how much autonomy an individual faculty member can have in targeting certain disciplinary concepts to the exclusion of others. A faculty member may not unilaterally be able to reduce the number of topics or concepts he or she addresses in a course if his or her colleagues are counting on him or her to cover others. Ideally, such differences can be worked out in the context of unit-level discussions about curriculum, but many academic units lack well-functioning mechanisms to discuss curriculum.

Measuring College Learning

The tuning approach sees statements of learning outcomes—what graduates with a particular degree should know and be able to do—as ends in themselves. To be sure, faculty involved in tuning are keenly aware of the ways in which it can be used for institutional purposes at some distance from the faculty's intellectual work in defining core ideas and competencies in their fields. During her tenure as president of the American Historical Association, Gabrielle Spiegel drew attention to what she called the "triple 'A' threat": accountability, assessment, and accreditation.[4] Writing in 2008, just two years after the release of the Spellings Commission report, she noted that the zeitgeist was demanding assessment and that if faculty didn't take the lead in designing assessments of students' learning of history, then the state and its bureaucrats would doubtless step in—and get it wrong.[5]

She wasn't the only one worried. Richard Arum and Josipa Roksa saw the reactions to their book *Academically Adrift,* which rode the wave of rising concern about student learning and the student experience in college.[6] They noted that external accountability and assessment could easily supersede that of the faculty who constituted the academic core of colleges and universities. They were alarmed by this possibility, as they believed faculty should be in the driver's seat in setting learning outcomes and in developing appropriate assessments of those outcomes.

In this stance, Arum and Roksa went beyond the tuning process, which was not intended to result in common assessments. Unlike the tuning projects, which saw the specification of what students should know and be able to do with a particular credential in a specific major or field of specialization as an end in itself, for Arum and Roksa, specifying learning outcomes was a means to an end: developing disciplinary assessments.

Among the many criticisms made of *Academically Adrift* was that contra what Arum and Roksa claim, the Collegiate Learning Assessment, the general-purpose tool developed to measure problem solving, quantitative reasoning, and critical reading skills, does not assess the learning of disciplinary knowledge.[7] In a subsequent piece, "Defining and Assessing Learning in Higher Education, they acknowledged this. "College-level courses are, by and large, discipline specific," they write. "This means that students, to the extent that they are developing broader skills such as analysis, writing, and critical thinking, are developing them in discipline-specific contexts. Learning how to think critically, write analytically, and problem solve in the disciplines is crucial, not only because it will enable students to be skilled disciplinary actors, but also because it will give them a foundation that can potentially be transferred to a range of other domains."[8] This realization has led to greater attention to the learning of disciplinary knowledge and how that learning might be assessed.

Arum and Roksa believed that once disciplinary communities had reached some consensus on what students should learn in an introductory course in a particular subject and what they should know and be able to do upon completing an undergraduate major, a logical next step would be to develop common assessments that would enable academic units and institutions to benchmark their students' performance against the performance of students in other institutions.

To this end, they, with their colleague Amanda Cook, sought and were awarded funds from the Gates Foundation to convene teams of faculty in six subject areas: biology, history, sociology, economics, communication, and business.[9] In many respects, their work paralleled that being carried out in tuning projects, though they gave less attention to stakeholders other than faculty with disciplinary expertise. Over a two-year period, these teams, often with the support of the staff of professional associations, deliberated on the desired learning outcomes for students enrolled in the field's introductory course, as well as the desired outcomes for students completing a major in the field.

Drawing on prior work in biology, each team articulated a set of essential concepts (i.e., the big ideas and ways of thinking at the heart of the discipline) and essential competencies (i.e., the practices and skills needed to apply the discipline within and outside of the academy). Identifying these concepts and competencies, the project leaders believed, could serve as a foundation for developing standardized assessments aligned to these concepts and competencies.

The volume emerging from this project detailed both the promise and challenge of identifying core competencies in the disciplines that could undergird assessments of student learning. The organization of knowledge in some disciplines resulted in greater consensus among the faculty in some fields about what "counts" as essential than among the faculty in other fields.[10] Nevertheless, we believe that the notion of essential concepts and competencies can orient college teachers in the disciplines to the most important content for them to teach and for students to learn. Even though the essential competencies were frequently phrased in language that could apply to many fields of study—applying quantitative reasoning, or constructing models of natural phenomena, or evaluating the quality of evidence that is used to support claims—these competencies are developed in discipline-specific contexts.

As part of their charge, the six working groups examined existing standardized learning outcomes assessments. They all came to the same dismal conclusion: nothing off the shelf seemed remotely satisfactory for measuring the kinds of disciplinary knowledge and know-how they deemed important for students to master. The reaction of the economics team as they reviewed the ninety-item Major Field Test marketed by the Educational Testing Service was typical. "Economists do not answer multiple-choice questions," they sniffed. "They formulate productive questions, and they convey their analyses in short and long form. They interpret data and construct and deconstruct arguments that explain observed phenomena. Communication is part of this process."[11]

The historians posed a different critique. The study of history, they said, does not lend itself easily to multiple-choice assessment items about historical content knowledge. There's too much history to go around, they added, and whose knowledge counts? Is it post-Reconstruction US history? Or the history of social revolutions in Europe? "Any attempt to build a test on a particular national history or to privilege particular regions or periods likely would meet with significant controversy," they argued further.[12] Conversely, though, some said that historical thinking requires content knowledge—that is, knowledge of specific historical facts. How, then, could one develop an assessment that draws on such facts when there is no guarantee that all students will have been exposed to them in the classes taken for their undergraduate history major? The field's coverage of multiple historical periods and geographical areas is not a bug; it's a feature.

Ultimately, the measuring college learning project faltered, though not for lack of interest among the working groups, nor because the project leaders were unskilled at herding faculty. Instead, the Gates Foundation lost interest, and when it failed to support the design and implementation of new disciplinary learning assessments, the project drew to a close. It's possible that the ambivalence of so many participants about standardized assessments as tools for assessing student learning signaled to the foundation that the eventual payoff would be modest. There could be many other explanations for the withdrawal of support.

In this section, we are mostly skirting thorny problems of assessment, beyond noting the common recognition that the assessments that are helpful in a formative sense to individual faculty as they teach their classes through a semester may not be the assessments that are helpful to a department or an institution trying to make sense of the overall level of learning that students are experiencing, either in a particular class or through the full length of an undergraduate program.

DBER

One might think that teaching improvement centered on the teaching and learning of disciplinary subjects might be addressed by professional associations of disciplinary practitioners. For the most part, this has not been the case, though a few disciplinary associations and communities have taken up the challenge.[13] Although scholars have strong identifications with their disciplines (and perhaps, by extension, their disciplinary professional associations), curricula and courses are local and customized within institutions. If organizing academics can be likened to herding cats, imagine trying to herd many groups of cats at once. A vivid and promising example, waged mainly via federal agencies such as the National Science Foundation, is the DBER community devoted to strengthening learning and teaching in that swath of disciplines encompassing science and engineering.

According to a 2012 report by the National Research Council's Committee on the Status, Contributions, and Future Directions of Discipline-

Based Education Research, DBER seeks to "combine the expertise of scientists and engineers with methods and theories that explain learning."[14] With support from the National Science Foundation, DBER scholars seek to understand and improve undergraduate students' learning and instructors' teaching of science and engineering in ways that reflect each "discipline's priorities, worldview, knowledge, and practices."[15] DBER's goals are to understand how people learn the concepts, practices, and ways of thinking of science and engineering; understand the nature and development of expertise in a discipline; help identify and measure appropriate learning objectives and instructional approaches that advance students toward those objectives; contribute to the knowledge base in a way that can guide the translation of DBER findings to classroom practice; and identify approaches to make science and engineering education broad and inclusive.[16]

As an emerging professional movement, DBER reflects some of the strengths we've previously identified in the SEI. First, the goals of DBER align well with the view of good teaching promoted by the learning sciences, and especially practice-based research on the teaching and learning of disciplinary subjects. Second, perhaps by virtue of their scientific training, DBER scholars value assessment and research; DBER-derived findings have significant credibility. Third, DBER's bottom-up quality, originating within the instructional experiences of teacher-researchers, suggests that these individuals' research questions will go to the heart of their teaching practices. Fourth, DBER's anchoring in practice also may allow for its rapid spread across the country—onto campuses and into some professional associations and, possibly, to even have an effect on the faculty staffing patterns of some undergraduate science programs.[17] Fifth, faculty members' voluntary and seemingly uncompensated contributions to DBER signal its sustainability. DBER's aims and interests closely parallel those of convergent teaching's emphasis on the targeting of disciplinary knowledge to be learned and taught.

As expected, questions and challenges remain. First, we identified no extant efforts to examine the quality of DBER products (e.g., research reports, documented pedagogical improvements, etc.), especially to ensure their grounding in current research-based conceptions of teaching and learning. Although the publications and websites of prominent agencies (e.g., National Research Council, National Academy of Sciences) proclaim an alignment between DBER and the learning sciences research literature, it will be important to assess the extent to which aspirations match up with reality.[18] Second, we cannot discern the amount or quality of interaction between the learning sciences community and the DBER community. DBER's impact on undergraduate teaching will be greatest if the two communities collaborate and learn from one another.

The National Research Council followed its original report on DBER with a consensus panel report on effective instruction in undergraduate science and engineering.[19] Of particular note is a chapter on building a culture that can support research-based teaching and learning in the STEM fields. As the SEI revealed, the department is a key unit for curricular change and instructional improvement, and the prospects for meaningful change are greatest when a large number of department faculty work together on teaching and learning matters, and when the department's efforts cover larger introductory courses and other widely subscribed undergraduate courses.

At the campus level, the second National Research Council report offers a set of recommendations that parallel our own. For the most part, they are not specific to the STEM fields, despite the fact that DBER originated in the sciences and engineering. These include creating graduate or postdoctoral fellowships to assist faculty with teaching reform and improvement, allowing team teaching or coteaching so as to facilitate the efficient sharing of pedagogical ideas and practices, and offering faculty release time from teaching to redesign courses.[20]

The notion of a DBER community need not be limited to science and engineering; these subjects became the center of gravity for DBER largely because of national interests in cultivating our collective capacity in the STEM fields in order to promote national economic competitiveness and development. Similar communities committed to teaching improvement should be constructed for the arts and humanities and the social sciences, whether in relation to the science and engineering versions of DBER or independently. It's possible that improvement in teaching might materialize more productively at the level of disciplinary sectors (the arts and humanities, the social sciences, the sciences and engineering) than at the level of the constituent disciplines. Opportunities for cross-sector conversations might also be explored.

We cannot, however, count on the National Science Foundation as the primary funder of such an effort to expand DBER's disciplinary purview, because it emphasizes the teaching and learning of STEM subjects, and the likelihood of it expanding its mission beyond STEM to the arts and humanities and the social sciences is slim. Instead, we must look to the philanthropic community to pick up the mantle and open its pocketbooks to extend DBER to other fields of study. We hope that the value of doing so is clear.

We have so far described several disciplinary groupings and movements directed at teaching improvement: tuning, measuring college learning, and DBER. In different ways, each promises to support practices associated with subject-matter targeting, the first principle of convergent teaching. While such efforts hold promise, we note that none speak quite as directly to the second principle of convergent teaching, the surfacing of learners' prior knowledge and the range of diverse understandings that this may encompass. And without attention to surfacing, the third principle, navigating between subject matter and students' prior knowledge, cannot be undertaken.

Although we can only touch on this point, we note that in American higher education, attention to students' experiences, in class and out, has largely been relegated to student affairs professionals—college specialists and administrators highly knowledgeable about and responsive to student development that takes place outside of students' interactions with subject matter in classrooms.[21] There is a stark separation between academic affairs and student affairs on most campuses, which creates the unfortunate possibility that few on campus can guide students in joining their prior personal knowledge to the disciplinary knowledge that their teachers and texts offer. Only faculty are positioned to bridge this, but it may require some reconfiguring of professional roles and responsibilities. Consider the case of Adina's response to the concept of Cartesian doubt in chapter 4. It took Sofia, a subject matter expert—in this case, a philosopher deeply attuned to Descartes' existential crisis and to how her students might respond to it—to assure that Adina came to understand the concept. We recall this case and the larger matter of higher education's inattention to learners' prior knowledge and to its juxtaposition with subject matter as a challenge for future reform attuned to postsecondary teaching improvement.

The Risk and the Promise

In this concluding section, we discuss our deepest fears regarding the future of undergraduate teaching in the United States and our grandest hopes with respect to its improvement. Our entry into this topic is a snapshot amid a series of moving pictures playing at the US higher education multiplex.[22] There are many initiatives aimed at undergraduate teaching improvement, and we have only discussed a handful of them—though we obviously chose those that we thought were most relevant to our argument.

The Risk

A big risk is that undergraduate teaching improvement will not be taken up in a serious way. We obviously think the improvement of undergraduate teaching is important; we would not have written this book otherwise. Nevertheless, we know that instructional reform efforts often falter, and we need to acknowledge that. Here, we point to two specific risks. First, college teachers may enact superficial reforms in their teaching practice, while believing that they are engaged in something much more ambitious. Second, undergraduate teaching improvement as a systemic reform may fail due to the current social, economic, and political context of higher education.

Cognitive scientist Richard Mayer shows how classroom teaching reforms can sidestep meaningful learning. Mayer distinguishes between the science of learning and the science of instruction. (He also addresses the science of assessment.) He characterizes the science of learning as the scientific study of how people learn. In contrast, the science of instruction is the scientific study of how teachers can help people learn. The two are related, and Mayer describes the most productive relationship between the two as a "two-way street" in which each informs the other.

Writing for a nontechnical audience, Mayer draws on three principles from the science of learning: dual channels, limited capacity, and active processing. Dual channels refers to the fact that people process verbal material and visual material differently, using different parts of the brain and different representations in the mind.[23] Limited capacity states that individuals can only process a small amount of material in either channel at one time. Our brains set natural limits on how much material we can take in and store in our working memory, where we can then attend to it and organize and interpret it. Finally, active processing is the principle that meaningful learning occurs when learners engage in a sequence of mental steps, including attending to the relevant material, organizing it in the mind into a coherent model (sometimes called a schema) or other representation, and integrating it with relevant prior knowledge that is drawn from their long-term memory.

There is, of course, much more that could be said about these principles, and active processing is perhaps most closely aligned with the three convergent teaching principles of targeting, surfacing, and navigating that we have articulated, because prior knowledge plays such a central role in active processing and in learning in general. But here's the rub: active processing is a principle of learning, whereas targeting, surfacing, and navigating are principles of teaching. The extant literature on undergraduate teaching has taken a *learning* principle, active processing, and transmuted it into a *teaching* principle, often referred to as active learning. The term takes on many meanings and expands or contracts depending on context. Although the concept implies a set of instructional practices that engage students in the learning process, operationally, active learning is usually understood as a set of practices that engage students with the course content by having them do things—discuss, teach peers, write short reflections, solve problems in small groups, or use classroom technologies such as clickers to respond to instructor questions about course content.

For a cognitive scientist such as Mayer, active learning refers to engagement in the cognitive processes of selecting incoming words and pictures, organizing them into a mental model or representation, and connecting these representations to one another and with prior knowledge that resides in long-term memory. But he cautions that active teaching techniques may not lead to the active processing and active learning that is so desirable. It's possible to have a high level of behavioral activity in the classroom and a relatively low level of cognitive activity. If one is not thoughtful, it is easy to mistake one for the other.

This is the lesson of a line of research by our colleague, Corbin Campbell, who has been studying teaching practices in college classrooms. Observing 150 classes at two eastern research universities, Campbell and her colleagues coded the teaching practices they observed and correlated them with the cognitive complexity of the course, defined as teaching practices and coursework that challenge learners to sustain a deep connection to the subject matter and to think in increasingly complex ways about the course content and its applications. Using a common definition of active learning rooted in behaviors such as group work, case studies, and class discussions, they found that there was only a moderate relationship between teachers' use of active learning practices (observed in about 70% of the classroom observations) and the cognitive complexity of the course.[24]

Having championed Scott Freeman and his colleague's prominent meta-analysis of active learning effects on student performance in chapter 1, we are not about to dismiss active learning techniques, even though they can be enacted in ways that are indifferent to the principles of convergent teaching.[25] The problem is that the term "active learning" has become institutionalized in higher education in a way that leads everyone to believe that it's a good thing—and that they're already doing it.

But for the most part, they're not—at least, not in a way that involves fundamental changes to pedagogical practice. Careful studies of how ambitious K–12 curriculum standards are translated into classroom practice have revealed that most teachers endorse such standards and believe that they are already implementing classroom practices that are consistent with them. But direct observation of teachers' classrooms revealed a yawning gap between what teachers *said* they were doing and what observers *saw* them doing.[26] The missing critical link between the standards and actual classroom practices was that school districts did not sufficiently educate teachers about the new standards or provide enough professional development opportunities for teachers to relate the standards to their existing instructional practices.

This, then, plays into our biggest fear: efforts to reform undergraduate teaching may fall flat. This risk is presaged by David K. Cohen and Jal Mehta's thoughtful analysis of the conditions under which school reforms in the United States have fizzled out or persisted.[27] They suggest that there are several characteristics of successful reforms. First, the reform must be understood as a solution to a problem that the targets of the reform want to solve, either because the problems are long standing or because the reform proposal creates a new urgency about a previously ignored problem of practice. Second, the reform must satisfy external demands being placed on the schools by governments or other stakeholders. Third, the reform must provide tools to enable educators to put the reform into practice, either by long-term capacity building, or direct materials and guidance, or both. And finally, successful reforms are aligned with the values of those affected, including educators but also students, parents, and other stakeholders.

The obverse of this is that if a reform is not seen as a solution to an important problem, no one is going to bite, and the reform will not be sustained. Unsuccessful reforms "offered solutions to problems that educators did not think they had, they met no felt need for most of the people who would implement them, they illuminated no problem of practice for many practitioners, or they offered no solutions for the people who would implement them," Cohen and Mehta note, adding that "still others failed either because they satisfied no demands that arose from the political, economic, or social circumstances of education; provoked hostility from influential actors in the environment; or failed to convince parents and students of their value."[28]

A critical point here is that reforms are likely to fail if the people whose behavior must change don't think there's a problem. Our fear is that most college teachers think they are doing okay in the classroom; they don't see a problem with their own practices or, to the extent that they bother to look around, with those of their disciplinary and institutional colleagues. There is no internal pressure to change. And people who are only faced with external pressures in the form of mandates or incentives can be very skilled at finding work-arounds and ways to game the system, including those systems that seek fundamental changes in how they teach. This, coupled with the public's focus on other aspects of higher education—e.g., access, costs, affordability, employment prospects, and the student success agenda—may not provide conditions for sustaining undergraduate teaching reform.

The Promise

The promise of undergraduate teaching improvement is that it might succeed as a "stealth reform." Over time, the institutionalization of practices can reorient values, conditions, and commitments in ways that build the capacity for undergraduate teaching improvement in general and for convergent teaching in particular to take hold.

Issues rarely rise to the top of anyone's policy agenda if they are not perceived as a serious problem affecting a large (or socially important) group of people. Convincing the public that good teaching matters is hard to do from the inside. Governments and philanthropic foundations, however, can invest in educating the public on what good college teaching looks like, perhaps in the form of cross-institutional, annotated galleries of the good teaching of core disciplinary concepts. Along with offering these representations of good teaching, we must shift rhetorical frames away from affordability and cost and move them to focus on learning. This is a challenge, because cost and affordability are more tangible and more on the minds of students and their families. Moreover, it is easier to fashion policies that address the costs of college than to invest in the longer-term challenge of improving undergraduate teaching.

We've already noted that it's hard to conceive of American higher education as a system given the diversity of institutional types and decentralization of governance (including the important divide between public and private institutions). Although we believe that undergraduate teaching can improve throughout the more than four thousand US institutions of higher education, we think it unlikely that there will be a systemic reform. There are few examples of systemic reforms of higher education in the United States, and the most salient call to arms of the recent past, the Spellings Commission report issued in 2006, has had limited impact.[29] The most recent blue-ribbon report, issued by the American Academy of Arts and Sciences Commission on the Future of Undergraduate Education, had the misfortune of arriving in the midst of extraordinary turmoil in the federal government, and although it is a bold call for action, it is too soon to judge its eventual uptake.[30]

An alternative to systemic reform is what Cohen and Mehta call "niche reform." In this view, the field of education can be classified and subdivided into distinctive organizational niches.[31] The inhabitants of organizational niches may share one or more identities that are associated with the features of the niche and its location in relation to other niches.[32] Cohen and Mehta describe niche reforms as "school systems that create a space in the education sector by defining a novel and specialized mission and mobilizing resources to support and sustain it."[33] Niches are internally coherent, because they share a common purpose, build shared identities, and typically involve self-selection into the niche.

Different niches in American higher education may serve as distinctive sites for undergraduate teaching improvement efforts that focus on different aspects of teaching and teaching improvement. Because they are small and coherent, there is greater likelihood that they will share teaching reform agendas, forge partnerships, and identify resources available in the niche's external environment. We have in mind several niches as prospects: community colleges, private liberal arts colleges, research universities, and particular fields of study.

Community colleges. As we note in chapter 1, community colleges serve approximately 40% of American undergraduates, and more than two-thirds of the faculty in community colleges are in part-time, contingent appointments. The community college thus has a specialized niche but also bears the challenge of a highly mobile teaching force and constant resource stress.

One effort to join forces around pedagogical practice in community colleges has been led by Gail Mellow, president of LaGuardia Community College, along with Diana Woolis, a founding partner of Knowledge in the Public Interest, and Gerardo de los Santos, former president of the League for Innovation in the Community College. With support from private philanthropies, the team has supported two national cohorts of community college faculty to work collaboratively on pedagogical problems using online tools. The first cohort of twenty-four faculty members were full-time faculty teaching developmental courses in math and English. The second cohort of twenty-four faculty included six adjunct faculty.[34] The initiative is, in our view, a proof of concept that it's possible to organize around a niche, in this case, the teaching of developmental education classes in community colleges. Scalability and incorporating greater numbers of adjunct faculty are ongoing challenges.

Private liberal arts colleges. The shared mission of a liberal education can serve as an organizing framework for consortia of private liberal arts colleges to support undergraduate teaching in general and convergent teaching in particular. There are precedents in the form of the Wabash National Study of Liberal Arts Education, led by Charles Blaich of the Center of Inquiry at Wabash College. A total of forty-nine institutions, including more than thirty small liberal arts colleges, participated in the Wabash study, which surveyed student experiences and gathered data on student outcomes over the course of a student's four years on campus.[35] A parallel exercise in gathering student outcome data across a range of institutions was undertaken by the Council of Independent Colleges Consortium using the Collegiate Learning Assessment as a means of gauging student learning outcomes. The consortium includes more than six hundred independent liberal arts colleges and universities, and the forty-seven institutions participating in the assessment between 2008 and 2011 were a mixture of liberal arts colleges and universities that offer few masters and doctoral degrees.

We acknowledge that the Wabash study and the consortium assessment did not, for the most part, work with the faculty of the participating institutions.[36] And doing so would mean expanding the purpose of these consortia. Nevertheless, we cite these as evidence that liberal arts colleges *could* serve as a niche within which improved undergraduate teaching could be cultivated systematically.

Research universities. One of the distinctive features of the research university is that it is the site from which most college instructors emerge. If the vast majority of college teachers have obtained advanced degrees from such universities, then they represent a potential venue for preparing college teachers. For some research universities, there is a direct benefit to placing graduate students in programs to prepare them to teach undergraduates, as these students may have some teaching responsibilities as teaching assistants or instructors in their home departments during their graduate studies.

In chapter 5, we discussed PPF programs and graduate certificates in college teaching. Graduate student participation in these initiatives typically is optional, and the uptake is small relative to the number of graduate students who will eventually be "instructors of record" either in the institution in which they study or in institutions that employ them after they complete their graduate studies. We believe that the graduate schools in universities preparing their doctoral students for academic careers must expand programs to prepare students for the classroom.

It's hard to quantify how many students should be enrolled in such initiatives, as there will be some fields of study in which doctoral graduates are unlikely to enter the college classroom and others in which that outcome is taken for granted. Presumably participation should be proportional to the career destinations of the students. We do hope, though, that faculty and administrators can disabuse students of the notion that preparing to teach is in conflict with the common goal of the production of new knowledge via research. Our own work has shown that, among mid-career faculty, teaching is a site for sustained and renewed engagement with one's subjects of study and a source of continued scholarly learning.[37]

And our view of the process of learning the concepts and tools of a discipline means that as doctoral students construct new representations of the knowledge of a field for pedagogical purposes, they engage with their prior knowledge of the field, creating new understandings. Put simply, doctoral students can learn new things about their subjects of study by preparing to teach them. In this sense, programs that prepare doctoral students to teach may be of value to *most* doctoral students and especially for the institutions that might employ them as teachers.

Particular fields of study. Earlier in this chapter, we outlined faculty efforts in various fields to identify a disciplinary core of what students should know and be able to do after a major program of study. We might envision a particular discipline as a niche that is a site for undergraduate teaching improvement. There are some things that disciplinary associations are able to do more successfully than individual campuses (though we recognize that the campus is the site where teaching and teaching improvement occur). Beyond establishing consensus panels regarding the disciplinary core that can be tuned to local institutional contexts, disciplinary associations can develop discipline-specific undergraduate teaching resources to support the teaching of core disciplinary ideas. They also can develop discipline-specific banks of formative and summative assessments of student learning to support research on effective pedagogical practices. These of course ought not be prescriptive, and care should be taken to avoid their co-optation for use in high-stakes accountability and accreditation processes.

Nevertheless, there's no reason that individual faculty should be continually reinventing the wheel, since their disciplinary associations can serve as repositories for field-specific resources for teaching, learning, and assessment in their disciplines. Finally, disciplinary associations may also be able to develop protocols for college classroom observations in particular fields of study. This is more speculation than recommendation, as we are not entirely sure what this might look like.

We close this volume with some thoughts about the promise of undergraduate teaching improvement for the careers of individual faculty. Faculty cannot, of course, unilaterally change the reward and recognition structures of their institutions or give themselves release time to reflect on and redesign their teaching in a sustained way. These are institutional responsibilities, as is the campus-level design of professional development initiatives such as those we have described. Without a doubt, exploring campus-based resources is an important first step, and a campus teaching and learning center is often the best place to start. Beyond that, though, we have a number of suggestions for individual faculty members who want to improve how they help their students learn.

Acknowledge that teaching can be improved with effort, ingenuity, and practice. Although some individuals have a knack for connecting and communicating with others, good college teachers are not born; rather, they are created, with much of that creation originating in their intellectual and professional interests and commitments. Adopting a growth mindset and a penchant for reflection opens the door to developing one's

qualities as a classroom teacher and to cultivating the pedagogical principles of convergent teaching we detail in part II.[38] Whether or not one is
successful in helping students learn is not an intrinsic attribute of the self
but rather a function of the situation. Recognizing this fact of institutional
life allows for the possibility of faculty members learning how to teach
through deliberate practice. Experimentation is one important strategy,
and college faculty should seek out teaching center staff, peers, and senior
colleagues to discuss how they can safely and productively experiment
with teaching practices in their classrooms. In brief, be open to the idea
that your teaching can get better, but that getting there takes effort and
thought.

Interview your students. As we note in part II, surfacing students' prior
knowledge is a critical step in convergent teaching. There can be a dramatic difference between what college teachers know and what their students know for many reasons. The mental representations of subject
matter constructed by college teachers, as experts, may be more coherent
and more accurate than those of students, who are relative novices to the
subject of study. Moreover, there may be substantial social distance between college teachers and their students; they are likely to be different
in age, race, or ethnicity, and perhaps social class as well. Cultural practices and common cultural touchstones that could be used as pedagogical devices may differ too.

Taking a couple of students out for coffee or lunch can be a way to get
to know not just those specific students but others like them. We are not
suggesting that such conversations should lead to faculty taking on responsibility for addressing the life challenges that students might describe; ideally, their college or university would have a robust set of services to support students. Rather, interviews—or more simply, humane
conversations—are a way for faculty to become sensitized to the realities
of students' lives, as well as a way to bolster their understanding of what
students know, or think they know, about matters that can be used to navigate toward the desired learning.

*Use teaching as a site to learn ever more deeply about the subjects that
you care about.* Most faculty study and teach subjects that they have
purposefully brought into their lives; those subjects often are a source

of intense curiosity and usually passion.[39] Recognizing that teaching can be a site for your own scholarly learning, even as you help students to develop the habits of mind and curiosities that you bring to your subject, can motivate your efforts to improve your teaching practice. We acknowledge that faculty cannot always teach those subjects that inspire their passions, but even those in neighboring subject-matter domains can induce surprising insights. And it need not take the teaching of advanced seminars to make this happen: your deep and probing thought of how to teach a core idea in a large introductory class can spur new and imaginative ways to think through complex ideas that are foundational to an area of study.[40]

Make your teaching practice more public.[41] If teaching takes place behind closed doors, with few opportunities to interrogate it, it is unlikely to improve. Talk about teaching with your colleagues. Garner feedback from teaching assistants, students, and peers. Invite colleagues to visit your classroom informally. Opening up your classroom and your teaching practices can open your mind to new possibilities for your teaching. Making yourself vulnerable to critique can feel risky; therefore you will feel most comfortable amid trusted colleagues and, where appropriate, teaching center specialists and administrators.

Learn to observe other teachers. Many college teachers never see what their colleagues are doing in the classroom. Probationary faculty may be observed, but rarely have the opportunity to observe others, as most teaching observations occur in the context of summative evaluations connected to reappointment, promotion and tenure processes. Observing teaching, guided either by institution-specific rubrics or more general ones drawn from the literature, can be a source of new knowledge about teaching that can be integrated with what faculty members think they already know. Importantly, such observations need not be done in the context of mandatory or high-stakes observations.

In many institutions, the volume of peer observations is just a trickle. If the only people being observed are probationary faculty and the only observers are colleagues at a higher academic rank and the expected frequency of observation is but once a year, not much peer observation is happening (and faculty might not be called on to observe another's teaching more than once every several years). Observing on such an infrequent basis is unlikely to be a reliable and sustained source of new knowledge for teaching practice. But taking the initiative in training to observe and then observing both disciplinary and nondisciplinary colleagues may pay off handsomely.

Identify expert teachers on campus and seek their advice. Whether or not nearby faculty are in your own department, you can learn from their orientations and practices. Ask if you can sit in on a class or two and discuss what you saw. Or, alternatively, ask if they'll come visit your classes and tell you about what they observed. Discussions with faculty recognized as expert teachers are a great way to learn more about your own practice.

Document your teaching practice. Some documentation of teaching is driven by periodic reviews, such as those for reappointment, promotion, and tenure. But as anyone who has gone through such processes can attest, pulling together the requisite materials is much easier when they have already been assembled for formative purposes. Archive your syllabi, course assignments, exam and paper topics and instruction sheets, and samples of student work and note how and why these have evolved in particular ways.[42] Take the time, ideally after each class you to teach, to articulate what went well or poorly in class, why you think so, and what it means to you and your teaching. Then write this down in specific terms, noting specific actions, images, words, and resources that you might want to redeploy in future versions of the class, including what probably should be changed or, perhaps, not repeated. If new ideas come to you as you do this, write these down too.

Seek out disciplinary resources on teaching. Many disciplinary professional associations have sections devoted to the teaching of the discipline, and some also sponsor professional journals on teaching in the discipline that offer insights into curriculum and teaching practice. Because these are rooted in specific disciplines, they hold the promise of addressing the teaching and learning of specific disciplinary ideas, which we've placed at the center of our definition of convergent teaching. Resources developed through the national DBER community are also good prospects for ideas about teaching practice, though they will likely need to be modified for application to teaching in the social sciences, arts, and humanities.

Use what is helpful to you from the three principles of convergent teaching to construct and guide your own teaching improvement agenda. Bring what you know already from the conceptual layout of your field into your teaching. Emphasize the core and foundational concepts that frame your field and consider how those concepts open doors to still others and why. Draw on this landscape to develop your courses, realizing that you can't include everything. Give special attention to the sequencing of concepts and topics. Get to know your students, especially what they know and value and what their lives are like in and out of school. Use this knowledge to envision how students' lives and prior knowledge may feed and support and at times misdirect their learning. Plan all of the elements of your classes, including course readings, in-class activities, and projects and exams, and think about what you will likely say and do in class and why. Be prepared, then, to revise and improvise; be flexible, but keep an eye on where you know you'd like your class to go. Keep your focus on helping students learn the subject matter that you deem most important.

Bear in mind that you won't get all of this done, that some of it won't work, and that you'll want to write your own recommendations. You'll make mistakes, but remember that by trying out new ideas, even if they flop, you too will be learning.

Coda

In this book, we've argued that current debates about the future of undergraduate education have, in recent times, lost sight of the heart and soul of a college education: the teaching and learning of disciplinary knowledge. We've sought to lift up good college teaching as an endeavor around which faculty, campus leaders, and policy makers can organize. We've presented examples of convergent teaching and the pedagogical principles that are central to it and have discussed strategies to cultivate, recognize, and reward good college teaching via professional development, personnel policies, and individual faculty initiative.

All of this is necessary but not sufficient. What's missing is a way of persuading a broader audience that good teaching matters and helping that audience understand what good teaching looks like. The challenge these days is getting beyond the cult of personality, which leads to good teaching being equated with an engaging TED talk and entertainment trumping substance. Good teaching is far more. Adults who recall their past teachers can attest to this. What we've advocated for classroom teaching applies to learning outside of school too. Educating people outside of the academy about the nature of good college teaching requires surfacing their prior knowledge and orchestrating a path from that prior knowledge to a new conception of the centrality of good undergraduate teaching that can guide policy and practice.

Part I · A Roadmap

1. Unlike the cases presented in chapters 2 through 4, the case of Chris Felton and Roseville University are fictitious, though it draws on stories we've heard for nearly three decades.

2. William T. Grant Foundation 2015.

3. For an excellent overview of a broad range of issues regarding undergraduate education, see American Academy of Arts and Sciences 2017.

4. Consistent with popular usage, we use phrases such as "higher education," "postsecondary education," and "college and university education" to refer to undergraduate studies specifically. Undergraduate education in the United States is the sole focus of this volume, though some of what we say may apply to graduate and professional education and to education in other countries. We also underline the tentativeness of many of our claims, as we are necessarily selective in the research and commentaries on which we draw.

5. In doing so, we join a good number of authors who have offered excellent advice to college teachers. See, e.g., Lang 2016, Ambrose et al. 2010, Eng 2017, and Brown, Roediger, and McDaniel 2014.

Chapter 1 · American Ambivalence and College Teaching

1. Luttrell 1997.

2. Berger 1963.

3. Hofstadter 1963.

4. See, e.g., Bissinger 1990.

5. Pallas, Boulay, and Karp 2003.

6. Labaree 1997a.

7. Semega, Fontenot, and Kollar 2017.

8. See census.gov/data/tables/2013/demo/wealth/wealth-asset-ownership.html.

9. Darity et al. 2018.

10. National Center for Education Statistics 2018, tables 326.10 and 326.20.

11. National Center for Education Statistics 2018, tables 326.10 and 326.20.

12. US Census Bureau 2018.

13. See Beck 1992, Brückner and Mayer 2005, and Giddens 1990.

14. See, e.g., Carnevale, Hanson, and Gulish 2013.

15. Beck 1992.

16. See Armstrong and Hamilton 2013 for examples of how college-going women can fall off a pathway to professional careers.

17. Tamborini, Kim, and Sakamoto 2015.

18. Messacar 2017; Feinstein et al. 2006.

19. Bureau of Labor Statistics 2017.

20. Tamborini, Kim, and Sakamoto 2015.

21. Bureau of Labor Statistics 2017.

22. Katz and Krueger 2017.

23. Manyika et al. 2016.

24. Manyika et al. 2016.

25. The average annual Social Security benefit for retired workers in 2018 is projected to be about $17,000. To achieve the maximum Social Security benefit of about $44,000, a retiree must have earned the taxable maximum income in at least thirty-five different years, and wait until age seventy to claim Social Security. Very few Social Security beneficiaries meet these criteria. See Frankel 2017.

26. Rosenbaum and Kariya 1989.

27. Brinton 2010.

28. Pew Research Center 2017.

29. The wording of these public opinion questions does not provide much guidance about the value of education. For a sharper account, see Drezner, Pizmony-Levy, and Pallas 2018.

30. Newport and Busteed 2017.

31. Carnevale, Rose, and Cheah, 2013.

32. These are our tabulations, which we arrived at using the Bureau of Labor Statistics' employment projections (www.bls.gov/emp/home.htm).

33. OECD 2016a.

34. American Academy of Arts and Sciences 2017; Snyder, de Brey, and Dillow 2018, table 303.25.

35. Baum, Ma, Pender, and Libassi 2018.

36. American Academy of Arts and Sciences 2016.

37. Baum, Ma, Pender, and Libassi 2018.

38. OECD 2016b.

39. Loveless 2007.

40. For example, the scoring rubric for analysis and problem solving states that a score of three on the scale from one to six indicates that the test taker "states or implies a decision/conclusion/position" and "provides some valid support" but "omits or misrepresents critical information, suggesting only superficial analysis and partial comprehension of the documents" and "may not account for contradictory information (if applicable)."

41. Astin 2011.

42. Dede 2010.

43. Becher 1989.

44. Lamont and Molnár 2002.

45. Becher and Trowler 2001.

46. Pallas 2001.

47. Pallas 2001.

48. Schwab 1964; Turner 2017; Becher 1989.

49. These are sometimes referred to as "threshold concepts," in recognition of the fact that they are "transformative, integrative, irreversible, and potentially troublesome." See, e.g., Land, Meyer and Smith 2008.

50. Becher and Trowler 2001.

51. Darling-Hammond 2003.

52. Bruner 1960, 12.

53. Goldstein 2018.

54. Less-than-two-year institutions offer at least a one-year program of study creditable toward a degree.

55. Hussar and Bailey 2018.

56. National Center for Education Statistics 2018, table 303.25.

57. Special focus institutions are two- and four-year institutions that award a high concentration of their degrees in a single field. The Carnegie classification does not cover less-than-two-year institutions.

58. See carnegieclassifications.iu.edu/classification_descriptions/basic.php.

59. Ruef and Nag 2015.

60. Only three of the top twenty-five national universities in the US News rankings are public institutions; see www.usnews.com/best-colleges/rankings/national-universities.

61. Witteveen and Attewell 2017.

62. National Center for Education Statistics 2018, table 303.25.

63. Snyder, de Brey, and Dillow 2018, table 101.10.

64. Snyder, de Brey, and Dillow 2018 table 306.10.

65. Snyder, de Brey, and Dillow 2018, table 306.50.

66. Ginder, Kelly-Reid, and Mann 2018.

67. These are our tabulations, which we calculated using Radwin et al. 2018.

68. Radwin et al. 2018, table 311.40.

69. Scott-Clayton, Crosta, and Belfield 2014.

70. Scott-Clayton and Rodriguez 2015.

71. Ginder, Kelly-Reid, and Mann 2018.

72. Curtis 2014.

73. See Ginder, Kelly-Reid, and Mann 2018; US Government Accountability Office 2017.

74. US Government Accountability Office 2017.

75. US Government Accountability Office 2017.

76. US Government Accountability Office 2017.

77. Eagan et al. 2014.

78. Eagan et al. 2014.

79. Satel and Lilienfeld 2013.

80. Menary et al. 2013; Ursache, Noble, and the Pediatric Imaging, Neurocognition and Genetics Study 2016.

81. Craig 2015.

82. Craig 2015, 91.

83. DeMillo 2015.

84. DeMillo 2015, 123.

85. Hoxby 2019; Hollands and Tirthali 2015; Head 2017.

86. Goodman, Melkers, and Pallais 2019.

87. Xu and Jaggars 2013.

88. Xu and Jaggars 2014.

89. Hoxby 2019.

90. See Roth 2014, Deresiewicz 2014, and Zakaria 2015.

91. Roth 2014, 163.

92. Roth's reference to Du Bois and Dewey in this context indicates that the tension between vocationalism and liberal education is nothing new but has coursed through the history of American higher education.

93. Roth 2014, xiii.
94. See Nussbaum 1997.
95. Attewell 2011.
96. Caplan 2018.
97. Labaree 1997b.
98. Kosslyn and Nelson 2017.
99. Kosslyn and Nelson 2017. The founders report that in the fall of the first year of study, the freshmen in Minerva's first class scored at the ninety-ninth percentile of freshmen nationally on the Collegiate Learning Assessment(CLA+), a measure of critical thinking skills. Since scores on the CLA+ are moderately to highly correlated with traditional college entrance exams such as the SAT and ACT, this is a very select group indeed.
100. See nces.ed.gov/collegenavigator/?q=minerva&s=all&id=484844#enrolmt.
101. Mayhew et al. 2016, 592.
102. A crude predecessor to this literature was initiated with research on K–12 school effects in the 1966 report Equality of Educational Opportunity. See Coleman et al. 1966.
103. This seems like a lot of money, but it's about $12,000 per student over the roughly forty-year working life of the student, or roughly $300 per year per student.
104. Jackson 2018; Blazar and Kraft 2017.
105. We note in passing that it is difficult to identify specific K–12 teaching practices that are consistently associated with improved student test performance. The Measures of Effective Teaching project, the Gates Foundation's large-scale effort to identify the elements of effective K–12 teaching, found modest correlations between observational ratings of teachers' classroom practices and their value-added scores on standardized tests of student achievement. See, e.g., Bill & Melinda Gates Foundation 2012.
106. Freeman et al. 2014, 8413–14.
107. An effect size of zero means that the two groups have the same mean performance; the two groups essentially overlap completely. There is no upper bound to the effect size, but it's rare for student-level education interventions at scale to demonstrate an effect size as large as 1.0 (which would imply that a typical individual in one group would perform at the eighty-fourth percentile of the performance of the other group).
108. Hill et al. 2008. One way of interpreting the magnitude of this effect size is to imagine randomly choosing a student from the traditional lecturing condition and one from the active learning condition. What is the probability that the student from the active learning condition scored higher on the course assessment than the traditional lecturing condition? With an effect size of .47, that probability is estimated as 63%.
109. We revisit the notion of active learning in chapter 6.
110. See swarthmore.edu/institutional-research/doctorates-awarded.
111. Fligstein 2012.
112. Reed College 2007.
113. Reed College 2007.
114. Reed College 2006.
115. See Shulman 1987 for a summary listing of the seven forms of knowledge. The article introduces the idea of pedagogical content knowledge as well as discusses its origins and provides a conceptualization of it.
116. Gonzalez, Moll, and Amanti 1992; Moll 1992.
117. Ladson-Billings 1995.
118. She also noted the importance of students developing competencies to negotiate both their local culture and the dominant culture.

119. Ladson-Billings 1995, 475.

120. Gutiérrez 2008.

121. See Valenzuela 1999 and Gonzalez, Moll, and Afanti 1992.

122. Paris and Alim 2017.

123. Paris and Alim 2014.

124. Lee 2007, 111.

125. For a powerful exposition of this idea in the context of reading comprehension, see Anderson and Pearson 1984.

126. Willingham 2009, 67. See also Ambrose et al. 2010.

Part II · Convergent Teaching

1. See Schwab 1978b. In identifying the "commonplaces" of teaching and learning—teacher, learner, subject matter, and milieu—Schwab set the foundation for much of the research and theory that supports this work.

2. Each principle summarizes a conglomerate of interrelated practices, meaning that teachers' enactments of any one principle will vary in light of the particular subjects being taught, variances in teachers' knowledge and in students' interests and proclivities as teachers understand these, specifics of time and place, availability of technological resources for teaching, policy and accountability imperatives, and so on. A principle can then be viewed as orienting and anchoring any number of more specific practices for instantiating it. We make no effort to differentiate the quality of delivery of such practices, such as whether and how much students learn, the quality and appropriateness of "moves" in use, the stage of instructors' development as teachers, and so on, viewing these as starting points for future research.

3. We explain in chapter 1 that convergent teaching draws heavily on Lee Shulman's conception of pedagogical content knowledge, as well as the learning dimension of Gloria Ladson-Billings's theory of culturally relevant pedagogy, and Carol Lee's concept of cultural modeling. See Shulman 1986, 1987, 2004a, and 2004b, Ladson-Billings 1995, and Lee 2007.

4. The Metropolitan Colleges Institute for Teaching Improvement (MetroCITI) is a cross-institution initiative to improve teaching in general education courses in two- and four-year institutions enrolling racially, culturally, and socioeconomically diverse students in the New York City metro area. MetroCITI is directed by Anna Neumann. See metrociti .pressible.org.

5. Schwab 1978b.

6. For insights into strategies for eliminating stereotyping and bias, creating inclusive college classrooms, and otherwise heightening equity in postsecondary teaching, see Bensimon 2007, Dowd and Bensimon 2015, Engberg, 2004; Enright 2016, Nuñez, Ramalho, and Cuero 2010, Steele 2010, and Yeager et al. 2014. For research on multiculturalism in education broadly, see Banks 2015; for philosophical analysis, see Nussbaum 1997. For discussions of civic learning, with implications for teaching, see Colby et al. 2007, Colby et al. 2003, Hurtado 2007, Kanter and Schneider 2013, and Nussbaum 2012. Classic texts pertaining to ethical thinking and college teaching include Callahan and Bok 1980, Hansen 2001, and Nussbaum 1997. Broader approaches include Delpit 2006, Freire 2000, hooks 1994, and Rose 1989.

7. For a comprehensive guide, see Svinicki and McKeachie 2011.

8. This theme has been prominent in British sociology of education. See, e.g., Bernstein 1975 and Young 2008.

Chapter 2 · Targeting: Carving Out What's To Be Taught

1. Blake's "Auguries of Innocence" describes a grain of sand as a miniature of the world and a "wild flower" as a model of heaven. Miniaturization renders a phenomenon accessible to inquiry in ways that the larger reality, which it represents, cannot. A microcosm, then, is a miniature of a larger reality, mirroring its distinctive features and forms. We view a core concept as a microcosmic representation of a discipline's unique substantive interests and its deep "syntactical structure" (see Schwab 1978a, 246); thus core ideas differ, one from another, in much the same way as do the larger disciplines they represent. Our use of the microcosm concept and references to the Blakean imagery derive from Parker Palmer's discussion of "teaching from the microcosm" in "subject-centered classrooms" (see Palmer 1998, 120–21). We note the growing prominence of related efforts by expert panels to distill "essential concepts" and "essential competences" for particular disciplines and fields (see Arum, Roksa, and Cook 2016). However, we know of no systematic efforts to survey the applicability of the "core concept" heuristic across fields, and suspect that other forms of knowledge warrant equal attention in studies of teaching.

2. For an overview of core ideas in other fields, see Arum, Roksa, and Cook 2016 and Neumann and Campbell 2016.

3. For a compelling example of how an instructor can go about selecting and sequencing texts so as to maximize students' opportunities of learning a core concept in a high school English literature class, see Lee 2007.

4. Schwab 1978a; Becher and Trowler 1989.

5. The level of measurement for years is ratio level, because there is a true zero point, which means that eight years is twice as much as four years.

6. The value of using tables and graphs to reduce the complexity of a batch of data can be more easily seen when there are more pieces of data in the distribution, as would be the case in a class of thirty-five students.

7. Although the quotes in this section are drawn from a transcript of an audio recording of the class session, they are not verbatim and have been edited for clarity. We have made similar adjustments in other sections where individuals are quoted.

8. Names of MetroCITI Fellows, here enacting the student role, are pseudonyms per pledges of research confidentiality. Only Aaron's name is real.

9. See Neumann 2009a, which presents case data in support of this claim, offering the possibility that students' interpretations of core disciplinary ideas can serve as sites for envisioning familiar content in novel ways, worthy of experts' consideration. Aaron had anticipated the see-saw image in planning the lesson on the statistical middle. However, the "parceling out" image, offered by a student amid class conversation, came by surprise some years later. Aaron now offers "parceling out" alongside the see-saw as ways to envision "middle" as a statistical core idea; he has found both to be pedagogically useful.

10. The colleague was renowned mathematics educator Deborah Ball.

11. With the exception of the final case (Sofia, teaching philosophy), all instructor names in chapters 2 through 4 are real. All granted permission to be identified as shown; all reviewed their own cases, granting permission for them to be documented.

12. See laguardia.edu/uploadedFiles/Main_Site/Content/IT/2018-Institutional-Profile .pdf.

13. See Schwab 1978a and Becher and Trowler 1989. Though fields vary internally, between-field differences pose distinctive challenges for students who, in their first two years of college, use general education requirements and sometimes elective structures to sample coursework across multiple fields. For a comprehensive overview of the undergraduate curriculum, see Lattuca and Stark 2009.

14. Wineburg 2001.

15. These quizzes were administered primarily to promote student reading of assigned texts. In the course, Tony required students to complete multiple short historical research papers, four to five pages long, in which they were required to ask and answer a historical question, using primary and secondary sources to support their answers, and to take a final exam.

16. Voelker 2008.

Chapter 3 · Surfacing: Unearthing Students' Prior Knowledge to Foster Learning

1. Bransford, Brown, and Cocking 1999.

2. Shulman 1999, 11.

3. When instructors present subject matter assuming that students will, in Shulman's terms, take it in, while ignoring "getting out" what students know already, students' learning may not go well. For descriptions of learning that "doesn't go well," see Shulman 1999. In this article, Shulman also discusses why and how prior knowledge matters to the learning of new content: "Any new learning must, in some fashion, connect with what learners already know. Of course, that is an oversimplification, but it is what I mean by 'getting the inside out.' As teachers, unless we can discover ways of getting the inside out and looking jointly at their prior knowledge with our students, taking seriously what they already know and believe, instruction becomes very difficult. Our first principle, therefore, begins with the assertion that we must take seriously what the students have already learned" (12).

4. Moses and Cobb 2001.

5. Moses and Cobb 2001, 195–220.

6. nces.ed.gov/collegenavigator/?q=long+island+university&s=all&id=192448.

7. In a 2005 Gallup survey, 25% of American adults reported believing in astrology, or that the position of the stars and planets can affect people's lives, and 21% reported believing in witches (Moore 2005).

Chapter 4 · Navigating: Orchestrating Subject-Matter Concepts and Students' Prior Knowledge

1. For a vivid critique of the five-paragraph essay, see Labaree 2017.

2. Flower 1997. As previously noted and as is common in community colleges, Allie taught several sections of this course in fall 2014. She made the teaching change described here in all of them.

3. The "believing and doubting" exercise is drawn from Elbow and Belanoff 1999.

4. See Harding 1986.

5. For an earlier discussion of this teaching challenge, see Gamson and associates 1984. See also Castillo-Montoya 2013 and Neumann 2009b.

6. Unlike in the earlier cases, here we use pseudonyms to mask the teacher's, students', and university's real names; we also shield other identifying features in line with promises to research participants. In the study, conducted in spring 2011, we made weekly class observations of two sections of Sofia's introductory philosophy class; we also audiorecorded one of the sections observed and then transcribed it, conducted multiple interviews with the instructor, and collected and reviewed pertinent documents, including class texts assigned to students. An earlier version of this case was presented in Anna Neumann's presidential address to the Association for the Study of Higher Education, November 2012, Las Vegas, Nevada, and subsequently published in elaborated form in Neumann 2014. The version here has been slightly modified to fit this book's form.

7. This is not a verbatim quote from *Meditations*. It is a summation of how the observer, Anna, heard Sofia and her students enter the text, with Sofia leading students to wonder out loud what exactly Descartes was struggling with—what he was asking himself.

8. See Bransford, Brown, and Cocking 1999 and Shulman 2004a and 2004b.

9. A similar analysis can be projected as to what a teacher like Sofia does as she plans out her course, well before classroom teaching begins. Indeed targeting, via principle 1, happens there and openly so; we can imagine that targeting is where class planning begins. But interviews with Sofia reveal that even as she plans her classes, she works at principle 2, for example, anticipating how her students might respond to Descartes (relishing his ideas, questioning his common sense or sanity, debating him, struggling, shutting down), then crafting various ways she could respond.

10. For a similar cases of the peer culture at work in high school literature classrooms, see Lee 2007.

11. For a brief lesson on the physics behind Adina's claim, see Minute Physics, "What Is Touch?," youtube.com/watch?v=BksyMWSygnc.

Part III · Policies and Practices

1. As is true of the Chris Felton case that opens the book, the case of Alejandra Garcia is fictitious, but her narrative is similar to many we've heard.

2. Several interesting initiatives are in their early stages, including the Bay View Alliance, which features the University of Massachusetts at Amherst, the University of Kansas, and the University of Colorado at Boulder; the Department of Earth, Ocean, and Atmospheric Science at the University of British Columbia; and the international group U21, which has a project on teaching indicators. Our thanks to Mary Taylor Huber for drawing these new efforts to our attention.

Chapter 5 · Campus-Level Supports for Convergent Teaching

1. These domains are not mutually exclusive; for example, professional development at the institutional level may be entwined with institutional personnel policies, as formative and summative judgments about teaching quality are central to both.

2. Brint 2009 and 2019.

3. Waller 1932; Babcock and Marks 2011.

4. Feldman and Pentland 2003; Lewis and Diamond 2015.

5. Birnbaum 1988.

6. O'Meara and Bloomgarden 2011.

7. Delaney 2015.

8. Bolitzer 2017.

9. On the importance of professional development resources and improved working conditions for contingent faculty, see Kezar and Maxey 2014, Kezar and Sam 2013, and Kezar 2012.

10. If a campus has approximately the same number of contingent and noncontingent faculty and the contingent faculty are currently ignored, then service provision for double the number of faculty would likely double the costs.

11. We do not wish to appear to paper over this challenge. Few institutions have slack resources, and there are inevitable trade-offs, as increasing investments in activities associated with one part of an institution's mission may require decreasing them in others. There is always the lure of external funds to support new initiatives—quite a few institutions have launched campus teaching centers with the support of private and philanthropic gifts—and these can create momentum for expanded professional development and

recognition and reward structures. Eventually, though, external funds go away and must be supplanted by operating funds.

12. Bowen and McPherson 2016.

13. Boyer 1990.

14. Neumann 2009a.

15. Neumann 2009b.

16. MLA Office of Research 2017.

17. See www.preparing-faculty.org.

18. See gs.howard.edu/graduate-programs/college-and-university-faculty-preparation.

19. We refer to this knowledge as "foundational"; it complements approaches to the teaching of specific subject matter, the focus of our definition of convergent teaching. Many scholars and expert teachers have offered excellent insights into these foundational features of teaching. See, e.g., Svinicki and McKeachie 2011.

20. See Garfield and Ben-Zvi 2008.

21. Beach et al. 2016; Cook and Kaplan 2011.

22. Beach et al. 2016.

23. Beach et al. 2016.

24. Plank and Kalish 2010.

25. Haras et al. 2017.

26. Cook and Kaplan 2011; Haras et al. 2017. The staff of the Center for Research on Learning and Teaching at the University of Michigan also recommend avoiding the administration of mandatory or regulatory activities, as these too diffuse the mission and may undermine faculty trust.

27. Beach et al. 2016.

28. Haras et al. 2017.

29. Beach et al. 2016.

30. Cook and Kaplan 2011.

31. Wieman 2017.

32. Haras et al. 2017.

33. Haras et al. 2017, ix.

34. Calder and Steffes 2016.

35. Beach et al. 2016.

36. Cook and Kaplan 2011.

37. Condon et al. 2016.

38. Condon et al. 2016, 43.

39. See, e.g., Frechtling 2007.

40. See Haras et al. 2018.

41. Haras et al. 2018, 7.

42. Council of Independent Colleges 2018.

43. MacCormack et al. 2018.

44. Wieman 2017.

45. Wieman 2017.

46. We note that reappointment, promotion and/or tenure procedures for tenure-track faculty are far more institutionalized than for contingent faculty. Much of what we have to say about the evaluation of faculty teaching applies to both groups.

47. Linse 2017.

48. The more modern version of this, according to a good friend who will remain nameless, is to invite one's students to one's home for the final class and then ask them to complete their evaluations on line while plying them with alcohol.

49. We cannot be sure that the results generalize to butter cookies or oatmeal raisin cookies, but the results are suggestive.

50. They also considered the provision of cookies as evoking a norm of reciprocity whereby students would provide enhanced evaluations as a way of reciprocating for the chocolate cookies.

51. Arbuckle and Williams 2003.

52. Naftulin, Ware, and Donnelly 1973.

53. A link to the video of the lecture is available in Simkin 2011.

54. Benton and Cashin 2014.

55. T. Ryan Gregory, tweet, May 2, 2018 4:21 pm, twitter.com/TRyanGregory/status /991819905677881344.

56. Hammer, Peer, and Babad 2018.

57. Hammer, Peer, and Babad forthcoming.

58. Benton and Cashin 2014.

59. Linse 2017.

60. Benton and Cashin 2014, 280–81.

61. Uttl, White, and Gonzalez 2017.

62. Bill & Melinda Gates Foundation 2012.

63. Espeland and Sauder 2016.

64. Flaherty 2018.

65. See Van Note Chism 2007 for detailed examples and discussions of peer observation protocols.

66. See academicaffairs.appstate.edu/sites/academicaffairs.appstate.edu/files/peer -review-of-teaching.pdf.

67. Doxsee 2016.

68. DeZure 1999.

69. Bill & Melinda Gates Foundation 2010.

70. See Bernstein et al. 2006.

71. See Pallas 2001 and Wenger 1998.

72. College teachers could, of course, create course portfolios for each of their courses, but that's a substantial time investment.

73. Whereas a benchmark portfolio is a snapshot of a course at a specific moment in time, an inquiry portfolio can draw on multiple semesters of the course as sites for changed practice, which introduces a longitudinal element.

74. See Bernstein et al. 2006. And since the book chronicling the UNL experience was published in 2006, the size of an appropriate stipend easily could have doubled.

75. Hatch and Grossman 2009. See also Lampert and Ball 1998.

76. Hatch and Grossman 2009.

77. Although most faculty view active learning as a desirable feature of classroom instruction, it can be enacted superficially. Corbin Campbell and her colleagues, for example, found evidence of courses enacting active learning practices without engaging student's prior knowledge. See Campbell et al. 2017.

78. See provost.umich.edu/programs/thurnau.

79. See provost.virginia.edu/faculty-teaching-awards/alumni-association-distinguished -professor-award.

80. See seminolestate.edu/foundation/giving/et-chairs.

81. Zamora 2017.

82. See icc.edu/faculty-staff/organizational-learning/awards/endowed-teaching-chair.

Chapter 6 · *Supporting Convergent Teaching beyond the Campus*

1. See www.unideusto.org/tuningeu/home.html.

2. Tuning is now subsumed under a different Lumina initiative, the Degree Qualifications Profile, which also relies on faculty and other stakeholders to collaborate in discerning what graduates at various degree levels should know and be able to do in areas of learning such as specialized knowledge, broad and integrative knowledge, intellectual skills, applied and collaborative learning, and civic and global learning.

3. See historians.org/teaching-and-learning/tuning-the-history-discipline/2016-history -discipline-core.

4. Spiegel 2008.

5. See US Department of Education 2006.

6. See Campbell 2015 for an overview of the tensions surrounding assessment in higher education.

7. See Pallas 2011.

8. Roksa, Arum, and Cook 2016, 20.

9. Aaron Pallas was part of the sociology working group.

10. It did not surface in this project, but there also is evidence that there can be cross-national differences in the knowledge structures in particular disciplines. See, e.g., Fourcade 2009.

11. Allgood and Bayer 2016, 126.

12. Calder and Steffes 2016, 57.

13. See Arum, Roksa, and Cook 2016.

14. Singer, Nielsen, and Schweingruber 2012, 1.

15. Singer, Nielsen, and Schweingruber 2012, 1.

16. Singer, Nielsen, and Schweingruber 2012, 1, 9.

17. The first thirty hits of a Google search on DBER yielded notices of DBER interest group meetings on several university campuses (University of Nebraska, University of Colorado, Michigan State University, Rochester Institute of Technology, George Mason University) and two professional associations (National Association of Geosciences Teachers), along with a job description for a tenure-track assistant professor in "Earth, Ocean or Environment Discipline-Based Education Research (DBER)."

18. For an example of engineering education research that draws heavily on the learning sciences, see Litzinger et al. 2011.

19. National Research Council 2015.

20. National Research Council 2015.

21. A significant exception is the combined intellectual and personal mentoring with which the teaching of faculty in liberal arts institutions has historically been associated. For a broader discussion, see Gamson and associates 1984.

22. Some in 3-D and IMAX, too.

23. This has nothing to do with "learning styles," a popular view about the nature of learning that refuses to die. See Willingham 2009.

24. It was not possible in the context of this study to link classroom practices to student learning outcomes. See Campbell and Dortch 2018.

25. Freeman et al. 2014.

26. See Spillane 2004.

27. See Cohen and Mehta 2017.

28. Cohen and Mehta 2017, 646.

29. See Zemsky 2009 for an insider's view of the Spellings Commission and why its recommendations were unlikely to gain traction.

30. See American Academy of Arts and Sciences 2017.

31. Here, a niche is defined by organizations' relationships with the other organizations that make up their external environments. See Hannan, Carroll, and Pólos 2003.

32. Hannan, Carroll, and Pólos 2003. In classical organizational ecology, niches are defined as the region of a resource space in which one or more entities can persist in the absence of competition.

33. Cohen and Mehta 2017, 665.

34. For a comprehensive account of the initiative, see Mellow et al. 2015.

35. For a brief summary of the Wabash study results, see Pascarella and Blaich 2013.

36. For an interesting analysis of faculty reactions to the CIC/CLA project, see Delaney 2015.

37. Neumann 2009a.

38. On fixed versus growth mindsets, see Dweck 2016.

39. Neumann 2006.

40. Neumann 2006.

41. Hatch et al. 2005.

42. These processes are fundamental to constructing the types of teaching portfolios we discussed earlier.

Allgood, Sam, and Amanda Bayer. 2016. "Measuring College Learning in Economics." In *Improving Quality in American Higher Education: Learning Outcomes and Assessments for the 21st Century*, edited by Richard Arum, Josipa Roksa and Amanda Cook, 87–134. San Francisco: Jossey-Bass.

Ambrose, Susan A., Michael W. Bridges, Michele DiPietro, Marsha C. Lovett, and Marie K. Norman. 2010. *How Learning Works: Seven Research-Based Principles for Smart Teaching*. San Francisco: Jossey-Bass.

American Academy of Arts and Sciences. 2016. *A Primer on the College Student Journey*. Cambridge, MA: American Academy of Arts and Sciences.

American Academy of Arts and Sciences. 2017. *The Future of Undergraduate Education: The Future of America*. Cambridge, MA: American Academy of Arts and Sciences.

Anderson, Richard C., and P. David Pearson. 1984. "A Schema-Theoretic View of Basic Processes in Reading Comprehension." In *Handbook of Reading Research*, edited by P. David Pearson, Rebecca Barr, Michael L. Mosenthal, and Peter Kamil, 255–91. New York: Longman.

Arbuckle, Julianne, and Benne D. Williams. 2003. "Students' Perceptions of Expressiveness: Age and Gender Effects on Teacher Evaluations." *Sex Roles* 49 (9): 507–16.

Armstrong, Elizabeth A., and Laura T. Hamilton. 2013. *Paying for the Party: How College Maintains Inequality*. Cambridge, MA: Harvard University Press.

Arum, Richard, Josipa Roksa, and Amanda Cook, eds. 2016. *Improving Quality in American Higher Education: Learning Outcomes and Assessments for the 21st Century*: San Francisco: Jossey-Bass.

Astin, Alexander W. 2011. "In 'Academically Adrift,' Data Don't Back Up Sweeping Claim." *Chronicle of Higher Education*, February 14. chronicle.com/article/Academically-Adrift -a/126371.

Attewell, Paul. 2011. "Riddle Remains in *Academically Adrift*." *Society* 48 (3): 225–26.

Babcock, Philip, and Mindy Marks. 2011. "The Falling Time Cost of College: Evidence from Half a Century of Time Use Data." *Review of Economics and Statistics* 93 (2): 468–78.

Banks, James A. 2015. *Encyclopedia of Diversity in Education*. Edited by James A. Banks. Thousand Oaks, CA: Sage.

Baum, Sandy, Jennifer Ma, Matea Pender, and C. J. Libassi. 2018. *Trends in Student Aid 2018*. New York: College Board.

Beach, Andrea L., Mary Deane Sorcinelli, Ann E. Austin, and Jaclyn K. Rivard. 2016. *Faculty Development in the Age of Evidence.* Sterling, VA: Stylus.

Becher, Tony. 1989. *Academic Tribes and Territories: Intellectual Enquiry and the Culture of Disciplines.* Buckingham, UK: Open University Press.

Becher, Tony, and Paul R. Trowler. 2001. *Academic Tribes and Territories: Intellectual Enquiry and the Cultures of Disciplines.* 2nd ed. Buckingham, UK: Open University Press.

Beck, Ulrich. 1992. *Risk Society: Towards a New Modernity.* London: Sage.

Bensimon, Estela Mara. 2007. "The Underestimated Significance of Practitioner Knowledge in the Scholarship on Student Success." *Review of Higher Education* 30 (4): 441–69.

Benton, Stephen L., and William E. Cashin. 2014. "Student Ratings of Instruction in College and University Courses." In *Higher Education: Handbook of Theory and Research,* edited by Michael B. Paulsen, 279–326. New York: Springer.

Berger, Bennett. 1963. "Adolescence and Beyond: An Essay Review of Three Books on the Problems of Growing Up." *Social Problems* 10 (4): 394–408.

Bernstein, Basil. 1975. *Class, Codes and Control.* Vol. 3: *Towards a Theory of Educational Transmissions.* London: Routledge and Kegan Paul.

Bernstein, Daniel, Amy Nelson Burnett, Amy Goodburn, and Paul Savory. 2006. *Making Teaching and Learning Visible: Course Portfolios and the Peer Review of Teaching.* San Francisco: Jossey-Bass.

Bill & Melinda Gates Foundation. 2010. *Learning about Teaching: Initial Findings from the Measures of Effective Teaching Project.* Seattle, WA: Bill & Melinda Gates Foundation.

Bill & Melinda Gates Foundation. 2012. *Gathering Feedback for Teaching: Combining High-Quality Observations with Student Surveys and Achievement Gains.* Seattle, WA: Bill & Melinda Gates Foundation.

Birnbaum, Robert. 1988. *How Colleges Work: The Cybernetics of Academic Organization and Leadership.* San Francisco: Jossey-Bass.

Bissinger, H. G. 1990. *Friday Night Lights: A Town, a Team, and a Dream.* New York: Addison-Wesley.

Blake, William. 1868. "Auguries of Innocence." In *Songs of Innocence and of Experience,* 96–101. London: Basil Montagu Pickering.

Blazar, David, and Matthew A. Kraft. 2017. "Teacher and Teaching Effects on Students' Attitudes and Behaviors." *Educational Evaluation and Policy Analysis* 39 (1): 146–70.

Bok, Derek. 2006. *Our Underachieving Colleges: A Candid Look at How Much Students Learn and Why They Should Be Learning More.* Princeton, NJ: Princeton University Press.

Bolitzer, Liza A. 2017. "Adjuncts as Teachers: A Study of How and What Adjunct Faculty Learn while Teaching General Education Courses to Diverse Undergraduate Students." EdD diss., Teachers College, Columbia University.

Bowen, William G., and Michael S. McPherson. 2016. *Lesson Plan: An Agenda for Change in American Higher Education.* Princeton, NJ: Princeton University Press.

Boyer, Ernest L. 1990. *Scholarship Reconsidered: Priorities of the Professoriate.* Princeton, NJ: Carnegie Foundation for the Advancement of Teaching.

Bransford, John D., Ann L. Brown, and Rodney R. Cocking. 1999. *How People Learn: Brain, Mind, Experience, and School.* Washington, DC: National Academy Press.

Brint, Steven. 2009. "Focus on the Classroom: Movements to Reform College Teaching and Learning, 1980–2008." In *The American Academic Profession: Transformation in Contemporary Higher Education,* edited by Joseph C. Hermanowicz, 44–91. Baltimore, MD: Johns Hopkins University Press.

Brint, Steven. 2019. *Two Cheers for Higher Education: Why American Universities Are Stronger Than Ever—and How to Meet the Challenges They Face.* Princeton, NJ: Princeton University Press.

Brinton, Mary C. 2010. *Lost in Transition: Youth, Work, and Instability in Postindustrial Japan.* New York: Cambridge University Press.

Brown, Peter C., Henry L. Roediger, and Mark A. McDaniel. 2014. *Make It Stick: The Science of Successful Learning.*

Brückner, Hannah, and Karl Ulrich Mayer. 2005. "The De-Standardization of the Life Course: What It Might Mean and If It Means Anything Whether It Actually Took Place." In *Advances in Life Course Research.* Vol. 9: *The Structure of Life Course,* edited by Ross Macmillan, 27–54. Amsterdam: Elsevier.

Bruner, Jerome S. 1960. *The Process of Education.* Cambridge, MA: Harvard University Press.

Bureau of Labor Statistics. 2017. "Number of Jobs, Labor Market Experience, and Earnings Growth among Americans at 50: Results from a Longitudinal Survey." bls.gov/news .release/pdf/nlsoy.pdf.

Calder, Lendol, and Tracy Steffes. 2016. "Measuring College Learning in History." In *Improving Quality in American Higher Education: Learning Outcomes and Assessments for the 21st Century,* edited by Richard Arum, Josipa Roksa and Amanda Cook, 37–86. San Francisco: Jossey-Bass.

Callahan, Daniel, and Sissela Bok, eds. 1980. *Ethics Teaching in Higher Education.* New York: Plenum.

Campbell, Corbin M. 2015. "Serving a Different Master: Assessing College Educational Quality for the Public." In *Higher Education: Handbook of Theory and Research,* edited by Michael B. Paulsen, 525–579. Switzerland: Springer.

Campbell, Corbin, Alberto Cabrera, Jessica Ostrow Michael, and Shikha Patel. 2017. "From Comprehensive to Singular: A Latent Class Analysis of College Teaching Practices." *Research in Higher Education* 58: 581–604.

Campbell, Corbin M., and Deniece Dortch. 2018. "Reconsidering Academic Rigor: Posing and Supporting Rigorous Course Practices at Two Research Institutions." *Teachers College Record* 120 (5): 1–42.

Caplan, Bryan. 2018. *The Case against Education: Why the Education System Is a Waste of Time and Money.* Princeton, NJ: Princeton University Press.

Carnevale, Anthony P., Andrew R. Hanson, and Artem Gulish. 2013. Failure to Launch: Structural Shift and the New Lost Generation. Washington, DC: Georgetown University.

Castillo-Montoya, Milagros. 2013. "A Study of First-Generation African American and Latino Undergraduates." EdD diss., Teachers College, Columbia University.

Chetty, Raj, John N. Friedman, and Jonah E. Rockoff. 2014. "Measuring the Impacts of Teachers II: Teacher Value-Added and Student Outcomes in Adulthood." *American Economic Review* 104 (9): 2633–79.

Cohen, David K., and Jal D. Mehta. 2017. "Why Reform Sometimes Succeeds: Understanding the Conditions That Produce Reforms That Last." *American Educational Research Journal* 54 (4): 644–90.

Colby, Anne, Elizabeth Beaumont, Thomas Ehrlich, and Josh Corngold. 2007. *Educating for Democracy: Preparing Undergraduates for Responsible Political Engagement.* San Francisco: Jossey-Bass.

Colby, Anne, Thomas Ehrlich, Elizabeth Beaumont, and Jason Stephens. 2003. *Educating Citizens: Preparing America's Undergraduates for Lives of Moral and Civic Responsibility.* San Francisco: Jossey-Bass.

Coleman, James S., Ernest Q. Campbell, Carol J. Hobson, James McPartland, Alex M. Mood, Frederick D. Weinfeld, and Robert L. York. 1966. *Equality of Educational Opportunity*. Washington, DC: US Department of Health, Education, and Welfare, Office of Education.

Condon, William, Ellen R. Iverson, Cathryn A. Manduca, Carol Rutz, and Gudrun Willett. 2016. *Faculty Development and Student Learning: Assessing the Connections*. Bloomington, IN: Indiana University Press.

Cook, Constance, and Matthew Kaplan, eds. 2011. *Advancing the Culture of Teaching on Campus: How a Teaching Center Can Make a Difference*. Sterling, VA: Stylus.

Council of Independent Colleges. 2018. "Council of Independent Colleges, Association of College and University Educators Partner to Create New Consortium Focused on Preparing Faculty with Career Advising Skills." cic.edu/n/p/Documents/CIC -Instructional-Excellence-2018.pdf.

Craig, Ryan. 2015. *College Disrupted: The Great Unbundling of Higher Education*. New York: St. Martin's Press.

Curtis, John W. 2014. *The Employment Status of Instructional Staff Members in Higher Education, Fall 2011*. Washington, DC: American Association of University Professors.

Darity, William, Jr., Darrick Hamilton, Mark Paul, Alan Aja, Anne Price, Antonio Moore, and Caterina Chiopris. 2018. *What We Get Wrong about Closing the Racial Wealth Gap*. Durham, NC: Samuel DuBois Cook Center on Social Equity, Insight Center for Community Economic Development, Duke University.

Darling-Hammond, Linda. 2003. *The Learning Classroom: Theory into Practice*. South Burlington, VT: Annenberg/CPB.

Dede, Chris. 2010. "Comparing Frameworks for 21st Century Skills." In *21st Century Skills: Rethinking How Students Learn*, edited by James Bellanca and Ron Brandt, 51–75. Bloomington, IN: Solution Tree Press.

Delaney, Esther Hong. 2015. "The Professoriate in an Age of Assessment and Accountability: Understanding Faculty Response to Student Learning Outcomes Assessment and the Collegiate Learning Assessment." PhD diss., Teachers College, Columbia University.

Delpit, Lisa D. 2006. *Other People's Children: Cultural Conflict in the Classroom*. New York: New Press.

DeMillo, Richard. 2015. *Revolution in Higher Education: How a Small Band of Innovators Will Make College Affordable and Accessible*. Cambridge, MA: MIT Press.

Denecke, Daniel, Julia Michaels, and Katherine Stone. 2017. *Strategies to Prepare Future Faculty to Assess Student Learning*. Washington, DC: Council of Graduate Schools.

Deresiewicz, William. 2014. *Excellent Sheep: The Miseducation of the American Elite and the Way to a Meaningful Life*. New York: Free Press.

Descartes, René. 1993. *Meditations on First Philosophy*. Translated by Donald A. Cress. 3rd ed. Indianapolis, IN: Hackett.

DeZure, Deborah. 1999. "Evaluating Teaching through Peer Classroom Observation." In *Changing Practices in Evaluating Teaching: A Practical Guide to Improved Faculty Performance and Promotion/Tenure Decisions*, edited by Peter Seldin, 70–96. San Francisco: Jossey-Bass.

Dowd, Alicia C., and Estela Mara Bensimon. 2015. *Engaging the "Race Question": Accountability and Equity in U.S. Higher Education*. New York: Teachers College Press.

Doxsee, Kenneth M. 2016. *Post-Tenure Review: Guidelines for Unit Policy Development*. Eugene, OR: Office of Academic Affairs, University of Oregon.

Drezner, Noah D., Oren Pizmony-Levy, and Aaron M. Pallas. 2018. *Americans' Views of Higher Education as a Public and Private Good.* New York: Teachers College, Columbia University.

Dweck, Carol S. 2016. *Mindset: The New Psychology of Success.* New York: Ballantine.

Eagan, Kevin, Ellen Bara Stolzenberg, Jennifer Berdan Lozano, Melissa C. Aragon, Maria Ramirez Suchard, and Sylvia Hurtado. 2014. *Undergraduate Teaching Faculty: The 2013–2014 HERI Faculty Survey.* Los Angeles: Cooperative Institutional Research Program at the Higher Education Research Institute at UCLA.

Ehrlich, Thomas. 2000. *Civic Responsibility and Higher Education.* Lanham, MD: Rowman and Littlefield.

Elbow, Peter, and Pat Belanoff. 1999. *Sharing and Responding.* 3rd ed. New York: McGraw-Hill.

Eng, Norman. 2017. *Teaching College: The Ultimate Guide to Lecturing, Presenting, and Engaging Students.* New York: Norman Eng.

Engberg, Mark E. 2004. "Improving Intergroup Relations in Higher Education: A Critical Examination of the Influence of Educational Interventions on Racial Bias." *Review of Educational Research* 74 (4): 473–524.

Enright, Esther. 2016. "Teaching to the "Good Ones"? Examining the Relationship Between Inequity and the Practice of and Preparation for Postsecondary Mathematics Instruction." PhD diss., University of Michigan.

Espeland, Wendy, and Michael Sauder. 2016. *Engines of Anxiety: Academic Rankings, Reputation, and Accountability.* New York: Russell Sage Foundation.

Feinstein, Leon, Ricardo Sabates, Tashweka M. Anderson, Annik Sorhaindo, and Cathie Hammond. 2006. "What Are the Effects of Education on Health?" In *Measuring the Effects of Education on Health and Civic Engagement: Proceedings of the Copenhagen Symposium*, 171–353. Paris: Organization of Economic Cooperation and Development.

Feldman, Martha S., and Brian T. Pentland. 2003. "Reconceptualizing Organizational Routines as a Source of Flexibility and Change." *Administrative Science Quarterly* 48 (1): 94–118.

Flaherty, Colleen. 2018. "Teaching Eval Shake-Up." *Inside Higher Education*, May 22. insidehighered.com/news/2018/05/22/most-institutions-say-they-value-teaching-how-they-assess-it-tells-different-story.

Fligstein, Neil. 2012. "Obituary: John Pock, 1926–2012." *ASA Footnotes*, April. asanet.org/sites/default/files/savvy/footnotes/apr12/obit_0412.html#obit_2.

Flower, Linda S. 1997. *Problem-Solving Strategies for Writing in College and Community.* New York: Wadsworth.

Fourcade, Marion. 2009. *Economists and Societies: Discipline and Profession in the United States, Britain, and France, 1890s to 1990s.* Princeton, NJ: Princeton University Press.

Frankel, Matthew. 2017. "This is the Maximum Social Security Retirement Benefit Payable in 2018." Motley Fool, December 1. fool.com/retirement/2017/12/01/this-is-the-maximum-social-security-retirement-ben.aspx.

Frechtling, Joy A. 2007. *Logic Modeling Methods in Program Evaluation.* San Francisco: Jossey-Bass.

Freeman, Scott, Sarah L. Eddy, Miles McDonough, Michelle K. Smith, Nnadozie Okoroafor, Hannah Jordt, and Mary Pat Wenderoth. 2014. "Active Learning Increases Student Performance in Science, Engineering, and Mathematics." *Proceedings of the National Academy of Sciences* 111 (23): 8410–15.

Freire, Paolo. 2000. *Pedagogy of the Oppressed.* New York: Continuum.

Gamson, Zelda F., and associates. 1984. *Liberating Education.* San Francisco: Jossey-Bass.

Garfield, Joan, and Dani Ben-Zvi. 2008. *Developing Students' Statistical Reasoning: Connecting Research and Teaching Practice.* New York: Springer.

Giddens, Anthony. 1990. *The Consequences of Modernity.* Stanford, CA: Stanford University Press.

Ginder, Scott A., Janice E. Kelly-Reid, and Farrah B. Mann. 2018. *Enrollment and Employees in Postsecondary Institutions, Fall 2017, and Financial Statistics and Academic Libraries, Fiscal Year 2017 (Preliminary Data).* Washington, DC: National Center for Education Statistics.

Goldstein, Dana. 2018. "Lawsuit Says Rhode Island Failed to Teach Students to be Good Citizens." *New York Times,* November 29, 2018. nytimes.com/2018/11/28/us/civics-rhode-island-schools.html.

Gonzalez, Norma, Luis Moll, and Cathy Amanti, eds. 2005. *Funds of Knowledge: Theorizing Practices in Households, Communities, and Classrooms.* New York: Routledge.

Goodman, Joshua, Julia Melkers, and Amanda Pallais. 2019. "Can Online Delivery Increase Access to Education?" *Journal of Labor Economics* 37 (1): 1–34.

Gutiérrez, Kris D. 2008. "Developing a Sociocritical Literacy in the Third Space." *Reading Research Quarterly* 43 (2): 148–64.

Hammer, Ronen, Eyal Peer, and Elisha Babad. Forthcoming. "Faculty Alleged 'Myths' about Student Evaluation of Teaching: An Empirical Assessment." *Journal of Education Psychology.*

Hammer, Ronen, Eyal Peer, and Elisha Babad. 2018. "Faculty Attitudes about Student Evaluations and Their Relations to Self-Image as Teacher." *Social Psychology of Education* 21 (3): 517–37.

Hannan, Michael T., Glenn R. Carroll, and László Pólos. 2003. "The Organizational Niche." *Sociological Theory* 21 (4): 309–40.

Hansen, David. 2001. *Exploring the Moral Heart of Teaching: Toward a Teacher's Creed.* New York: Teachers College Press.

Haras, Catherine, Margery Ginsberg, Emily Daniel Magruder, and Todd Zakrasjek. 2018. *A Beta Faculty Development Center Matrix.* Washington, DC: American Council on Education.

Haras, Catherine, Steven C. Taylor, Mary Deane Sorcinelli, and Linda von Hoene, eds. 2017. *Institutional Commitment to Teaching Excellence: Assessing the Impacts and Outcomes of Faculty Development.* Washington, DC: American Council on Education.

Harding, Sandra G. 1986. *The Science Question in Feminism.* Ithaca, NY: Cornell University Press.

Hatch, Thomas, Dilruba Ahmed, Ann Lieberman, Deborah Faigenbaum, Melissa Eiler White, and Desiree H. Pointer Mace, eds. 2005. *Going Public with Our Teaching: An Anthology of Practice.* New York: Teachers College Press.

Hatch, Thomas, and Pam Grossman. 2009. "Learning to Look Beyond the Boundaries of Representation: Using Technology to Examine Teaching (Overview for a Digital Exhibition: Learning From the Practice of Teaching)." *Journal of Teacher Education* 60 (1): 70–85.

Head, Karen J. 2017. *Disrupt This! MOOCs and the Promises of Technology.* Lebanon, NH: University Press of New England.

Hessler, Michael, Daniel M Pöpping, Hanna Hollstein, Hendrik Ohlenburg, Philip H. Arnemann, Christina Massoth, Laura M Seidel, Alexander Zarbock, and Manuel Wenk. 2018. "Availability of Cookies during an Academic Course Session Affects Evaluation of Teaching." *Medical Education* 52 (10): 1064–72.

Hill, Carolyn J., Howard S. Bloom, Alison Rebeck Black, and Mark W. Lipsey. 2008. "Empirical Benchmarks for Interpreting Effect Sizes in Research." *Child Development Perspectives* 2 (3): 172–77.

Hill, Heather C., Brian Rowan, and Deborah Loewenberg Ball. 2005. "Effects of Teachers' Mathematical Knowledge for Teaching on Student Achievement." *American Educational Research Journal* 42 (2): 371–406.

Hofstadter, Richard. 1963. *Anti-Intellectualism in American Life*. New York: Knopf.

Hollands, Fiona, and Devayani Tirthali. 2015. *MOOCs in Higher Education: Institutional Goals and Paths Forward*. New York: Palgrave Macmillan.

hooks, bell. 1994. *Teaching to Transgress: Education as the Practice of Freedom*. New York: Routledge.

Hoxby, Caroline. 2019. "Online Postsecondary Education and Labor Productivity." In *Education, Skills, and Technical Change: Implications for Future US GDP Growth*, edited by Charles R. Hulten and Valerie A. Ramey, 401–64. Chicago: University of Chicago Press.

Hurtado, Sylvia. 2007. "Linking Diversity with the Educational and Civic Missions of Higher Education." *Review of Higher Education* 30 (2): 185–96.

Hussar, William J., and Tabitha M. Bailey. *Projections of Education Statistics to 2026*. Washington, DC: National Center for Education Statistics.

Jackson, C. Kirabo. 2018. "What Do Test Scores Miss? The Importance of Teacher Effects on Non-Test Score Outcomes." *Journal of Political Economy* 126 (5): 2072–2107.

Kanter, Martha, and Carol Geary Schneider. 2013. "Civic Learning and Engagement." *Change: The Magazine of Higher Learning* 45 (1): 6–14.

Katz, Lawrence F., and Alan B. Krueger. 2017. *The Rise and Nature of Alternative Work Arrangements in the United States, 1995–2015*. National Bureau of Economic Research Working Paper Series. Cambridge, MA: National Bureau of Economic Research.

Kezar, Adrianna. 2012. *Embracing Non–Tenure Track Faculty*. New York: Routledge.

Kezar, Adrianna, and Dan Maxey. 2014. "Faculty Matter: So Why Doesn't Everyone Think So?" *Thought and Action* (Fall): 29–44.

Kezar, Adrianna, and Cecile Sam. 2013. "Institutionalizing Equitable Policies and Practices for Contingent Faculty." *Journal of Higher Education* 84 (1): 56–87.

Kosslyn, Stephen M., and Ben Nelson, eds. 2017. *Building the Intentional University: Minerva and the Future of Higher Education*. Cambridge, MA: MIT Press.

Labaree, David F. 1997a. *How to Succeed in School without Really Learning: The Credentials Race in American Education*. New Haven, CT: Yale University Press.

Labaree, David F. 1997b. "Public Goods, Private Goods: The American Struggle over Educational Goals." *American Educational Research Journal* 34 (1): 39–81.

Labaree, David F. 2017. "The Five-Paragraph Fetish." *Aeon*, February 15. aeon.co/essays/writing-essays-by-formula-teaches-students-how-to-not-think.

Ladson-Billings, Gloria. 1995. "Toward a Theory of Culturally Relevant Pedagogy." *American Educational Research Journal* 32 (3): 465–91.

Lamont, Michèle, and Virág Molnár. 2002. "The Study of Boundaries in the Social Sciences." *Annual Review of Sociology* 28 (1): 167–95.

Lampert, Magdalene, and Deborah Ball. 1998. *Teaching, Multimedia, and Mathematics: Investigations of Real Practice*. New York: Teachers College Press.

Land, Ray, Jan Meyer, and Jan Smith. 2008. *Threshold Concepts within the Disciplines*. Rotterdam: Sense Publishers.

Lang, James M. 2016. *Small Teaching :Everyday Lessons from the Science of Learning*. New York: Wiley.

Lattuca, Lisa R., and Joan S. Stark. 2009. *Shaping the College Curriculum: Academic Plans in Context.* 2nd ed. San Francisco: Jossey-Bass.

Lee, Carol. 2007. *Culture, Literacy, and Learning: Taking Bloom in the Midst of the Whirlwind.* New York: Teachers College Press.

Levine, Donald N. 2006. *Powers of the Mind: The Reinvention of Liberal Learning in America.* Chicago: University of Chicago Press.

Lewis, Amanda E., and John B. Diamond. 2015. *Despite the Best Intentions: How Racial Inequality Thrives in Good Schools.* New York: Oxford University Press.

Linse, Angela R. 2017. "Interpreting and Using Student Ratings Data: Guidance for Faculty Serving as Administrators and on Evaluation Committees." *Studies in Educational Evaluation* 54 (3): 94–106.

Litzinger, Thomas A., Lisa R. Lattuca, Roger G. Hadgraft, and Wendy C. Newstetter. 2011. "Engineering Education and the Development of Expertise." *Journal of Engineering Education* 100 (1): 123–50.

Loveless, Tom, ed. 2007. *Lessons Learned: What International Assessments Tell Us about Math Achievement.* Washington, DC: Brookings Institution Press.

Luttrell, Wendy 1997. *Schoolsmart and Motherwise: Working-Class Women's Identity and Schooling.* New York: Routledge.

MacCormack, Penny, Meghan Snow, Jonathan Gyurko, and Julianne Candio Sekel. 2018. *Connecting the Dots: A Proposed Accountability Method for Evaluating the Efficacy of Faculty Development and its Impact on Student Outcomes.* New York: ACUE.

Manyika, James, Susan Lund, Jacques Bughin, Kelsey Robinson, Jan Mischke, and Deepa Mahajan. 2016. *Independent Work: Choice, Necessity, and the Gig Economy.* McKinsey Global Institute.

Mayer, Richard E. 2010. *Applying the Science of Learning.* Boston: Pearson/Allyn & Bacon.

Mayhew, Matthew J., Alyssa N. Rockenbach, Nicholas A. Bowman, Tricia A. Seifert, Gregory C. Wolniak, Ernest T. Pascarella, and Patrick T. Terenzini. 2016. *How College Affects Students: 21st Century Evidence that Higher Education Works.* Vol. 3. San Francisco: Jossey-Bass.

Mellow, Gail O., Diana D. Woolis, Marisa Klages-Bombich, and Susan G. Restler. 2015. *Taking College Teaching Seriously: Pedagogy Matters!* Sterling, VA: Stylus.

Menary, Kyle, Paul F. Collins, James N. Porter, Ryan Muetzel, Elizabeth A. Olson, Vipin Kumar, Michael Steinbach, Kelvin O. Lim, and Monica Luciana. 2013. "Associations between Cortical Thickness and General Intelligence in Children, Adolescents and Young Adults." *Intelligence* 41 (5): 597–606.

Messacar, Derek. 2017. *The Effects of Education on Canadians' Retirement Savings Behaviour.* Ottawa: Statistics Canada.

MLA Office of Research. 2017. "The Upward Trend in Modern Language PhD Production: Findings from the 2015 Survey of Earned Doctorates." *Trend*, July 6. mlaresearch.mla .hcommons.org/2017/02/06/the-upward-trend-in-modern-language-phd-production -findings-from-the-2015-survey-of-earned-doctorates.

Moll, Luis C., Cathy Amanti, Deborah Neff, and Norma Gonzalez. 1992. "Funds of Knowledge for Teaching: Using a Qualitative Approach to Connect Homes and Classrooms." *Theory Into Practice* 31 (2): 132–41.

Moore, David W. 2005. "Three in Four Americans Believe in Paranormal." Gallup News Service, June 16. news.gallup.com/poll/16915/three-four-americans-believe-paranormal .aspx.

Moses, Robert P., and Charles E. Cobb Jr. 2001. *Radical Equations: Civil Rights from Mississippi to the Algebra Project.* Boston: Beacon Press.

Naftulin, Donald H., John E. Ware, Jr., and Frank A. Donnelly. 1973. "The Doctor Fox Lecture: A Paradigm of Educational Seduction." *Journal of Medical Education* 48 (7): 630–35.

National Academies of Sciences, Engineering, and Medicine. 2018. *The Integration of the Humanities and Arts with Sciences, Engineering, and Medicine in Higher Education: Branches from the Same Tree.* Edited by David Skorton and Ashley Bear. Washington, DC: National Academies Press.

National Center for Education Statistics. 2018. *Digest of Education Statistics 2017.* Washington, DC: US Department of Education.

National Research Council. 2015. *Reaching Students: What Research Says About Effective Instruction in Undergraduate Science and Engineering.* Washington, DC: National Academies Press.

Neumann, Anna. 2006. "Professing Passion: Emotion in the Scholarship of Professors at Research Universities." *American Educational Research Journal* 43 (3): 381–424.

Neumann, Anna. 2009a. *Professing to Learn: Creating Tenured Lives and Careers in the American Research University.* Baltimore, MD: Johns Hopkins University Press.

Neumann, Anna. 2009b. "Protecting the Passion of Scholars in Times of Change." *Change: The Magazine of Higher Learning* 41 (2): 10–15.

Neumann, Anna. 2014. "Staking a Claim on Learning: What We Should Know about Learning in Higher Education, and Why." *Review of Higher Education* 37 (2): 249–67.

Neumann, Anna, and Corbin Campbell. 2016. "Homing in on Learning and Teaching: Current Approaches and Future Directions for Higher Education Policy." In *American Higher Education in the 21st Century*, edited by Michael Bastedo, Phillip Altbach, Robert Berdahl, and Patricia Gumport, 401–31. Baltimore, MD: Johns Hopkins University Press.

Newport, Frank, and Brandon Busteed. 2017. "Why Are Republicans Down on Higher Ed?" Gallup News Service, April 16. news.gallup.com/poll/216278/why-republicans-down -higher.aspx.

Nuñez, Anne-Marie, Elizabeth Murakami Ramalho, and Kimberley K. Cuero. 2010. "Pedagogy for Equity: Teaching in a Hispanic-Serving Institution." *Innovative Higher Education* 35 (3): 177–90.

Nussbaum, Martha Craven. 1997. *Cultivating Humanity: A Classical Defense of Reform in Liberal Education.* Cambridge, MA: Harvard University Press.

Nussbaum, Martha Craven. 2012. *Not for Profit: Why Democracy Needs the Humanities.* Princeton, NJ: Princeton University Press.

OECD. 2016a. *Education at a Glance 2016: Education Indicators.* Paris: OECD Publishing.

OECD. 2016b. *Skills Matter: Further Results from the Survey of Adult Skills.* Paris: OECD Publishing.

O'Meara, KerryAnn, and Alan Bloomgarden. 2011. "The Pursuit of Prestige: The Experience of Institutional Striving from a Faculty Perspective." *Journal of the Professoriate* 4 (1): 39–73.

Pallas, Aaron M. 2001. "Preparing Education Doctoral Students for Epistemological Diversity." *Educational Researcher* 30 (5): 6–11.

Pallas, Aaron M. 2011. "Assessing the Future of Higher Education." *Society* 48 (3): 213–15.

Pallas, Aaron M., Matthew Boulay, and Melinda Mechur Karp. 2003. "On What Is Learned in School: A Verstehen Approach." In *Stability and Change in Education: Structure, Processes, and Outcomes*, edited by Maureen T. Hallinan, Adam Gamoran, Warren Kubitschek and Tom Loveless, 17–40. New York: Percheron Press.

Palmer, Parker J. 1998. *The Courage to Teach: Exploring the Inner Landscape of a Teacher's Life.* San Francisco: Jossey-Bass.

Paris, Django, and H. Samy Alim. 2014. "What Are We Seeking to Sustain through Culturally Sustaining Pedagogy? A Loving Critique Forward." *Harvard Educational Review* 84 (1): 85–100.

Paris, Django, and H. Samy Alim, eds. 2017. *Culturally Sustaining Pedagogies: Teaching and Learning for Justice in a Changing World.* New York: Teachers College Press.

Pascarella, Ernest T., and Charles Blaich. 2013. "Lessons from the Wabash National Study of Liberal Arts Education." *Change: The Magazine of Higher Learning* 45 (2): 6–15.

Pew Research Center. 2017. *Sharp Partisan Divisions in Views of National Institutions.* Washington, DC: Pew Research Center.

Plank, Kathryn M., and Alan Kalish. 2010. "Program Assessment for Faculty Development." In *A Guide to Faculty Development,* edited by Kay J. Gillespie, Douglas L. Robertson and Associates, 135–49. San Francisco: Jossey-Bass.

Radwin, David, Conzelmann, Johnathan G., Nunnery, Annaliza, Lacy, T. Austin, Wu, Joanna, Lew, Stephen, Wine, Jennifer, and Siegel, Peter. 2018. *2015–16 National Postsecondary Student Aid Study.* Washington, DC: National Center for Education Statistics, Institute of Education Sciences.

Rebell, Michael A. 2018. *Flunking Democracy: Schools, Courts, and Civic Participation.* Chicago: University of Chicago Press.

Reed College. 2006. "How to Mark a Family Legacy." *Reed Magazine,* summer. reed.edu /reed_magazine/summer2006/columns/supporting_reed/legacy.html.

Reed College. 2007. "New Chair Named for Sociology Professor John Pock." *Reed Magazine,* autumn. reed.edu/reed_magazine/autumn2007/columns/NoC/pock.html.

Roksa, Josipa, Richard Arum, and Amanda Cook. 2016. "Defining and Assessing Learning in Higher Education." In *Improving Quality in American Higher Education: Learning Outcomes and Assessments for the 21st Century,* edited by Richard Arum, Josipa Roksa and Amanda Cook, 1–36. San Francisco: Jossey-Bass.

Rose, Mike. 1989. *Lives on the Boundary: A Moving Account of the Struggles and Achievements of America's Educationally Underprepared.* New York: Penguin.

Rosenbaum, James, and Takehiko Kariya. 1989. "From High School to Work: Market and Institutional Mechanisms in Japan." *American Journal of Sociology* 94 (6): 1334–65.

Roth, Michael S. 2014. *Beyond the University: Why Liberal Education Matters.* New Haven, CT: Yale University Press.

Ruef, Martin, and Manish Nag. 2015. "The Classification of Organizational Forms: Theory and Application to the Field of Higher Education." In *Remaking College: The Changing Ecology of Higher Education,* edited by Michael Kirst and Mitchell Stevens, 84–109. Stanford, CA: Stanford University Press.

Satel, Sally, and Scott O. Lilienfeld. 2013. *Brainwashed: The Seductive Appeal of Mindless Neuroscience.* New York: Basic Books.

Schwab, Joseph J. 1964. "Structure of the Disciplines: Meaning and Significance." In *The Structure of Knowledge and Curriculum,* edited by Gervais W. Ford and Lawrence Pugno, 6–30. Chicago: Rand-McNally.

Schwab, Joseph J. 1978a. "Education and the Structure of Disciplines." In *Science, Curriculum, and Liberal Education,* edited by Ian Westbury and Neil J. Wilkof, 229–69. Chicago: University of Chicago Press.

Schwab, Joseph J. 1978b. "The Practical: Translation into Curriculum." In *Science, Curriculum, and Liberal Education,* edited by Ian Westbury and Neil J. Wilkof, 365–84. Chicago: University of Chicago Press.

Scott-Clayton, Judith, Peter M. Crosta, and Clive R. Belfield. 2014. "Improving the Targeting of Treatment: Evidence From College Remediation." *Educational Evaluation and Policy Analysis* 36 (3): 371–93.

Scott-Clayton, Judith, and Olga Rodriguez. 2015. "Development, Discouragement, or Diversion? New Evidence on the Effects of College Remediation Policy." *Educational Finance and Policy* 10 (1): 4–45.

Semega, Jessica L., Kayla R. Fontenot, and Melissa A. Kollar. 2017. *Income and Poverty in the United States: 2016*. Washington, DC: US Census Bureau.

Shulman, Lee S. 1986. "Those Who Understand: Knowledge Growth in Teaching." *Educational Researcher* 15 (2): 4–14.

Shulman, Lee S. 1987. "Knowledge and Teaching: Foundations of the New Reform." *Harvard Educational Review* 57 (1): 1–23.

Shulman, Lee S. 1999. "Taking Learning Seriously." *Change: The Magazine of Higher Learning* 31 (4): 10–17.

Shulman, Lee S. 2004a. *Teaching as Community Property: Essays on Higher Education*. San Francisco: Jossey-Bass.

Shulman, Lee S. 2004b. *The Wisdom of Practice: Essays on Teaching, Learning, and Learning to Teach*. San Francisco: Jossey-Bass.

Simkin, Mikhail. 2011. "PhDs Couldn't Tell an Actor from a Renowned Scientist." *Significance*, July 4. significancemagazine.com/science/437-phds-couldn-t-tell-an-actor -from-a-renowned-scientist.

Singer, Susan, Natalie Nielsen, and Heidi Schweingruber. 2012. *Discipline-Based Education Research: Understanding and Improving Learning in Undergraduate Science and Engineering*. Washington, DC: National Academies Press.

Snyder, Thomas D., Cristobal de Brey, and Sally A. Dillow. 2018. *Digest of Education Statistics 2016*. Washington, DC: National Center for Education Statistics, Institute of Education Sciences, US Department of Education.

Spiegel, Gabrielle M. 2008. "A Triple 'A' Threat: Accountability, Assessment, Accreditation." *Perspectives on History* 46 (3). historians.org/publications-and-directories /perspectives-on-history/march-2008/a-triple-a-threat-accountability-assessment -accreditation.

Spillane, James P. 2004. *Standards Deviation: How Schools Misunderstand Education Policy*. Cambridge, MA: Harvard University Press.

Steele, Claude. 2010. *Whistling Vivaldi: And Other Clues to How Stereotypes Affect Us*. New York: Norton.

Svinicki, Marilla D., and Wilbert James McKeachie. 2011. *McKeachie's Teaching Tips: Strategies, Research, and Theory for College and University Teachers*. 14th ed. Belmont, CA: Wadsworth.

Tamborini, Christopher R., ChangHwan Kim, and Arthur Sakamoto. 2015. "Education and Lifetime Earnings in the United States." *Demography* 52 (4): 1383–1407.

Turner, Stephen. 2017. "Knowledge Formations: An Analytic Framework." In *The Oxford Handbook of Interdisciplinarity*, edited by Robert Frodeman, 9–20. New York: Oxford University Press.

US Census Bureau. 2018. *2017 Annual Social and Economic Supplement of the Current Population Study*. Washington, DC: US Census Bureau.

US Department of Education. 2006. *A Test of Leadership: Charting the Future of U.S. Higher Education*. Washington, DC: US Department of Education.

US Government Accountability Office. 2017. *Contingent Workforce: Size, Characteristics, Compensation, and Work Experiences of Adjunct and Other Non-Tenure-Track Faculty*. Washington, DC: US Government Printing Office.

Ursache, Alexandra, Kimberly G. Noble, and Pediatric Imaging, Neurocognition, and Genetics Study. 2016. "Socioeconomic Status, White Matter, and Executive Function in Children." *Brain and Behavior* 6 (10): e00531.

Uttl, Bob, Carmela A. White, and Daniela Wong Gonzalez. 2017. "Meta-Analysis of Faculty's Teaching Effectiveness: Student Evaluation of Teaching Ratings and Student Learning Are Not Related." *Studies in Educational Evaluation* 54: 22–42.

Valenzuela, Angela. 1999. *Subtractive Schooling: U.S.-Mexican Youth and the Politics of Caring.* Albany: State University of New York Press.

Van Note Chism, Nancy. 2007. *Peer Review of Teaching: A Sourcebook.* 2nd ed. San Francisco: Jossey-Bass.

Voelker, David J. 2008. "Assessing Student Understanding in Introductory Courses: A Sample Strategy." *History Teacher* 41 (4): 505–18.

Waller, Willard. 1932. *The Sociology of Teaching.* New York: Wiley.

Wenger, Etienne. 1998. *Communities of Practice : Learning, Meaning, and Identity.* Cambridge: Cambridge University Press, 1998.

Wieman, Carl. 2017. *Improving How Universities Teach Science: Lessons from the Science Education Initiative.* Cambridge, MA: Harvard University Press.

William T. Grant Foundation. 2015. *Measuring Instruction in Higher Education: Summary of a Convening.* New York: William T. Grant Foundation.

Willingham, Daniel T. 2009. *Why Don't Students Like School? A Cognitive Scientist Answers Questions about How the Mind Works and What It Means for the Classroom.* New York: Wiley.

Willingham, Daniel T. 2018. "Does Tailoring Instruction to 'Learning Styles' Help Students Learn?" *American Educator* 42 (2): 28–33.

Wineburg, Samuel S. 2001. *Historical Thinking and Other Unnatural Acts: Charting the Future of Teaching the Past.* Philadelphia: Temple University Press.

Witteveen, Dirk, and Paul Attewell. 2017. "The Earnings Payoff from Attending a Selective College." *Social Science Research* 66: 154–69.

Xu, Di, and Shanna Smith Jaggars. 2013. "The Impact of Online Learning on Students' Course Outcomes: Evidence from a Large Community and Technical College System." *Economics of Education Review* 37: 46–57.

Xu, Di, and Shanna Smith Jaggars. 2014. "Performance Gaps between Online and Face-to-Face Courses: Differences across Types of Students and Academic Subject Areas." *Journal of Higher Education* 85 (5): 633–59.

Yeager, David Scott, Valerie Purdie-Vaughns, Julio Garcia, Nancy Apfel, Patti Brzustoski, Allison Master, William T. Hessert, Matthew E. Williams, and Geoffrey L. Cohen. 2014. "Breaking the Cycle of Mistrust: Wise Interventions to Provide Critical Feedback across the Racial Divide." *Journal of Experimental Psychology: General* 143 (2): 804–24.

Young, Michael. 2008. "From Constructivism to Realism in the Sociology of the Curriculum." *Review of Research in Education* 32 (1): 1–28.

Zakaria, Fareed. 2015. *In Defense of a Liberal Education.* New York: Norton.

Zamora, Alyssa. 2017. "Miami Dade College Announces 2017 Endowed Teaching Chairs." Miami Dade College Foundation.

Zemsky, Robert. 2009. *Making Reform Work: The Case for Transforming American Higher Education.* New Brunswick, NJ: Rutgers University Press.

Wabash National Study of Liberal Arts
  Education, 194
Washington State University, 144–46
wealth gap, 10
Westchester Community College, 81–82
Wieman, Carl, 151–53
Willingham, Dan, 59
Wineburg, Sam, 84

Woolis, Diana, 193
writing assignments: authenticity of, 106;
  navigating example for, 100–108; targeting
  example for, 77–81

Xu, Di, 38

Zakaria, Fareed, 39